# GREAT
# DOCUMENTS
## OF THE WORLD

πάντα γὰρ καιρῷ καλά.  EVERYTHING IS MADE CLEAR IN TIME.

Sophocles, *Oedipus the King*

# FRIEDRICH HEER
## IN COLLABORATION WITH XAVER SCHNIEPER

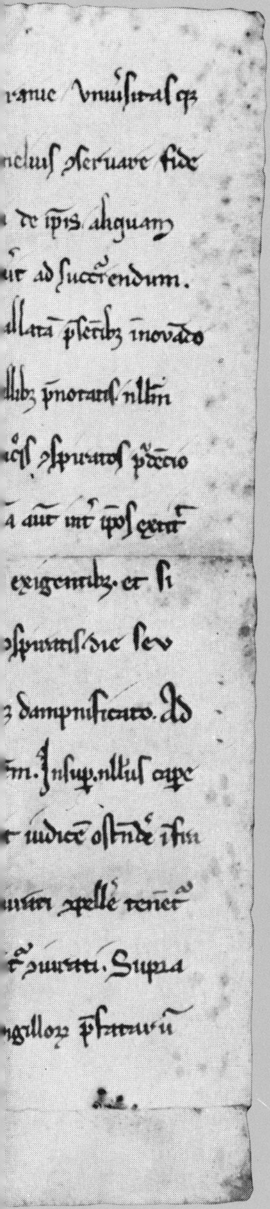

# GREAT DOCUMENTS OF THE WORLD
*Milestones of Human Thought*

EDITED BY PIERRE SCHWOB

DESIGNED BY ROBERT TOBLER

McGRAW-HILL BOOK COMPANY

NEW YORK   SAN FRANCISCO   ST. LOUIS   KUALA LUMPUR

MONTREAL   SÃO PAULO   TORONTO

*Title page:* The Swiss "Bundesbrief" of August 1291 is the historically authentic "birth certificate" of the Swiss defense league or Confederation. It is considered the oldest existing document of the founding of a state, one that has succeeded in maintaining its independence uninterruptedly for nearly seven hundred years.

*Right:* Before the Americans declared their independence, they made one last effort to settle the differences with the mother country. In 1775 they sent King George III a message that John Adams called the "Olive Branch Petition." The bearer of the "Olive Branch" was not received by the king. Twenty-five of the same men who signed this petition *(right)* put their names, one year later, to the American Declaration of Independence.

A McGraw-Hill Co-Publication

Library of Congress
Cataloging in Publication Data
Great documents of the world.
  Bibliography
  Includes index.
  1. Civilization—History—Sources. I. Heer, Friedrich, 1916–
CB5.G7   909   77-8160
ISBN 0-07-027780-X

Original Concept: EMIL M. BÜHRER
Editor: DAVID BAKER
Managing Editor: FRANCINE PEETERS
Picture Procuration: ROSARIA PASQUARIELLO
Production Manager: FRANZ GISLER

This book was manufactured
entirely in Switzerland:

Printed by: POLYGRAPHISCHE GESELLSCHAFT, LAUPEN
Bound by: SCHUMACHER AG, SCHMITTEN
Composition by: FILMSATZ STAUFFER + CIE., BASEL
Photolithography by: KREIENBÜHL AG, LUCERNE

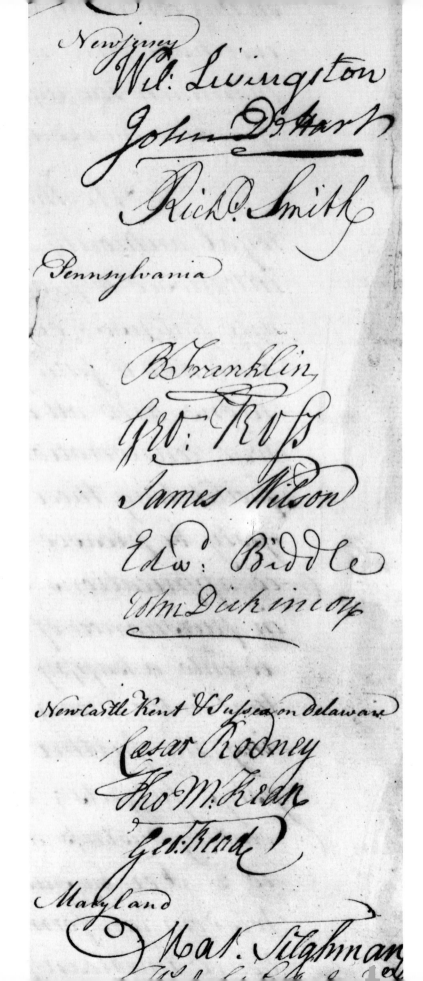

# CONTENTS

Man is an ultimately untamable creature.

So says the Bible, so everyone has said from Hammurabi to Emperor Hirohito, every lawgiver, legal thinker, sage, philosopher, and doctor who has ever decided to assume responsibility for the life —and in practical terms that has always meant also the survival —of mankind in its children and in its children's children.

For *such is man,* seeking over and over again to tame the untamable, to take this never entirely governable animal and train and educate him with the instruments of culture, civilization, legal systems, and peace treaties. And at the same time psychologists recognize that full "domestication" would mean the end of man's humanity, neutralizing all the tensions that drive him on.

*Being human means living with the conflicts that each self, each society, each nation, each period bears within it.*

Some conflicts pass away if dealt with patiently enough, cast off like a god's old robes, like the religious conflicts that led particularly in Europe to so much suffering. (The United States owes its existence to these "Old World" passions and persecutions, which in an exodus lasting several centuries drove wave after wave of refugees across the oceans to America.)

There is a whole series of conflicts, however, that do not pass away, that are inherent in the system, be it a particular society, a particular religion, or a particular church, conflicts to do with "capitalism" and "socialism" (if for a moment we accept those mythic codewords), conflicts that go even farther and belong to a particular civilization (and who would deny that both Americans and Russians belong to a "white man's civilization"?), to a particular period, to an era.

These conflicts have to be lived with. They need to be watched; sometimes they can be kept under control; they can be "governed"— but with kid gloves, if they are not to spark off explosions. Ultimately they are conflicts between powers, opposing powers that yet need to coexist.

It is this that gives these documents of mankind—our history as the story of the "Family of Man" (the title of a justly famous American photographic exhibition that toured the world in 1955)—their importance: they take account, in all their ideas, laws, contracts, and covenants, of the fact that man is a highly complex creature who lives in and through his conflicts, a dangerous creature who is continually threatening himself, a creature who lives in society, i.e. in a context of conflicting interests. Man is a creature who is daily inclined to suicide and murder, to civil war and wars of aggression. Yet this selfsame creature, man, can be helped by legal systems and peace treaties, by thought, particularly forethought, and by having others share his sufferings, by the spiritual and intellectual help of sages, trailblazers on the long journey through the wasteland of history and the jungle of the soul. Such men are like beacons, like lighthouses in the dark reaches of the self and of society, showing men the "way" to happiness, beatitude, personal fulfillment.

*Man has a right, his human right, to be happy, to be allowed to grow unhindered into the rich maturity shown us in the* tao *of Lao-tse, the* sophrosyne *of Plato's Socrates, the "fullness" of Paul's Christ, and in the equivalent Indian, Buddhist, and Japanese sources of philosophic wisdom.*

But how does it work, this spirit of man we call "mind"? We do not even know what it is. Nor, however, do we know what electricity is, and we still find a million uses for it. It is more important for us to know what mind is not. It is not God's mind; it is not the "spirit of history." It is a concept that philosophers, theologians, and politicians are fond of appropriating, in

From the beginning, man has been a murderer of his fellows—from the stone spear *(far left)* to the Nike Zeus rocket *(left)*.

effect giving us their own mind as the spirit informing the whole, taking over the role of producer of history, of all "reality." At least since his shaman days in the caves of the Ice Age, man has been tempted to put forward his "spirit," his mental experience, as the first and last voice of the godhead.

*What is mind, the spirit of man? We do not know, but we recognize it by its fruits; we know the products and achievements of its force and energy.*

These are first of all the myths and legends, then the folk tales and fairy stories, the sagas and epics that, concentrated and compressed like millennia-old segments of rock, earth, and sand in the Omo Valley, the Gobi Desert, and the soil of Mesopotamia and India, hand down and keep alive the experience of mankind.

Myths and sagas and tales and, from first to last, song (which as far back as the threshers of ancient Egypt could already be protest song) recall what countless generations before our folksingers—ten, fifteen centuries before Christ —went through on their life's journey.

The winds of this spirit blow where they will. Mind, in terms of the tangible output of poets, prophets, philosophers, and scientists, is as influential consciously as unconsciously, performing in glaring contradictions, balking at no suspension of self. Persecuted, eventually "forgotten," it goes underground—often for centuries, even

millennia (the work of the Indian king Ashoka is a prime example). Then up it wells again, as fresh as a spring, like a river that for a few hundred miles (or years) has flowed on beneath the surface of the earth, hidden from man's eyes.

The living fire of mind creates traditions that last as long as one man continues to give another his hand and heart, passing on his experience and his intellectual joy and freedom; traditions that can die out overnight when the younger generation turns its back on its spiritual forebears; traditions that just as "suddenly" reappear, often already in the grandchildren. This is always happening to mind among the capricious race of men—and the result is always another "Passion." Re-ignited in a young man, in a holy man such as Francis of Assisi, in a young poet, in a young scientist (whose vision of a new theory—literally "way of beholding"—deeply upsets his scientific rivals), in a community, a group, a commune, the fire is quickly stamped out and its vessels fall victim to persecution, execution, inquisition, or banishment. Franciscans persecuted for their non-conformity fled as far as the court of the Great Khan of the Mongols; banished Buddhists fled through the depths of Asia; pious men and women left Europe from the sixteenth to the twentieth century and fled to the two Americas.

This "going underground," this acceptance of the rags of beggarhood, of pilgrims and fools (God's fools, *jurodivij,* in Russia) and clowns, has had the effect of continually removing mind from the reach of rulers who wanted to get hold of and make use of it.

*Man's spirit is "eternal" primarily by virtue of its transformations and compressions, its ability to assume different shapes and forms in different people, periods, and civilizations.*

Let us briefly recall one or two reincarnations of that spirit and one or two of the compressions it has undergone in the context of "white" civilization. In Plato —and also in Aristotle for example —not only did the knowledge of ancient Egypt and Mesopotamia find expression but also the wisdom of Magi handed down from time immemorial. In Hegel, the intellectual father of Marx and Lenin, some highly archaic modes of thought crop up such as Augustine's theory of *alienatio* or alienation, a theory that, in conjunction with insights gained from depth psychology, has led to the symbiosis of Marx and Freud favored by the Hegelians of today's Left. And the life of the mind today? Bertolt Brecht, an "atheist" poet who called himself a Marxist, also ironically claimed to be "the last Catholic poet" (aware of the greater communion appealed to by Goethe), and in his songs he can in fact only be understood biblically—as a reader of and disciple of the Psalmist. James Joyce, the anti-Catholic, anti-Irish, Catholic Irish patriot, condensed the six thousand years of "our" ex-

8

# The Axial Period

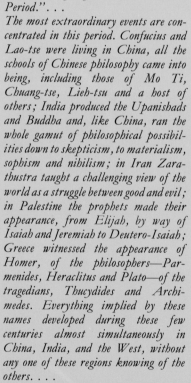

Buddha

Confucius

Heraclitus

The Prophet Jeremiah

Lao-tse

Homer

Zarathustra

*An axis of world history, if such a thing exists, would have to be discovered* empirically, *as a fact capable of being accepted as such by all men. . . . It would seem that this axis of history is to be found in the period around* 500 B.C., *in the spiritual process that occurred between* 800 *and* 200 B.C. *It is there that we meet with the most deepcut dividing line in history. Man, as we know him today, came into being. For short we may style this the "Axial Period.". . .*
*The most extraordinary events are concentrated in this period. Confucius and Lao-tse were living in China, all the schools of Chinese philosophy came into being, including those of Mo Ti, Chuang-tse, Lieh-tsu and a host of others; India produced the Upanishads and Buddha and, like China, ran the whole gamut of philosophical possibilities down to skepticism, to materialism, sophism and nihilism; in Iran Zarathustra taught a challenging view of the world as a struggle between good and evil; in Palestine the prophets made their appearance, from Elijah, by way of Isaiah and Jeremiah to Deutero-Isaiah; Greece witnessed the appearance of Homer, of the philosophers—Parmenides, Heraclitus and Plato—of the tragedians, Thucydides and Archimedes. Everything implied by these names developed during these few centuries almost simultaneously in China, India, and the West, without any one of these regions knowing of the others. . . .*
*In this age were born the fundamental categories within which we still think today, and the beginnings of the world religions, by which human beings still live, were created. The step into universality was taken in every sense.*

Karl Jaspers, from *The Origin and Goal of History* (translated by Michael Bullock)

perience of life's journey through the hells of men from Gilgamesh to Homer and Virgil into his *Ulysses,* a work in which the whole of history is compressed into a single day. And it all takes place in Dublin, which stands for Babylon and Rome and Jerusalem and all the other holy and unholy cities of the world.

No less than in our sagas, legends, and accounts of creation by poets, theologians, and philosophers, the mind of man finds expression in the great natural scientists.

Kepler, father of the "Copernican revolution" (which Copernicus himself had not in fact completed), was deeply imbued with Platonic and even older visions of the sun as the deity of the cosmos.

In 1974 Raymond Ruyer (*La Gnose de Princeton,* Paris), an experienced student of the "Utopias" of our own history, investigated the ideological speculations of American natural scientists, particularly astronomers, physicists, chemists, biologists, and doctors, and showed how deeply they were still affected by age-old Near Eastern, Greek, Hellenistic, Gnostic, and neo-Platonic patterns and currents of thought.

This tremendous "radioactivity" of the human spirit that can flare up now in one place, now in another, often skipping whole centuries, even millennia, during which it continues underground, cannot be understood in simple mythical or magical terms as a kind of "bolt from the blue."

Barefoot and bareheaded, the spirit wanders through the millennia, covering many thousands of miles.

Then it puts on crude footgear such as peasants still wear in parts of the Balkans and in remote valleys of the Apennine and Iberian peninsulas. The tribes, peoples, and individuals of the millennia that lie behind us and that continue to leaven our intellectual and spiritual awareness were nomadic —like the hippies who migrate from California and Scandinavia to Eilat in Israel and on to Persia and India.

We know of the economic relations that existed between Greece, Egypt, the Middle East (Palestine), India, and China in the first millennium B.C. Excavations in the Arabian peninsula and around the shores of the Gulf of Aden and the Persian Gulf have found a series of commercial centers that from the very earliest times played a part in the great east-west trade between Europe and India, China, and the whole of the Far East.

Without those economic relations, one of the most stimulating phenomena of our intellectual history would probably defy comprehension, namely the "simultaneous" (i.e. between the eighth and second century B.C.) appearance of Mahavira and the Buddha in India, Lao-tse and Confucius in China, Homer in Greece, Jeremiah and Isaiah in Israel, the pre-Socratics, and Zoroaster. This *Axenzeit,* as Karl Jaspers called it, this "axial" or "pivotal" period, produced the first philosophers. "Men dared to take a look at themselves as individuals. Hermits and wandering thinkers in China, ascetics in India, philosophers in Greece, prophets in Israel—they all,

however different in faith, behavior, and inner disposition, belong together"; and "man succeeded inwardly in seeing himself as against the whole world. He discovered in himself the root out of which he rises above himself and the world."

Mind means, first and last: freedom and peace within. The man who possesses that freedom and that peace is above murderers and tyrants, above the taunts and spitefulness of his contemporaries; he is superior to "cruel" nature.

*Peace. We find the first rational thinking about peace almost simultaneously in East and West, in China and Greece; Chinese disarmament proposals dating from 546 B.C. parallel Greek attempts to use alliances to end internal wars and contain external ones.*

In Europe it was the Roman Stoa that first evolved a concept of world peace: one humanity was called and committed to reproduce the "great order" of the cosmos on earth. Marcus Aurelius, the philosopher-emperor who died in Vienna in 180 A.D., saw "all men [as] partners in a universal empire." The *Pax Romana,* here expressed in its exalted, Stoic form, was for some two thousand years prototype and pattern of a *closed* peace. Within its walls and frontiers a wide variety of peoples and groups lived under one law. Peace was for one's legal fellows within one's own system, one's own walls, one's own home. Peace was not for outsiders, for the "barbarian," the foreigner, the ignorant, the enemy. The equation was complete: "foreigner" = "enemy" (and even "wretch," because living in another country, he must be wretched!).

Other major and historically influential concepts of the closed peace are the Pax Hispanica, the Pax Americana, and the Pax Sovietica. The Spanish Peace meant *"paz entre cristianos y guerra contro los infieles"*—peace among Christians and permanent war on the unbeliever.

The Pax Americana is a name critics gave to the U.S. role in the Cold War and especially in Vietnam, as America sought to impose world "peace" on its own terms. But in fact the country has played

Satan" (the term Calvin used to condemn his "apostates" in Poland, Transylvania, and throughout Europe) and the "satellites" of Moscow. As early as 1945—i.e. long before Vietnam—Reinhold Niebuhr criticized this American concept of world peace, which in its historical heyday was backed by a genuine and powerful faith: the vocation of the Pax Americana was to bestow on all the peoples of this earth the blessings of democracy, freedom, and progress in the form of the "American way of life."

The Pax Sovietica was solemnly presented by Stalin and Brezhnev as the pacification of the peoples of its peace zone by means of schools, colleges, administrations, police, and armies; those peoples as well as each individual member of those

"freedom," and "progress." Again, very much an armed peace.

*The struggle today is gradually to overcome all closed peace systems by a great breakthrough to an open peace that will really have to do with people, making it possible for them to live, think, love, manage their economic affairs, and generally behave each in his own particular way.*

The great prophets of this kind of open peace in Asia were Buddha, Lao-tse, Mo Ti, the Emperor Ashoka—whose doctrines were given new life, two thousand years later, by Mahatma Gandhi in India. European prophets of peace

The Family of Man

policeman—and played God—for much of its history. The Pax Americana: the "children of light" at war with the "children of darkness," the latter being, in the seventeenth and eighteenth centuries, the "Papists," and subsequently the "Commies." The children of light fight the "satellites of

peoples was committed, as a result, to fight for that peace both at home and abroad. World peace grows as the territory covered by the Pax Sovietica grows.

Its peace mission involves making "friends for peace" who accept the language of that peace with its specific concepts of "democracy,"

include Erasmus of Rotterdam, the Spaniard Francisco de Vitoria, and the Dutchman Grotius, as well as the Christian non-conformists, men like Sebastian Franck in Germany (who inveighed against "bloodthirsty theologians" as ideologists of the "just war"), the Anabaptists, the Bohemian Brethren, the Brownists, and the Mennonites and the Sozzinians.

The heirs to these persecuted "brethren"—the first to give historical substance to the fraternity idea—were the Quakers. From 1660 onward they survived all persecutions and for a long time filled a lonely role on this earth—as the most daring advance units in the struggle for world peace. It was in 1660 that George Fox and eleven other Quakers published their famous declaration against war; all wars between men were civil wars, they said. The idea was taken further in Robert Barclay's *Apology* of 1676; its twin bases were the Sermon on the Mount and the guidance of the "Inner Light" that projects God into every *open* soul.

AND THE LORD GOD
COMMANDED THE MAN, SAYING,
OF EVERY TREE OF THE GARDEN
THOU MAYEST FREELY EAT:
BUT OF THE TREE OF THE KNOWLEDGE
OF GOOD AND EVIL,
THOU SHALT NOT EAT OF IT:
FOR IN THE DAY
THAT THOU EATEST THEREOF
THOU SHALT SURELY DIE.

Genesis 2: 16–17

Penn created a model for an open peace in his treaty with the Indians, made when founding his colony of Pennsylvania and enabling him to set up the first unarmed government on earth: "We meet on the broad pathway of good faith and good will. No advantage shall be taken on either side, but *all shall be openness and love*. We are all one flesh and blood." Penn paid the Indians for the land settled and ran the colony with the aid of an arbitration court of six colonists and six Indians. His treaty and his concept of peace came up again on the agenda of the Frankfurt Peace Conference of 1850—and the 1941 Atlantic Charter echoed Penn's words in speaking of the need to free men from oppression, fear, and want.

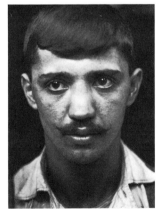

The link with the thought of Sebastian Franck and other modern pacifists was made in Holland by William Penn. Son of the great war hero Admiral Sir William Penn, young William found his true spiritual home with the Mennonites in his mother's Holland. In 1693 he published his *Essay towards the Present and Future Peace of Europe*.

An international court of ninety representatives, including Turks and Muscovites (ten years earlier, in 1683, the Turks had been at the gates of Vienna!), was to meet yearly and arbitrate on all international questions.

Whose vocation is it to make peace? Who can bestow peace? Every man? Every woman? Greek drama (Clytemnestra, Antigone, and their male counterparts) and the tragedies of our history show that it is often not easy. War grows out of civil war; war *is* civil war, a vendetta. A family feud.

The first great step toward containing war is to proscribe it within the family, the clan, the tribe, the nation. For a thousand years and more Europe was the scene of almost incessant clan warfare, until princes, kings, and emperors succeeded—by force—in depriving their nobles of the right to wage private wars. Our custom of shaking hands is a lasting reminder of the relinquishment of this right: the man who offers another his right hand foregoes the right to use it to reach for sword, dagger, or pistol.

To make peace, to bestow peace—this has been the achievement of the great lawgivers of mankind. Peace as a law for man (Hammurabi), peace as a covenant with God (Moses), peace as an inward state of the soul—that home, as Lao-tse, Confucius, Buddha, Plato, and all the great sages know, of the deepest discord.

To legislate is to create a time and place for law where there were no time and no place for law before. To bring peace where there was no peace.

*"God himself is law," said medieval Europe. Man's divinity emerges in his ability to create law, to set up legal systems, and to use laws, covenants, and "holy alliances" to bring peace.*

They are towering individuals, persons of "historical stature," these men who first prescribe laws. Their codes, legal systems, and verdicts incorporate in condensed form what actual people, actual classes of society fought for and won as their right in terms of concrete freedoms centuries, even millennia before.

The freedom of European man has grown painfully out of a thousand-year struggle for what at first were quite specific liberties: for the "freedom of the Church," which popes and monks sought to wrest from secular rulers, for the freedoms of cities, of "estates," of certain classes of privileged people. Later on, in the eighteenth, nineteenth, and twentieth centuries, freedoms for the underprivileged found their way onto the agendas of gatherings of the Family of Man: freedoms for women, for workers, for slaves, for children, for "colored" people. We in the last third of the twentieth century are deeply involved in this great struggle for law, for one legal system for mankind, for freedom as the freedom of all, for human rights for all, a struggle whose course up to now we can trace through the documents assembled in this volume.

The core of each of these major utterances of mankind is a challenge that says, "Bring me about!" These words cry out to be made flesh; they seek reincarnation —reiterated incarnation in each new generation, including the generations that are about to enter the third millennium of our era. For they are already born, the men and women who will bear the burden and wear the privilege of being human in the twenty-first century.

*In this sense each of these "words of man" is open—wide open. Each is an invitation, a summons here and now to carry the human cause a stage further. And to resist the daily temptations to drown the child of man in a bath of blood.*

Skeptics, cynics, self-haters—who attribute little good to man because they dare do little good themselves—may say: Well, what have they achieved, these mighty "words of man"? Do we not still live together in enmity like a pack of wolves, setting upon one another in our hunger and greed?

Yes: the possibility that we will set upon our fellows is still there; we are all still cavemen, with a caveman's instincts, and will remain so as long as we remain men.

And no: for as the heirs of Hammurabi and Moses, of Solon and Plato, we are the heirs to *one* civilization, one universal culture. We build orthogonal cities using the proportions of Babylon; we reckon our days with a seven-day calendar; we possess *one* common language, *one* alphabet—in which weights and measures, rights, freedoms, and orders are laid down for us to implement. We can do it. We can erect laws, admit rights; we are capable, we sons and daughters of the human race, of *bringing peace*. Not only is our future wide open but we have a powerful past behind us—as these documents bear compelling witness.

Friedrich Heer's reflections are based on the insights of a cultural historian who is deeply committed to a universal, open humanism. He sees the history of the human race as a continuing drama of emergent humanity—what he calls *Menschwerdung* or "becoming man." He stands for the conviction that human self-realization, "man's becoming man," is an ongoing process. This "optimism" is not as far as he is concerned the "blind faith" that doubting and despairing pessimists charge him with, but a sober recognition gained from his study of the wealth of documents that mark the different stages of man's historical development.

A number—necessarily a limited number—of those documents are reproduced in this book, together with brief commentaries. These documents, it can safely be said, represent landmarks in human history. Our selection is anything but dogmatic in character.

*Our intention throughout has been to offer the reader documents that altered, broadened, or intensified contemporary awareness at the time they came into being and so constituted lodestars, as it were, leading man into a new era of his history.*

We must be clear in our minds from the outset that although each of the documents that have come down to us was the product of a particular historical moment and most were the work of people who, intellectually speaking, stood head and shoulders above their contemporaries, they were preceded by intellectual processes and by very varied and complex individual and social experiences that then "condensed" in the form of the document concerned. Inevitably we who come after are inclined to see such a document as the "birth certificate" of a new age without going into too much detail about how the pregnancy came about, what forces influenced it, how long a maturation period was required, and what vicissitudes and reverses attended it. Understandably documents with a primarily political content are relatively easy for us to judge and evaluate in terms of their historical impact. This does not mean, however, that the purely political documents in our selection are not susceptible of a wide variety of interpretations.

Probably every reader will miss certain documents that from one or another point of view he quite rightly considers to be historically significant. Let him bear in mind that on the one hand any selection is inevitably governed by subjective criteria and that on the other hand—in view of the sheer mass of material available—economic imperatives have played their part. Nevertheless, all the political documents included were or are heavy with historical consequences of one sort or another. Documents that evince great political humanism but can hardly be described as universally influential have been deliberately omitted: for example the law abolishing serfdom passed by Czar Alexander III in 1861, or the Edict of Nantes—a document of enormous importance for France—that Henri IV signed on 30 April 1598. Some readers will doubtless be surprised to find no political document included from classical Rome, although Rome, above all the Rome of the Caesars, continues to shape Europe to this day, our legal systems particularly, not least through the medium of the nineteenth-century *Code Napoléon,* being still rooted in the Roman *corpus juris.*

There is, however, no single political document in which the political ideas of ancient Rome and its concept of empire are expressed with the brevity and intensity with which, for example, the Roman approach to life comes across in the *Odes* of Horace or in Virgil's *Georgics* and *Eclogues.* And incidentally "political" England, Magna Charta notwithstanding, nowhere finds such vivid expression as in Shakespeare's history plays. Where in the German-speaking world can we find a political document still alive in men's minds today that speaks authoritatively of the universality of the medieval Holy Roman Empire of the German nation? That universality is conveyed far more impressively by the French and German poets of the Middle Ages than by any dusty political document. Russia too has influenced the world not only by political documents but by the works of her great writers, and the American outlook on life, voiced in truly magnificent political documents, finds a fascinating parallel in Walt Whitman's *Leaves of Grass.*

*But if opinions can sincerely differ with regard to the significance of political documents, how much harder it is to evaluate documents from the fields of philosophy, religion, and intellectual history—fields that often overlap, not to say intermingle.*

This is true, for example, of Jesus of Nazareth's Sermon on the Mount, a literary and religious document advancing a "constitution for mankind" that in its radicalism, both moral and humane, has been surpassed by no other declaration of human rights since the day it was committed to writing. To speak of an immediate influence in social or political terms would be a mockery. Yet for nearly two thousand years Christians have been confronted with this statement, and who can say how great or small an indirect effect it has had on the formation of Christian society and above all on individual Christians, and how powerfully it has influenced the current of Christian thought?

The nearer we draw to modern times, the harder it becomes to select and evaluate those documents that have intellectually and politically shaped our awareness and the reality of our lives—bearing in mind, of course, the fact that for at least the last five hundred years the "common consciousness" of mankind has been a steadily fragmenting entity, so that one is today entitled to ask whether such a thing still in fact exists in any way that can be compared to medieval man's uniform understanding of the "cosmos." Even so theoretically straightforward a phenomenon as "democracy" is in practice still highly controversial; indeed the different interpretations of democracy are in some cases mutually exclusive. Historically the beginning of modern times is accepted to have been the Renaissance. Its great achievement, namely to have turned its face to nature and glimpsed and grasped the autonomy of the human person, is not to be found in any one comprehensive document.

*As to when in the dawning Renaissance nature was first thought of as an intrinsic value and man first seen as being answerable only to his conscience, one must surely point to Francis of Assisi.*

It was Jacob Burckhardt in *The Civilization of the Renaissance* who first recognized the unique novelty of the view of nature expressed in the "Canticle of the Sun." And it was in Francis of Assisi's will that liberty of conscience as against the claims of the Church received its first unequivocal manifestation. Thus in the evening of the Middle Ages, which when Francis wrote his hymn was bathing all Europe in a golden glow in the person of the young Hohenstaufen emperor Frederick II, and was about to give way to the Renaissance dawn, the "man responsible to himself," the man who during the Renaissance was to mount the stage of history and expand his world in every direction, was already "programmed."

Another point to bear in mind is that occasionally thinkers have produced works whose substance has not penetrated public awareness for centuries after they were written; the ideas and impulses contained in them, however, have enjoyed a certain "underground" influence without people being aware of where they originally came from. Of the wealth of possible examples we have chosen a document—*De Pace Fidei (Concerning Concord in Religious Belief)*, written by Nicholas of Cusa in 1453—the spiritual and political topicality of which is obvious today. Nicholas is difficult to place as a philosopher and theologian and his work was for centuries passed over in silence. Today progressive modern theologians tend to see him as their legitimate forbear, and modern philosophy is engaged in a stimulating discussion of his definition of God as *coincidentia oppositorum,* embodying the clash of opposites. For this reason we felt justified in including this controversial document concerning peace within the world religions, based on his conception of God. Like the rest of the documents collected in this book, it is one of those statements that have served to accelerate the intellectual, religious, and political forces that still color our outlook and form part of the generally accepted inheritance of our world and of our age, regardless of how widely they may diverge from one another or how divergently they may be interpreted.

DETRAHS DESCELERI
BAC TIONIBUS BUS TORMENTO
LIBER I LIBER II

I. TIT. De ecclesiis eticis rebus.
II. TIT. De donationibus generalibus.
III. TIT. De pagenosum donationibus.
IIII. TIT. De comutationibus et uendicationibus.
V. TIT. De pigneribus et debitis.
VI. TIT. De commendatis et comodo ducatis.
VIII. TIT. De liberationibus et libertatis.

I. TIT. De accusationibus criminosorum.
II. TIT. De maleficiis et consulentibus eisudeq beneficiis.
III. TIT. De queunenantibus patrusomitiu.
IIII. TIT. De concauimelio et uulnere et debilitacione hominu.
V. Ticulus detecede et mostre hominu.

# The Code of Hammurabi

The Code of Hammurabi, one of the earliest collections of laws we have, is not a manuscript in any modern sense, but rather a text carved on a stele or upright slab of diorite (a hard, greenish-black stone) measuring 2.25 meters in height. The stele was found beneath the acropolis of Susa, a ruined city in western Iran that was once the capital of the Persian kings, by a French expedition under Jean de Morgan in the winter of 1901–1902; it was taken back to France and is now preserved in the Louvre Museum. Written in Akkadian, a Semitic language that died out long before the Christian era, the Code comprises 282 paragraphs. At the top of the stele is a portrait of Hammurabi, shown holding the tokens of salvation, the staff and ring, while the sun god dictates the law to him. Hammurabi had the stele set up in a temple where everybody could see and refer to it. The engraved text begins with a preamble explaining the purpose of the Code:
"Before this portrait let every man

*Right:* Portrait of Hammurabi. It is thought the artist succeeded brilliantly in capturing the slightly resigned expression on the old king's face.

The text of Hammurabi's Code *(opposite)* is carved on a stone pillar or stele.

*Below:* Map of Hammurabi's kingdom.

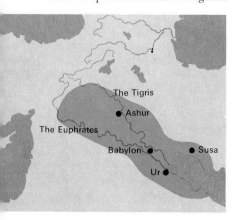

O Marduk, exalted Lord, keep me by your princely
　　word
Healthy and whole, that I may extol your divinity.
Heed and fulfill my desire, whatever I may wish for.
Fill my mouth with truth and my heart with gen-
　　erosity
That courtier and gateman may alike speak well of me.
My tutelary god shall walk beside me on my right
And my goddess shall take up her place here upon
　　my left.
May the god of my salvation be ever at my side.

A poet put these words into Hammurabi's mouth.

who has a legal dispute come forward, read this text, and heed its precious words. The stone tablet will enlighten him in his trouble, and thus may he find justice and breathe easier in his heart, speaking these words: 'Hammurabi is a king who cares for his people like a loving father.'"
Following the fall of the Old Babylonian Empire the stele was seized as booty by a victorious Elamite king around 1000 B.C. and dragged off to his court at Susa.

## KING OF JUSTICE

The great king Hammurabi, sixth ruler of the First Dynasty of Old Babylon, was born probably around 1750 B.C.; he reigned—this we know for certain—for forty-three years and died probably in 1686 B.C. These dates are based on the latest research.
It was not until the nineteenth century that Akkadian was deciphered; in our own century archaeologists are continually coming across material from the time of Hammurabi, particularly inscriptions on temple ruins, votive inscriptions, building inscriptions, and a large number of Hammurabi's letters to his governors and officials. All these finds together give us a historically reliable picture of a figure once distorted by legend. Hammurabi was a clear-thinking statesman, a calculating politician, an extremely talented strategist, and a soldier who combined courage with shrewd good sense. He was a pragmatist in every way, even his visions of greatness retaining a sense of proportion. These gifts enabled him to unite the mass of warring peoples and kingdoms that was Babylonia and weld it into a civilized and well-administered political entity: the Old Babylonian Empire, which stretched from the Persian Gulf up

*Right:* The Babylonian sun god Shamash, who because he sees everything that goes on during the day is also the god of justice and guardian of the law.

the Tigris and Euphrates rivers almost to the Mediterranean. Hammurabi's period must be thought of as one of high civilization, a civilization that grew organically out of the third millennium B.C. to reach full flower in the great king's reign. The principal witness to that civilization is the Code of Hammurabi, which shows us that the Old Babylonian Empire was in a very modern sense founded on justice and the rule of law. It seems likely that the Code in fact constitutes a *reform,* defining, modifying, or adding to a traditional body of legislation. Interestingly it is a purely secular, socially oriented document that leaves religious law entirely out of account. Hammurabi aimed at an improvement, clarification, and enrichment of the law of his day. He sought to safeguard small farmers, day laborers, and craftsmen against debt and exploitation and generally to protect the weaker members of society. Being an "imperial law" it meant—not of course for the three classes of "citizens," "semi-freedmen," and "slaves" but for the members of the various subject peoples and also for all "foreigners"—complete *equality before the law.* And paragraph 23, for example, is sensational even by modern standards, committing local authorities to compensating the burgled "for whatever was lost . . . if the brigand be not captured." Any kind of legal self-help is of course proscribed; only the royal judge can and may give the injured party satisfaction. A notable feature of the Code and one that was far in advance of its time is the way in which it protects women. On the other hand, the old Semitic talion of "an eye for an eye, a tooth for a tooth" still makes its presence felt in passages dealing with murder and bodily harm. Hammurabi's sense of mission comes out clearly in the epilogue to his Code:

"I, Hammurabi,
who was a perfect king
to the downtrodden people
entrusted to me by the god Enlil,
I who was, by Marduk's order,
their shepherd,
have never tarried, never rested.
I gave the people beautiful places,
kept all pressing needs far away,
and made their lives easier.
With the mighty weapons
given me by the gods
Zababa and Ishtar,
with the wisdom granted me by Ea,
with the powers I hold from Marduk,
I wiped out enemies on every side,
put an end to wars,
brought prosperity to our land,
allowed men to live in peace and let
no one fall upon them or harass them.
I was called by the great gods,
wherefore I became the good shepherd
whose staff is straight.
My righteous shadow has stretched
across my city, I have gathered
Sumer and Akkada in my arms,
that they might thrive
under my protection.
I shield them in my peace
and protect them in my wisdom.
That the strong
might not oppress the weak,
that the widow and orphan
might receive their due,
here in Babylon . . .
have I inscribed my precious words
on a memorial stone
and erected my statue
as King of Justice."

## The Laws

*The text consists of 282 paragraphs, which for practical purposes can be arranged as follows.*

### § 1–5
### Contempt of Court

*False accusation is severely punished:*

### § 1

If a man bring an accusation against a man, and charge him with a capital crime, but cannot prove it, he, the accuser, shall be put to death.

*Giving false testimony in a murder trial is also punishable by death (§ 3). In a civil case, the person giving the false testimony must suffer the penalty of the case (§ 4). A unique provision and one that is highly controversial as regards its legal interpretation is the celebrated paragraph 5, which prescribes that a judge who, having pronounced his sentence, subsequently declares it to be null and void must pay the claim at issue in the case twelve times over.*

### § 6–25
### Crimes against Property

*Paragraphs 6–8 lay down the penalties for temple and palace theft. In principle these are punishable by death:*

### § 6

If a man steal the property of a god (temple) or palace, that man shall be put to death; and he who receives from his hand the stolen property shall also be put to death.

*Paragraphs 9–13 deal with theft against private persons. The penalties are extremely severe: A thief is put to death even when he has returned what he had stolen. Theft is treated as "breach of the peace."*

*Paragraphs 14–20 lay down the penalties for those who abduct or steal slaves, paragraph 14 carrying the death penalty for a special case:*

### § 14

If a man steal a man's son, who is a minor, he shall be put to death.

*Paragraphs 21–25 deal with breaking and entering and burglary. Burglars and housebreakers are put to death without exception. Paragraph 23 is a famous one, laying down that, in the event a burglar is not caught, the authorities must compensate the burgled for everything taken from him.*

### § 26–126
### Civil Law

*Paragraphs 26–41 contain provisions regarding military personnel who have been enfeoffed with crown property and are in consequence obliged to answer the king's summons.*

*Paragraphs 42–47 govern the leasing of fields. Tenants are bound by law to cultivate the fields they hold under lease.*

*Paragraphs 48–52 are about mortgaging harvests. The following provision is instructive:*

### § 48

If a man owe a debt and Adad inundate his field and carry away the produce, or, through lack of water, grain have not grown in the field, in that year he shall not make any return of grain to the creditor, he shall alter his contract-tablet and he shall not pay the interest for that entire year.

*Paragraphs 53–56 are concerned with flood damage as a result of careless maintenance of dykes. Under Hammurabi the whole country was covered with a network of canals to irrigate pasture and arable land. That network could only function as long as the dykes remained intact. Hence these paragraphs:*

An extract from the Code of Hammurabi. The text, which is carved in the polished stone, is in Akkadian cuneiform. Cuneiform writing evolved from an originally pictographic script that had as early as *c.* 2000 B.C. become simplified into a system of vertical, horizontal, and oblique strokes or wedges (L. *cuneus*).

### § 53

If a man neglect to strengthen his dyke and do not strengthen it, and a break be made in his dyke and the water carry away the farm-land, the man in whose dyke the break has been made shall restore the grain which he has damaged.

### § 54

If he be not able to restore the grain, they shall sell him and his goods, and the farmers whose grain the water has carried away shall share the results of the sale.

*Paragraphs 57 and 58 protect landowners against unauthorized feeding down of their fields.*

*Paragraphs 59–65 protect orchard owners. Unlawful damaging of trees carries a stiff penalty:*

### § 59

If a man cut down a tree in a man's orchard, without the consent of the owner of the orchard, he shall pay one-half mana of silver.

*The remaining paragraphs in this section govern the legal relations between the orchard owner and his managing gardener. The main point at issue is the manager's liability to pay damages in the event of his failing or only partially succeeding in meeting his contractual obligations. For example:*

### § 65

If the gardener do not properly manage the orchard and he diminish the produce, the gardener shall measure out the produce of the orchard on the basis of the adjacent orchards.

*Paragraphs 66–99 have been chiseled away from the stele.*

*Paragraphs 100–107 are concerned with the relations between merchant and agent. An interesting paragraph from the religious and psychological points of view is this one:*

### § 103

If, when he goes on a journey, an enemy rob him of whatever he was carrying, the agent shall take an oath in the name of god and go free.

*Paragraphs 108–111 deal with women saloonkeepers and are concerned among other things to protect travelers against exorbitant wine prices. Evidently certain saloons were popular meeting places for "subversive elements," and one paragraph here has a distinctly modern ring:*

### § 109

If outlaws collect in the house of a wine-seller, and she do not arrest these outlaws and bring them to the palace, that wine-seller shall be put to death.

*Paragraph 110 is interesting in that it forbids priestesses to open a saloon or even enter one for the purposes of consuming wine.*

*Paragraph 112 is to do with misappropriation. Anyone failing to deliver to their destination goods with whose transport he has been charged must pay the owner the value of the misappropriated goods five times over.*

*Paragraphs 113–119 contain provisions regarding distraint and imprisonment for debt. Interestingly, self-help is expressly forbidden:*

### § 113

If a man hold a debt of grain or money against a man, and if he take grain without the consent of the owner from the heap or the granary, they shall call that man to account for taking grain without the consent of the owner from the heap or the granary, and he shall return as much grain as he took, and he shall forfeit all that he has lent, whatever it be.

*Not only goods can be distrained; so can relatives and slaves. But after three years' service in the distrainer's house, in the fourth year they must be set free.*

*Paragraphs 120–126 lay down rules governing objects delivered into safekeeping.*

### § 127–193
### THE FAMILY

*Paragraphs 127–132 relate to marriage. Hammurabi's desire to extend the law to all spheres of life is reflected in paragraph 128, which declares that a marriage is only valid when a marriage contract has been concluded. There is a clear intention of protecting women:*

### § 127

If a man point the finger at a priestess or the wife of another and cannot justify it, they shall drag that man before the judges and they shall brand his forehead.

*Paragraph 129 threatens adulterous couples with the death penalty. If, however, the husband forgives his wife, the king pardons the adulterer too. But a man who rapes a woman is put to death. The following paragraph strikes a very humane note:*

### § 131

If a man accuse his wife and she has not been taken in lying with another man, she shall take an oath in the name of god and she shall return to her house.

*Paragraphs 133–136 allow wives of missing persons to marry again. If a missing person comes back, however, the woman must return to her first husband, any children born in the meantime remaining with their father.*

*Paragraphs 137–143 govern divorce procedure. Only the man has the right to demand a divorce. If a woman is divorced through no fault of her own, she receives her dowry back; she is also granted the income from field, orchard, and other property with which to bring up her children. If the court finds a woman guilty of a matrimonial offense, her husband is entitled to divorce her without becoming liable to return her dowry; alternatively he* can keep her in the house as a slave. If a woman says she hates her husband and can advance valid reasons for doing so, she may return to her father's house and the husband must repay her dowry. The marriage is not formally dissolved, however, and the woman may not remarry.

*Paragraphs 144–147 contain provisions regarding childless wives. The husband of a childless wife is allowed to take a concubine:*

## § 145

If a man take a wife and she do not present him with children and he set his face to take a concubine, that man may take a concubine and bring her into his house. That concubine shall not rank with his wife.

*To prevent her husband from taking a concubine the childless wife can give him a maidservant. If the maidservant bears him children, he may no longer take a concubine.*

*Paragraphs 148 and 149 protect the sick wife:*

## § 148

If a man take a wife and she become afflicted with disease, and if he set his face to take another, he may. His wife, who is afflicted with disease, he shall not put away. She shall remain in the house which he has built and he shall maintain her as long as she lives.

## § 149

If that woman do not elect to remain in her husband's house, he shall make good to her the dowry which she brought from her father's house and she may go.

*Paragraph 150 allows the husband to give his wife gifts which she is then free to bequeath as she wishes.*

*Paragraphs 151 and 152 deal with the question of debts contracted before marriage. Both parties to a marriage are jointly liable for debts contracted during and prior to their marriage. They may,*

however, contractually exonerate each other from liability for premarital debts.

*Paragraphs 153–158 lay down penalties for offenses against morality. Since only husbands had the right to divorce, the wife might be tempted to gain her freedom by engineering her husband's death:*

## § 153

If a woman bring about the death of her husband for the sake of another man, they shall impale her.

*The death penalty also awaits any man who has sexual intercourse with his son's wife. The father who violates his daughter is banished from the city, but sexual intercourse between mother and son carries the death penalty for both.*

*Paragraphs 159–161 concern the annulment of betrothal. Paragraph 161 notably forbids a girl to marry the man who by defaming her betrothed provokes her father to cancel the match.*

*Paragraphs 162–164 govern inheritance following the wife's death, paragraphs 165–177 that following the death of the husband. The intention is unmistakably to divide the inheritance equally among the sons. There is no mention in these paragraphs of the capacity of daughters to inherit. A son who commits an offense against his father may be disinherited.*

*Paragraphs 178–184 deal with the right of inheritance of daughters who have entered the service of the temple. They inherit one third of a son's share.*

*Paragraphs 185–193 regulate the legal position of foster children, that is, children who could not be brought up by their own parents. Hammurabi's Code evinces a most humane concern for the welfare of such children.*

## § 194–214
## PENALTIES ON THE LEX TALIONIS PRINCIPLE

*This is the principle of exacting like compensation, the best-known formulation of*

which is the Old Testament's "an eye for an eye, a tooth for a tooth." Various paragraphs of the Code are unequivocally talionic:

## § 195

If a son strike his father, they shall cut off his fingers.

## § 196

If a man destroy the eye of another man, they shall destroy his eye.

## § 197

If one break a man's bone, they shall break his bone.

## § 200

If a man knock out a tooth of a man of his own rank, they shall knock out his tooth.

*The protection of pregnant women too is in part talionic:*

## § 209

If a man strike a man's daughter and bring about a miscarriage, the guilty one shall pay ten shekels of silver for her miscarriage.

## § 210

If that woman die, they shall put his daughter to death.

## § 215–227
## MEDICINE

*Doctors' fees are set out in detail in this section, with the poor having to pay less than the well-to-do:*

## § 215

If a physician operate on a man for a severe wound or make a severe wound upon a man with a bronze lancet and save the man's life; or if he open an abscess (in the eye) of a man with a bronze lancet and save that man's eye, he shall receive ten shekels of silver as his fee.

A relief at the top of the stele bearing the Code of Hammurabi shows the god Shamash transmitting the law to the king.

§ 216

If he be a freeman, he (the physician) shall receive five shekels.

*But the medical profession in Hammurabi's day carried risks that our own doctors are not exposed to:*

§ 218

If a physician operate on a man for a severe wound with a bronze lancet and cause the man's death; or open an abscess (in the eye) of a man with a bronze lancet and destroy the man's eye, they shall cut off his fingers.

*The physician may also become liable to pay damages. If for example a slave dies after an operation, he must provide the deceased's master with a new slave. The veterinary surgeon is also partially liable for any unfortunate consequences of his interventions:*

§ 225

If he operate on an ox or an ass for a severe wound and cause its death, he shall give the owner of the ox or ass one fourth its value.

§ 228–240
BUILDING

*Paragraphs 228–233 commit builders to the most extreme diligence:*

§ 229

If a builder build a house for a man and do not make its construction firm, and the house which he has built collapse and cause the death of the owner of the house, that builder shall be put to death.

*Builders' fees are laid down by law, as is their liability to pay damages in the event of structural faults occurring as a result of negligence.*

*Paragraphs 234–240 relate to shipbuilding and shipping. Essentially the same demands are made on the shipbuilder as on the housebuilder. If for example in the*

*year of its manufacture a ship puts to sea and is found to be unseaworthy, the shipbuilder must dismantle and rebuild it at his own expense.*

§ 241–271
AGRICULTURE

*Many of the paragraphs in this section set out the sums to be paid in cash or grain for services of an agricultural nature. A progressive measure is the one whereby the hirer of an animal or the shepherd cannot be held responsible for damage brought about by acts of God:*

§ 244

If a man hire an ox or an ass and a lion kill it in the field, it is the owner's affair.

*Acts of God also include bulls running amok in the street:*

§ 250

If a bull, when passing through the street, gore a man and bring about his death, this case has no penalty.

*Things are different, however, when a bull is known to be aggressive. The owner of such an animal is obliged to blunt its horns and hamper its movements. If he fails to do so and there is an accident, he is partially liable.*

§ 272–277
WAGE RATES FOR LABORERS
AND ARTISANS

*The purpose of these legally binding wage rates is to protect the small and economically dependent from exploitation by the economically powerful. They can be regarded as prototypes of our modern collective labor agreements.*

§ 278–282
SLAVERY

*It is clear from these five paragraphs that, as far as the law was concerned, slaves were chattels rather than people.*

## A LEGACY: THE CONSTITUTIONAL STATE

*Hammurabi's empire collapsed soon after his death. The Kassites, pushing down from the mountains of the northeast (what is now western Iran), and later the Hittites from northeast Asia Minor overran it and set up new states. But the peoples who colonized the Old Babylonian Empire themselves succumbed to the splendor of Babylonian culture, the magnetism of its center, the city of Babylon (literally "Gate of God"), and the efficacy of Hammurabi's reforming Code. How exactly the heritage of Babylonian law affected the Middle East and later, directly or indirectly, the Greeks and Romans is something we do not know in detail. It is surprising, for example, that Mosaic law shows hardly any Babylonian influence. What is important, however, is the prototype, for which we have to thank Hammurabi, of a state that, though anchored in God, bases its social organization unreservedly on a code of law—leaving no scope for tyranny on the part of those who wield political power. Hammurabi's ideal of a thoroughly constitutional state that would be not only a formal but also a social reality has lost none of its relevance today. In fact today more than ever the fuller realization of that ideal is the active concern of all who seek to bring law and, through law, justice increasingly into line with Hammurabi's great vision.*

# The Ten Commandments

The Ten Commandments form the basis of the collection of laws recorded in the Pentateuch or "Five Books of Moses." This Mosaic legislation, which Jews call the Torah (and every synagogue has its Torah scroll), to this day constitutes the religious bond uniting the world of Jewry. Devotion to the Torah and literal observance of its prescriptions and commandments are, as Judaism sees it, what make the Jew (or the convert) specifically Jewish.

The binding text of the Ten Commandments as far as Judaism is concerned can be found both in the Second Book of Moses, called Exodus, 20: 2–17, and in the Fifth Book of Moses, or Deuteronomy, 5: 6–21.

It was Early Christian theologians who gave the Ten Commandments the name "Decalogue," a Greek expression meaning literally "ten words." The historical background to the use of this term was an ancient Jewish tradition according to which the Ten Commandments had already existed in a primitive form, the text of which was then expanded on the occasion of the proclamation of the Mosaic

law on Mount Sinai. The version of the Ten Commandments propagated by the Christian churches from the very earliest days was this shorter, primitive form:

I am the Lord thy God:

1. Thou shalt have none other gods.
2. Thou shalt not make thee idols.
3. Thou shalt not take the name of the Lord thy God in vain.
4. Remember to keep the Sabbath day holy.
5. Thou shalt honor thy father and mother.
6. Thou shalt not kill.
7. Thou shalt not commit adultery.
8. Thou shalt not steal.
9. Thou shalt not bear false witness.
10. Thou shalt not covet thy neighbor's house.

Nowhere in the Bible are the Ten Commandments numbered. The numbering we use today goes back to the Hellenistic Jewish philosopher Philo, who lived in Alexandria between about 25 B.C. and 50 A.D.

## SLOW OF SPEECH AND TONGUE

Moses ("God . . . begot him," as the name means in conjunction with that of a god) is traditionally believed to have led the Israelites out of Egypt to the borders of the Promised Land, which he himself was permitted only to view from a distance. For early Judaism as well as for the New Testament tradition, Moses was *the* great mediator between God and his people, chosen by Yahweh to be their law-giver, judge, and deliverer.

We know little about the historical Moses. Martin Buber suggested that "historical legend" has heightened this enormously impressive figure; the nostalgia of centuries,

Mount Sinai *(above)*. A romantic lithograph from J.R. Wellsted's *Travels in Arabia,* published in London in 1838.

Moses. The statue by Michelangelo that adorns the tomb of Pope Julius II in the church of S.Pietro in Vincoli, Rome.

76
hic filii isrl dicunt
ad moysen omnia que
precepit dns faciemus
hic ubi offe
ret holocausta
TENTORIA FILIORUM
ISRL
IOSUE
MOYSES
NADAB
ABIU

Hebrew manuscript of the Pentateuch *(right)*. A sixteenth-century parchment scroll, 40 meters long, in the Papal Bible Institute, Rome.

indeed of millennia, has also "processed" him to produce the Moses of Michelangelo and of Sigmund Freud. The exodus from Egypt across the Red Sea and through the desert is usually dated between 1400 and 1200 B.C. Historically speaking, the tribes or clans that were to become Israel (the word means "striver with God") migrated to the Holy Land individually rather than under common leadership.

Moses is a man in the grip of the most explosive tensions. Hence his lack of skill in speech: "Oh, my Lord, I am not eloquent, either heretofore or since thou hast spoken to thy servant; but I am slow of speech and tongue. . . . Send, I pray, some other person."

The background to the Ten Commandments is a covenant between Yahweh and Israel, a protection agreement under which Yahweh is the giver and Israel the receiver. The essence of the Sinai covenant is the formula: "I will be your God, and you shall be my people." Covenant and law are inseparable. The purpose of the law is to prevent Israel from dropping out of the covenant by breaking faith with God.

Exceptional importance, particularly in view of the three-thousand-year history of the Jewish people, attaches to the first commandment. God is the Lord who has led his people out of Egypt. "Egypt" as *the* great temptation—"when we sat by the fleshpots"—has stood as a warning throughout the millennia to the Jews of all the host lands in which they have settled and from which they have been driven again in an ongoing exodus. Man must always be moving on in search of his true fatherland and in order to defend his incarnation. In this sense Jews today find that the Soviet Union, for example, is a country they must move out of because in it they are unable to serve their God as he requires.

"Thou shalt have none other gods before me"; "thou shalt not make thee any graven image, or any likeness . . ."; "thou shalt not bow down thyself unto them . . ." —these commandments occurred in a historical situation in which the Jews—not all of them, but a great many—were under great temptation to practice other cults. The "holy city" of Jerusalem itself had happily worshiped other gods for thousands of years before the advent of the Israelites. Yahweh came as a stranger to its pantheon. Solomon's temple contained plenty of heathen idols. Again and again the worship of some new "golden calf," some new "Baal," threatened to seduce Israel.

"Honour thy father and thy mother. . . ." It is no coincidence that in our own century it should have been Jewish depth psychologists who first came up with scientific proof of the fateful significance of this commandment: A young man or woman becomes a complete person, maturing to assume full possession of his intellectual, spiritual, and physical potential, only when he has been able to integrate these twin poles of his personality, male and female, father and mother. "Thou shalt not kill." *The* great promise—and one that mankind has still not made good.

## I AM THE LORD THY GOD

And Moses called all Israel, and said unto them, Hear, O Israel, the statutes and judgments which I speak in your ears this day, that ye may learn them, and keep, and do them.
The Lord our God made a covenant with us in Horeb.
The Lord made not this covenant with our fathers, but with us, even us, who are all of us here alive this day.
The Lord talked with you face to face in the mount out of the midst of the fire,
(I stood between the Lord and you at that time, to shew you the word of the Lord: for ye were afraid by reason of the fire, and went not up into the mount;) saying,

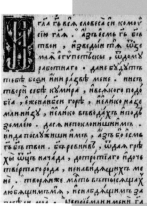

The Bible is one of the books that have been translated into more or less every language, major and minor. Above are four examples, each with the text of the Ten Commandments.
*From left to right:*
Latin, twelfth century.

Old Church Slavonic, 1580.
Arabic, 1622.
Chinese, 1826.

*Far right:* Angry at Israel's apostasy, Moses smashes the tablets of the law. Painting by Rembrandt.

I am the Lord thy God, which brought thee out of the land of Egypt, from the house of bondage. Thou shalt have none other gods before me. Thou shalt not make thee any graven image, or any likeness of any thing that is in heaven above, or that is in the earth beneath, or that is in the waters beneath the earth:

Thou shalt not bow down thyself unto them, nor serve them: for I the Lord thy God am a jealous God, visiting the iniquity of the fathers upon the children unto the third and fourth generation.

And shewing mercy unto thousands of them that love me and keep my commandments. Thou shalt not take the name of the Lord thy God in vain: for the Lord will not hold him guiltless that taketh his name in vain.

Keep the sabbath day to sanctify it, as the Lord thy God hath commanded thee.

Six days thou shalt labour, and do all thy work:

But the seventh day is the sabbath of the Lord thy God: in it thou shalt not do any work, thou, nor thy son, nor thy daughter, nor thy manservant, nor thy maidservant, nor thine ox, nor thine ass, nor any of thy cattle, nor the stranger that is within thy gates; that thy manservant and thy maidservant may rest as well as thou.

And remember that thou was a servant in the land of Egypt, and that the Lord thy God brought thee out thence through a mighty hand and by a stretched out arm: therefore the Lord thy God commanded thee to keep the sabbath day.

Honour thy father and thy mother, as the Lord thy God hath commanded thee; that thy days may be prolonged, and that it may go well with thee, in the land which the Lord thy God giveth thee.

Thou shalt not kill.

Neither shalt thou commit adultery.

Neither shalt thou steal.

Neither shalt thou bear false witness against thy neighbour.

Neither shalt thou desire thy neighbour's wife, neither shalt thou covet thy neighbour's house, his field, or his manservant, or his maidservant, his ox, or his ass, or any thing that is thy neighbour's.

These words the Lord spake unto all your assembly in the mount out of the midst of the fire, of the cloud, and of the thick darkness, with a great voice: and he added no more. And he wrote them in two tables of stone, and delivered them unto me.

And it came to pass, when ye heard the voice out of the midst of the darkness (for the mountain did burn with fire,) that ye came near unto me, even all the heads of your tribes, and your elders;

And ye said, Behold, the Lord our God hath shewed us his glory and his greatness, and we have heard his voice out of the midst of the fire: we have seen this day that God doth talk with man, and he liveth.

Now therefore why should we die? for this great fire will consume us: if we hear the voice of the Lord our God any more, then we shall die.

For who is there of all flesh, that hath heard the voice of the living God speaking out of the midst of the fire, as we have, and lived?

Go thou near, and hear all that the Lord our God shall say: and speak thou unto us all that the Lord our God shall speak unto thee; and we will hear it, and do it.

And the Lord heard the voice of your words, when ye spake unto me; and the Lord said unto me, I have heard the voice of the words of this people. O that there were such an heart in them, that they would fear me, and keep all my commandments always, that it might be well with them, and with their children for ever!

Go say to them, Get you into your tents again. But as for thee, stand thou here by me, and I will speak unto thee all the commandments, and the statutes, and the judgments, which thou shalt teach them, that they may do them in the land which I give them to possess it.

Ye shall observe to do therefore as the Lord your God hath commanded you: ye shall not turn aside to the right hand or to the left.

*Deuteronomy, Chapter 5*

## FROM COMMANDS TO APPEALS

*The Ten Commandments, as we have seen, formed the basis of the Torah. Adopted by Christianity, they came to be acknowledged throughout the world as Judaism's great contribution to human civilization. For at least two thousand years their influence has been strikingly evident in all Western as well as in all Islamic cultures.*

*The poor in their hovels, the oppressed in their prisons and concentration camps, Christian statesmen of all denominations from Thomas More to Dag Hammarskjöld, the Swedish secretary-general of the United Nations who was prepared to give his life in the service of peace and justice—all have found a renewal of their strength in daily confrontation with the Decalogue. Let one witness speak for them all: "This I hope: that we shall judge our personal conduct, our daily decisions, by the Commandments. It is what I have always tried to do myself, in my personal, professional, and*

*political life. Gradually I have come to understand that the unsophisticated language of the Ten Commandments ought not to deter us from reading them in the spirit of the 'Ten Appeals' . . ." (Dr. Gustav Heinemann, President of the German Federal Republic, Bonn, July 1973).*

内之客皆然益六日内神圭造

# The Laws of Solon

Solon (pronounced Sol'on) is the earliest of the Athenian city-state's lawgivers whom we can pin down historically. Around the middle of the seventh century B.C., before Athens had achieved the commanding position it was subsequently to enjoy within the Greek league of states, political and social conditions in the city came to a dangerous head. Political power was entirely in the hands of the aristocratic families, while the mass of the people, oppressed and exploited, saw their debts to the big landowners increasing to intolerable proportions. This explosive situation—and Athens really was on the brink of revolution—was defused by a man who was himself of noble birth but whose intellect and political acumen enabled him to rise above the tensions of the moment and see the solution in legal reform. The text of Solon's legislation, traditionally described as the "first Athenian constitution," has not come down to us. We do, however, have access to the way he thought through a number of poetic fragments, written probably some time after 600 B.C. We know them only as quotations in the works of later Greek authors. Yet they convey a striking impression of the purity and strength of Solon's personality and of his ethical and political thinking, making it easy to understand why he was numbered at a very early stage among the "seven wise men" whose sayings all Greeks knew by heart, some of them even being used as temple inscriptions.

## POET AND LAWGIVER

Solon was born in Athens around 640 B.C. into a family of the higher nobility that traced its descent back through the last king of Athens to the legendary sea god Poseidon. He died in his native city around

Bust in the Farnese Collection, National Museum, Naples.

Nothing to excess.
Flee desire, that fathers aversion.
Do not make friends rashly,
nor rashly abandon friendships once made.
When you have learned to obey,
then you will know how to command.
Give your fellow citizens not the most agreeable
but the best advice.
Be charitable to the members of your family.
Infer the invisible from the visible.

Sayings of "Solon the Wise"

560. He began his career as a merchant, traveling to North Africa, Egypt, and Asia Minor. In 594 he was elected to the archontate, the highest office in the Athenian state, and in view of the tense political situation was invested with special powers. He immediately set about the work of reform. His first measure was the so-called *seisachtheia*, the "shaking off of burdens," an ordinance relieving debts on land and persons. Solon was convinced that there was no sense in talking about "equality"—as is still done today in many formal democracies—unless you first created the economic conditions in which such a thing could exist. His legislative work shows him to have been one of the few statesmen to place the solution of economic problems before the drafting of a constitution.

Politically he replaced the privileges of a hereditary nobility with those of ownership. Citizens were divided into four classes on the basis of income. The wealthy were granted political privileges, but in return they had to do more for the state and the army. To pacify the hereditary nobility Solon retained the old Areopagus or senate of nobles, offsetting it with a new deliberative chamber, the Council of Four Hundred; at the same time he revived the people's assembly, the Ecclesia. This latter body was to play an important part in the development of democracy in Athens. It elected the archon and magistrates, supervised their adminis-

Relief of a horse and rider *(left)* from an Attic tomb stele. Marble, sixth century B.C., Barracco Museum, Rome. Solon's laws made knights the second highest class of citizens.

tration, took decisions in matters of war and peace, and constituted the supreme legislature as well as being responsible for criminal procedure. Theoretically Solon's Ecclesia was *the* power in the state. Even if over the years its actual scope fluctuated somewhat, it proved itself in the long run as the cornerstone on which the Athenian democracy was built.

In 575, after twenty-two years in office, Solon returned to private life. But before he went he made the magistrates swear that they would leave his laws in force and unchanged for the next ten years. With the famous dictum "I grow old, always learning many things," he revisited Egypt and then Cyprus and Lydia before returning to Athens in his last years.

Solon, an open yet cautious man, coupled a sophisticated rationalism and a mature sense of the possible with a fundamentally religious passion for politics. He had something one seldom finds in great states-

A coin (a silver stater) from Solon's time, stamped with a turtle. Found on Aegina, sixth century B.C.

Ruins of the Temple of Hera, Olympia. This holy place in the western Peloponnesus was sacred to Hera and Zeus, the queen of heaven and the father of the gods. It was here that the Olympic

men—a desire to be effective without the wish to dominate. He saw himself as the servant of his state and showed himself in his reforming work and in his life as the first great democrat of Western civilization.

Games were held, in which the tribes and states of Greece dropped their political squabbles for a brief demonstration of pan-Hellenic solidarity.

Splendid children of Memory and Olympian Zeus, give ear, Pierian Muses, unto my prayer. Grant me prosperity at the hands of the Blessed Gods, and good fame ever at the hands of men; make me, I pray You, sweet to my friends and sour unto my foes, to these a man reverend to behold, to those a man terrible. Wealth I desire to possess, but would not have it unrighteously; retribution cometh alway afterward; the riches that be given of the Gods come to a man for to last, from the bottom even to the top, whereas they which be sought by wanton violence come not orderly, but persuaded against their will by unrighteous works—and quickly is Ruin mingled with them; whose beginning is with a little thing as of fire, slight at the first, but in the end a mischief; for the works of man's wanton violence endure not for long, but Zeus surveyeth the end of every matter, and suddenly, even as the clouds in Spring are quickly scattered by a wind that stirreth the depths of the billowy unharvested sea, layeth waste the fair fields o'er the wheat-bearing land, and reaching even to the high heaven where the Gods sit, maketh the sky clear again to view, till the strength of the Sun shineth fair over the fat land, and no cloud is to be seen any more,—even such is the vengeance of Zeus; He is not quick to wrath, like us, over each and every thing, yet of him that hath a wicked heart is He aware alway unceasing, and such an one surely cometh out plain at the last. Aye, one payeth to-day, another to-morrow; and those who themselves flee and escape the pursuing destiny of Heaven, to them vengeance cometh alway again, for the price of their deeds is paid by their innocent children or else by their seed after them.

We mortal men, alike good and bad, are minded thus:—each of us keepeth the opinion he hath ever had till he suffer ill, and then forthwith he grieveth; albeit ere that, we rejoice open-mouthed in vain expectations, and whosoever be oppressed with sore disease bethinketh himself he will be whole; another that is a coward thinketh he be a brave man; or he that hath no comeliness seemeth to himself goodly to look upon; and if one be needy, and constrained by the works of Penury, he reckoneth alway to win much wealth. Each hath his own quest; one, for to bring home gain, rangeth the fishy deep a-shipboard, tossed by grievous winds, sparing his life no whit, another serveth them whose business lieth with the curvèd plowshare, plowing the well-planted land for them through-

Sophocles. It was in his tragedies that the spirit of Athens, which Solon's legislation made politically effective, achieved its highest and most memorable expression.

Sophocles. It was in his tragedies that the spirit of Athens, which Solon's legislation made politically effective, achieved its highest and most memorable expression.

out the year; one getteth his living by the skill of his hands in the works of Athena and the master of many crafts, Hephaestus, another through his learning in the gifts of the Olympian Muses, cunning in the measure of lovely art; others again as physicians, having the task of the Master of Medicines, the Healer—for these men too there's no end of their labors, for often cometh great pain of little and a man cannot assuage it by soothing medicines, albeit at other times him that is confounded by evil and grievous maladies maketh he quickly whole by the laying on of hands; another again the Far-Shooting Lord Apollo maketh a seer, and the mischief that cometh on a man from afar is known to him that hath the Gods with him, for no augury nor offering will ever ward off what is destined to be.

Aye, surely Fate it is that bringeth mankind both good and ill, and the gifts immortal Gods offer must needs be accepted; surely too there's danger in every sort of business; nor know we at the beginning of a matter how it is to end; nay, sometimes he that striveth to do a good thing falleth unawares into ruin great and sore, whereas God giveth good hap in all things to one that doeth ill. . . .

But Athens, albeit she will never perish by the destiny of Zeus or the will of the happy Gods immortal—for of such power is the great-hearted Guardian, Daughter of a Mighty Sire, that holdeth Her hands over us—, Her own people, for lucre's sake, are fain to make ruin of this great city by their folly. Unrighteous is the mind of the leaders of the commons, and their pride goeth before a fall; for they know not how to hold them from excess nor to direct in peace the jollity of their present feasting . . . but grow rich through the suasion of unrighteous deeds . . . and steal right and left with no respect for possessions sacred or profane, nor have heed of the awful foundations of Justice, who is so well aware in her silence of what is and what hath been, and soon or late cometh alway to avenge. This is a wound that cometh inevitable and forthwith to every city, and she falleth quickly into an evil servitude, which arouseth discord and waketh slumbering War that destroyeth the lovely prime of so many men. For in gatherings dear to the unrighteous a delightful city is quickly brought low at the hands of them that are her enemies. Such are the evils which then are rife among the common folk, and

Stone inscription of a Solonic text from the early fifth century B.C., probably from a temple or other public building.

many of the poor go slaves into a foreign land, bound with unseemly fetters, there to bear perforce the evil works of servitude. So cometh the common evil into every house, and the street-doors will no longer keep it out; it leapeth the high hedge and surely findeth a man, for all he may go hide himself in his chamber. This it is that my heart biddeth me tell the Athenians, and how that even as ill-government giveth a city much trouble, so good rule maketh all things orderly and perfect, and often putteth fetters upon the un-righteous; aye, she maketh the rough smooth, checketh excess, confuseth outrage; she straighteneth crooked judg-ments, she mollifieth proud deeds; she stoppeth the works of faction, she stilleth the wrath of baneful strife; and of her all is made wise and perfect in the world of men.

For I gave the common folk such privilege as is sufficient for them, neither adding nor taking away; and such as had power and were admired for their riches, I provided that they too should not suffer undue wrong. Nay, I stood with a strong shield thrown before the both sorts, and would have neither to prevail unrighteously over the other.

But as for me, why did I stay me ere I had won that for which I gathered the commons? Right good witness shall I have in the court of Time, to wit the Great Mother of the Olympian Gods, dark Earth, whose so many fixed land-marks I once removed, and have made her free that was once a slave. Aye, many brought I back to their God-built birthplace, many that had been sold, some justly, some unjustly, and others that had been exiled through urgent penury, men that no longer spake the Attic speech because they had wandered so far and wide; and those that suffered shameful servitude at home, trembling before the whims of their owners, these made I free men. By fitting close together right and might I made these things prevail, and accomplished them even as I said I would. And ordinances I wrote, that made straight justice for each man, good and bad alike. Had another than I taken the goad in hand, a foolish man and a covetous, he had not restrained the peo-ple; for had I been willing to do now what pleased this party and now what pleased the other, this city had been bereft of many men. Wherefore mingling myself strength from all quarters I turned at bay like a wolf among many hounds.

## A PRODUCTIVE MODEL

*Five hundred years after Solon a Roman orator, consul, and philosophic author Cicero was able to record that the Solonic laws still held good in Ath-ens—despite all the political upheavals, revolutions, and dictatorships that had begun even before Solon's death under the archontate of his nephew (or cousin) Pisistratus. And as has rightly been pointed out nearer our own day, "the remarkable thing was that in the very dawn of the intellectual, cultural, and social history of the world Solon created a positive, productive model of a modern form of society that antedates the efforts of the mighty but ultimately transient historical religions of Zoroastrianism, Judaism, Christianity, Islam, and Marxism from which the personalities and circumstances of contemporary socialism derive."*

*History has been influenced not by Solon's words but certainly by his deeds and intentions. To take just one exam-ple of how "modern" these were, in the year 594 B.C. he abolished debt bon-dage. It was not until well into the nine-teenth century that England—after Athens the home of European democ-racy—dropped the principle of putting people in prison when they could not meet their material liabilities, in other words stopped giving creditors the legal right to rob defaulting debtors of their freedom with the help of the state. Solon's ideals constitute a kind of yeast that is still working in our political his-tory today; indeed today more than ever we see the relevance of his insight that demands for "freedom," "justice," and "equality before the law" are doomed to remain fine-sounding but empty phrases as long as the economically underprivi-leged have no real possibility of effectively pressing such claims against the rich and powerful.*

The Parthenon, the most famous example of classical Greek architecture and a symbol of the whole civilization of ancient Athens. Dedicated to Athena, the Doric temple was built between 447 and 432 B.C. on the Acropolis in Athens. Solon the lawgiver, in approximately 590 B.C., had laid down the guidelines for classical Athenian society, a culture that reached its peak a century later in outstanding works of art, sculpture, architecture, political thought, poetry, and drama, and which continues to mold and influence our world.

Next day we set out early and saw the ruins of the Parthenon, the site of the old Theater of Bacchus, the Temple of Theseus, the sixteen pillars that survive from the divine Olympion; but I was most struck by the old gate that formerly led from the old city into the new, and where, at one time, a thousand beautiful people would greet one another in one day.

"Oh," I said, as we went on in our walk, "it's a splendid trick of Fate, to have torn down the temples here and given their broken stones to children to throw around, to have made the broken gods into benches in front of peasant huts and turned the gravestones into resting places for the grazing cattle; such extravagance is more regal than the wantonness of Cleopatra when she drank melted pearls."

Friedrich Hölderlin, *Hyperion or the Eremite in Greece,* Vol. I, Book 2

# ca. 500 B.C.

# Buddha: Truth and Enlightenment

The founder of Buddhism, whose real name was Prince Siddhartha Gautama (his family belonged to the higher nobility), was born in Kapilavastu in the central Ganges valley, probably in 550 B.C. At the age of sixteen he married the Shakya princess Yashodhara, who bore him a son, Rahula. Living in luxury, he undertook the four legendary expeditions on which he met an old man, a sick man, a dead man, and an ascetic. These impressed him so deeply that he left his family in secret and "went forth into homelessness." After seven years of ascetic existence the forty-year-old received enlightenment under the fig tree at Bodh Gaya. In the famous Benares sermon the

*Above:* Young Buddha during his *ascesis,* or ascetic withdrawal, in which he could not find salvation. Gandhoara, India. Second to third century.

*Above:* Head of a Buddha, influenced by classical Greek form. Fourth century.

*Right:* Buddha portrait in the style of Cambodian Khmer art. Twelfth century.

Enlightened One proclaimed for the first time his Four Noble Truths: all life is transitory; lust for life is the cause of suffering; knowledge and purification remove suffering; the path of knowledge is the "Eightfold Way" by which men, released from the suf-

Know, O monks,
that all existence is suffering.
Birth is suffering,
growing old is suffering,
death is full of suffering.

Buddha

fering of eternal rebirth, may finally enter Nirvana—"extinction."
Like Christ and Mohammed, the Buddha left no writings of his own. His communications with pupils and disciples were exclusively oral. The oldest surviving Buddhist documents are the *Tipitaka* or *Baskets of the Law,* originally compiled orally for the Buddhist Council of 241 B.C. and committed to writing in the Pali language around 80 B.C. They fall into three groups: the *Sutta-pitaka* or legends, the *Vinaya-pitaka* or rules of the monastic life, and the *Abid-*

*harma-pitaka* or teaching. So the generations who came after the Buddha worked over the content of the Buddhist tradition for a period of almost two centuries, stylizing and canonizing it.

## STRIVE WITHOUT CEASING

Our only avenue of approach to the authentic, historical Buddha is through the Suttas, and it is an open question how close they bring us to him. They take the form of messages that the Buddha's spiritual heirs preserved for posterity by oral transmission. This is why each text begins with the formula: "Thus have I heard: Once, when the Master was staying at . . ."

A particular situation is then described, and this is followed by a teaching dialogue between the Buddha and his "disciples," "brothers," and "monks." He recounts experiences, builds them up into parables, is interrupted by questions from the monks, answers them, and particularly encourages certain favorite disciples to speak at length. Nearly all the Suttas end with the affirmation: "Thus spake the Master. And those monks uplifted, rejoiced in the word of the Master."

In these dialogues (which also contain fragments of information about the Buddha's life and the scenes of his ministry) the Buddha puts forward his teaching in ever-changing form, calling for a renunciation of self and for an "overcoming of worldly desires and cares" while allowing "no nostalgia for the past and no hope for the future" in order that the "thirst for existence" may be extinguished.

The Buddha died near Kusinagara, the present-day Kasia, about 480 B.C. His last words were: "So, O disciples, I say to you: All that has come into being shall pass away, therefore strive without ceasing."

*Left to right:*
Buddha in the "Great Miracle." Afghanistan.
Japanese Buddha in the Horyu-ji Temple of the Nara region. Seventh to eighth century.
Seated Chinese Buddha. Bronze of the Sung dynasty (eleventh to twelfth century).
Indian Buddha from Pala. Tenth century.
Buddha's temptation. Buddha sits under the fig tree of enlightenment, in order to experience the great wisdom. Demons, sent by the Evil One (Mara), assail him with temptations. Stone relief. India. Second century.

*Knowledge, affections, ignorance,* are grouped
With *molding elements,* fifth *mind-at-work,*
*Touch, feeling, craving,* and *attachment,* then
*Zest-to-do, sustenance,* and *stir-and-moil,*
*Trust, form* and *truth* and *ill:* sixteen in all.

Thus have I heard:—Once, when the Master was staying near Savatthi, in East park at the storeyed house of Migara's mother, he sat in the open, surrounded by the order of the monks; and it was the fifteenth night of the Observance day and the moon was at full. And the Master, after gazing round on the order of monks, addressed them, saying:—

"Monks, if there should be questioners, asking: 'What is the reason for listening to these good teachings that are Ariyan, lead onward and reach to awakening?'—it would be proper to say to them: 'It is to know as such the extent of dual teachings.' And if you should say what dual?—'This is ill, this is ill's coming to be.' That is the first view-point. 'This is ill's end, this is the going thereto.' That is the second view-point.

"Verily, monks, when a monk dwells earnest, alert and resolute, viewing the dual thus rightly, one of two fruits is to be expected: Knowledge here and now; or, if attachment remain, the state of a Non-returner."

Thus spake the Master, and having thus spoken, the Well-farer spoke again as teacher:—

"Who know not ill nor how ill comes to be,
Nor where ill ceases wholly, utterly,
Nor know the way that leads to calming ill,
Lacking release by wisdom, mind's release,
They cannot end, but go to birth and eld.
But they who know ill, how ill comes to be,
And where ill ceases wholly, utterly,
And know the way that leads to calming ill,
They in release by wisdom, mind's release,
Can make an end, nor go to birth and eld.

"Monks, if there should be questioners, asking, 'May one even in another way view the dual rightly?'—it would be proper to say, 'One may.' And how? 'Whatsoever ill comes to be, all that is caused by affections.' That is the first view-point; 'By the utter ending and ceasing of affections, there is no coming to be of ill.' That is the second view-point. Verily, monks, when a monk . . . views the dual thus . . . he may attain . . .

Caused by affections ever grows
The multitude of worldly ills;
The fool who here unwittingly
Affection forms, meets ill again.
Hence wisely no affection form,
Perceiving thence grows birth and ill.

". . .'May one in another way view the dual rightly?'. . . One may: 'Whatsoever ill comes to be, all that is caused by ignorance.' That is the first view-point; 'By the utter ending and ceasing of ignorance, there is no coming to be of ill.' That is the second view-point . . .

Who run the round of birth and death
    and run
Again, becoming here or otherwhere.
Run long in leash from erring ignorance:
But beings, come to knowledge, come no
    more.

". . .'May there be another way . . .?' . . .'Whatsoever ill comes to be, all that is caused by molding elements.' That is the first view-point; 'By the utter ending and ceasing of the molding elements, there is no coming to be of ill.' That is the second view-point . . .

All ill that comes is caused by elements
That mold; by ending them, there
    comes no ill:
Knowing this bane: 'The molders cause
    the ill.'
Knowing this truly: 'By perception's end
All molding ceases, thus is ill destroyed!'
Great seers, wise by right knowledge,
    lore-adepts,

Victors o'er Mara's bondage, come no more.

". . .'May there be another way . . .?' . . .'Whatsoever ill comes to be, all that is caused by mind-at-work.' That is the first view-point; 'By the utter ending and ceasing of mind-at-work, there is no coming to be of ill.' That is the second view-point . . .

All ill that comes is caused by mind-at-
    work,
By ending mind-at-work there comes no
    ill;
Knowing this bane: 'Ill's caused by
    mind-at-work,'
A monk, completely calming mind-at-
    work,
Becomes from yearning free and wholly
    cool.

". . .'May there be another way . . .?' . . .'Whatsoever ill comes to be, all that is caused by touch.' That is the first view-point; 'By the utter ending and ceasing of touch, there is no coming to be of ill.' That is the second view-point . . .

Who fall to touch, follow becoming's
    stream,
Fare the false way, are far from fetters'
    end:
But they who fathom touch, touch mastering,
By knowledge come into the bliss of
    calm,
Become from yearning free and wholly
    cool.

". . .'May there be another way . . .?' . . .'Whatsoever ill comes to be, all that is caused by feeling.' That is the first view-point; 'By the utter ending and ceasing of feeling, there is no coming to be of ill.' That is the second view-point . . .

Both ease and ill, with neither-ill-nor-
    ease,
Within, without, whatever there be felt,
Knowing all that as ill, rotting and false,
Seeing all touch decays and loathing it,
A monk by quenching every feeling here
Becomes from yearning free and wholly
    cool.

". . .'May there be another way . . .?' . . .'Whatsoever ill comes to be, all that is caused by craving.' That is the first view-point; 'By the utter ending and ceasing of craving, there is no coming to be of ill.' That is the second view-point . . .

Long stretch the rounds of man who
    craving mates,
Becoming this or that, he passes not:
Knowing this bane: 'From craving
    cometh ill,'
Gone craving, grasping, moves the
    mindful monk.

". . .'May there be another way . . .?' . . .'Whatsoever ill comes to be, all that is caused by attachment.' That is the first view-point; 'By the utter ending and ceasing of attachment, there is no coming to be of ill. That is the second view-point . . .

Attachment forms becoming; man,
    become,
Fares ill; death follows birth; this is ill's
    cause:
Hence by right knowledge, by attach-
    ment's end,
Wise men, by knowing end of birth,
    come not.

". . .'May there be another way. . .?' . . .'Whatsoever ill comes to be, all that is caused by zest-to-do.' That is the first view-point; 'By the utter ending and ceasing of zest-to-do, there is no coming

Death of Buddha. Painting on silk.

to be of ill.' That is the second view-point . . .

All ill that comes is caused by zest-to-do,
By ending zest-to-do, there comes no ill:
Who knows this bane: 'Ill's caused by zest-to-do,'
Rid of all zest and zestless in release,
Calm monk, with craving and becoming cut.
Crossing the round of birth, cometh no more.

" . . .'May there be another way . . .?'
. . .'Whatsoever ill comes to be, all that is caused by sustenance.' That is the first view-point; 'By the utter ending and ceasing of sustenance, there is no coming to be of ill.' That is the second . . .

All ill that comes is caused by sustenance,
By ending sustenance there comes no ill:
Who knows this bane: 'Ill's caused by sustenance,'
Perceiving sustenance, with trust in none,

With cankers quenched, health by right knowledge won,
Discerning follower in Dharma poised,
That lore-adept goes to what none can sum.

" . . .'May there be another way . . .?'
. . .'Whatsoever ill comes to be, all that is caused by stir and moil.' That is the first view-point; 'By the utter ending and ceasing of stir and moil, there is no coming to be of ill.' That is the second view-point . . .

All ill that comes is caused by stir and moil,
By ending stir and moil there comes no ill:
Knowing this bane: 'Ill's caused by stir and moil,'
Ejecting moil, the molding forces held,
Still and detached moveth the mindful monk.

" . . .'May there be another way . . .?'
. . .'Whoso trusts, trembles.' That is the

first view-point; 'Whoso trusts not, trembles not.' That is the second view-point . . .

Whoso hath trust in naught, he trembles not;
Who trusteth, is attached, he passes not
The round, becoming here or otherwhere:
Knowing this bane: 'Danger abides in trust,'
Detached, with trust in naught, moves mindful monk.

" . . .'May there be another way . . .?'
. . .'The formless is a calmer state than form.' That is the first view-point. 'Ending is a calmer state than the formless.' That is the second view-point . . .

Beings form-bound, and formless dwellers too,
Not knowing 'ending,' come again, again:
But all who forms do comprehend, well poised

*Right:* Ashoka pillar, with lion figure, at Lauriya Nandangarh. Sandstone. Early Buddhist, third century B.C.

In formless things, in 'ending' all-
released,
They are the folk who have left death
behind.

". . . 'May there be another way . . .?'
. . . What the world with its devas,
Maras, Brahmas, recluses and brahmans,
the earth with its devas and men, hold to
be truth, that is well seen by Ariyans, by
right wisdom, as it is, to wit, as false.'
That is the first view-point. 'What the
world . . . and men hold to be false,
that is . . . seen by Ariyans . . . as truth.'
That is the second view-point . . .

See how the worlds, content with what is
not
The self, convinced by name-and-form,
hold it
As true! By this and that they hold it so—
Thereafter otherwise. Herein, forsooth,
Its falseness lies, false, fleeting thing it is!
'Tis no false thing the cool! That Ariyans
Find true, and as they surely master

'What the whole world . . . considers as
bliss, that is . . . well seen by Ariyans as
ill.' That is the first view-point; 'What
the whole world . . . considers as ill,
that . . . is well seen by Ariyans as bliss.'
That is the second view-point.
"Verily, monks, when a monk dwells
earnest, alert and resolute, viewing the
dual thus rightly, one of two fruits is to
be expected: Knowledge here and now;
or, if attachment remain, the state of a
Non-returner.
Thus spake the Master, and having thus
spoken, the Well-farer spoke again as
teacher:—

"How sweet and dear are winsome
forms, sounds, tastes,
Scents, touches, thoughts—all while one
says, 'They're here';
And all the world agrees, 'How blissful
they!'
And when they pass away, 'How sad is
that!'
'Tis bliss, think Ariyans when body's

Manuscript from the Tibetan *Tipitaka*.

truth,
Become from yearning free and wholly
cool.

"Monks, if there should be questioners,
asking, 'May one even in another way
view the dual rightly?'—it would be
proper to say, 'One may.' And how?

frame
Is seen to end: 'Alas!' sigh worldly-wise.
The 'bliss' of others Ariyans call 'ill':
The 'ill' of others Ariyans find 'bliss.'
Behold how hard is Dharma to be learnt,
Confounding those who see not clear
therein!
Gloom wraps the shrouded, darkness

36

*Right:* Lion capital from the Deer Park pillar in Sarnath, Uttar Pradesh, India. Manzia period. This capital served as the model for the state seal of modern India.

wraps the blind:
But for the wise there is an opening,
A very light for those with eyes, tho'
dolts,
Unskilled in Dharma, know it not as
nigh.
In those o'ercome by lust of life, who
drift
Along life's stream, to realm of Mara
gone,
This Dharma wakeneth not easily.
Who, verily, save Ariyans are ripe
To waken wholly to that lofty bourn,
That bourn which when they rightly
come to know,
They wholly cool become and canker-
less?"

Thus spake the Master. And those monks uplifted, rejoiced in the word of the Master. Now while this exposition was being spoken, the minds of more than sixty monks became without attachment, freed from the cankers.

*Above:* Script from the Delhi-Topra pillar of Ashoka.

*Right:* Mahatma Gandhi, who brought about a twentieth-century revival of Ashoka's pacifist teachings.

## PEACE TO ALL CREATURES

*Itinerant monks spread the Buddha's teaching throughout India. In 67* A.D. *the Chinese emperor Ming Ti invited monks to come and translate the Buddhist scriptures into Chinese. As the new religion of China, Buddhism continued to evolve there undisturbed until the year 900. Moving on through Korea, it reached the island kingdom of Japan in 538* A.D.

*The Buddhist World Conference held in Ceylon in 1950 launched a campaign to step up the Buddhist mission globally as an answer to the problems of today's world; Buddhism, the conference claimed, with its total indifference to everything worldly, was the only religion suited to modern man.*

*The strength of Buddhism lies not least in its unique openness. As its history in Asia shows, it has managed to adapt itself to the most disparate national, religious, political, and social circumstances. Strictly speaking it is an atheistic religion, recognizing no "other world" and no absolute gods. The Buddha, like Lao-tse and Jesus, seeks to repay evil with good, hatred with love; his exalted ethic demands that all life be protected in this world. It calls for "peace to all creatures" in order that they may find spiritual extinction in the fullness of the para-divine "void."*

*In India, the Buddha's homeland, Buddhism reached its apogee under Ashoka, the "apostle king" (c. 290–232* B.C.*; reigned from 269). Ashoka started out as a cruel warrior who, by means of brutality and massacre and with the aid of the notorious prisons known as "Ashoka's hells," united politically almost the whole of India. Around 250* B.C.*, however, there was a dramatic change in him: he was converted to Buddhism, became the first ruler in history wholly to renounce war as a means to power, took the title "Emperor of the Great Peace," an empire of tolerance and humanity, and began issuing his celebrated edicts. He had these carved on rocks and pillars all over India in the local dialect. Their joyful message was (Rock Edict XII):*
*"His holy and gracious majesty the king entertains respect for men of all faiths, ascetics and housefathers alike.... His holy majesty is concerned less with the externals of reverence, very much more with the growth of the inner substance of all religious beliefs."*

*Proof that these inscriptions really did stem from Ashoka only emerged in 1915. Gandhi cited Ashoka's belief in non-violence; the Indian nationalist movement hailed him as its hero. Ashoka became a symbol of India's reawakening, and since independence the Indian government has used a picture of the capital of one of his inscription pillars as its official seal.*

<table>
</table>

# ca. 480 B.C.

# The Great Wisdom of Confucius

We have nothing authentic written by Confucius himself. There is even uncertainty about the dates (551?–479? B.C.) between which the man responsible for the classical, two-thousand-year-old Chinese political and ethical order lived. Our document is made up of extracts from the dialogues of the "Great Master" as handed down in the twenty books of the *Lun Yü* or *Confucian Analects*. These consist of notes made by disciples that the scholar Dsong Hüan (A.D. 127–200) collected and edited from three ancient sources. There are other collections of the sayings, teachings, and anecdotes of "Master Kung" besides the *Lun Yü*, the most important being the "Discourses" or *Gia Yü*. The *Lun Yü*, in which the Master speaks in polished aphorisms that always go straight to the point, became known to the Chinese as *Ta Hsüe, The Great Learning*—a name also applied to a much shorter text in which the Master distills his advice to the seeker after truth.

## CONFUCIUS AND CONFUCIANISM

Historically, Confucius (as Jesuit missionaries to China and also his two great European admirers, Leibnitz and Voltaire, called "Master Kung" or "Master Kung Futse") was the son of a governor of Tsu in Lu county, southwest Shantung. He began his career as a minor official, turned to teaching, became a famous scholar, went into exile with his lord Ki in 517, returned in 501 to become among other things minister of public works and later minister of justice. He fell into disfavor in 497 and went into exile again, and following his return to Lu in 483 lived there quietly until his death, surrounded by the many disciples who had accompanied him during the years of banishment.

His power is like heaven and earth;
his profundity is unequaled in past and opposite.

Translation of the inscription in the painting above.

Confucius saw himself as breathing new life into China's most ancient philosophical tradition. His concern was with "right thinking," the guarantee of a good, moral, peaceful existence for everyone in the hierarchically ordered house of the cosmos: under the aegis of the Great Obedience, in the family, in the clan, and in a hierarchy that extended from the head of the clan right up to the emperor.

Confucius was one of humanity's greatest teachers. He devoted himself primarily to educating the sons of the ruling class because he was convinced that the prosperity or corruption of the state and of all social, intellectual, and spiritual relations depended on their success or failure in setting an example. This did not, however, mean that Confucius turned away pupils from less noble families or from the poorer classes of society.

From the phenomenon of Confucius it was an inevitable step to the phenomenon of Confucianism, although Chinese in fact has no word for Confucianism. The teaching of Confucius was called simply that—*Ju-Kiao* or *The Teaching*—and his school thus became known

38

as *Ju-Kia,* the school of scribes or men of letters. It was the Confucians who, as *the* men of letters in China, molded the intellectual and political character of the country right up into the twentieth century.

Following a struggle lasting for centuries they finally broke through in the Han period, half a millennium after Confucius. Book burnings and executions at the stake had only put off the moment of victory; they were powerless to prevent it. And having won, the men of letters used a blend of Confucian and other elements to erect a disciplined and disciplining philosophical structure, seeing themselves as the ideologists of the ruling class led by the emperor.

Actually the Confucian world view with its emphasis on the "noble" and "aristocratic" could also be understood apolitically. In this sense Western mysticism too speaks of "nobility of soul" as being a quality within the reach of every man. But the Confucians took the great idea of the "noble man" and gave it a thoroughly political, feudalistic interpretation: the aristocracy and the body of Confucian scholars known as the mandarins, who stood for an advanced form of hierarchically organized bureaucracy, were invested with the sacred right and duty of acting "in the name of Heaven," i.e. of the emperor, to protect the law and hold the peoples of the empire to obedience.

Two figures and their respective periods made their mark on Confucianism up until the revolution of 1912: Tung-king Shu as the "Confucius of the Han Dynasty" in the first century B.C., and Ku Hsi with his neo-Confucianism during the Sung period, A.D. 960–1290. It is a curious fact that hand in hand with this politicization came a deepening of sensibility, a refinement of taste, and not least a sophisticated eroticism.

## GREAT TEACHINGS

When Confucius was Great Director of Crimes of Lu, there were a father and a son who had a dispute and went to law. The Master held them in custody in the same prison and for three months he did not decide the case. Then the father begged to stop the lawsuit, upon which the Master pardoned them. Chi-sun upon hearing it was not pleased and said: "The Director of Crimes is fooling me. The other day he told me: in governing the state and families, always go by filial piety first. When I now would execute one who is not filial in order to teach the people filial conduct, would that not be in order? But instead he pardons him!"

Jan Yu told it to Confucius. The Master said with a deep sigh: "Alas! That a ruler, himself falling short of the Way, yet should kill his subjects for falling short, is contrary to reason. Without educating the people in filial piety only to judge their criminal cases,—this means to kill the innocent. If the three armies suffer a great defeat, they may not be beheaded, and likewise, if the prisons are not well-ordered, people may not be punished. Why? It is because, if the ruler's teaching is not put into effect, the guilt is not with the people. Now to be lax in giving orders and yet diligent in punishment,—this means injury. Collecting taxes and not observing the proper season,—this means oppression. Without warning beforehand yet to demand the completion of tasks,—this means cruelty. Only when a government lacks these three evils, punishments may be effected. . . .

"When a ruler displays the Way *(tao)* and moral power *(tê),* and thereby first tries to make the people follow it,—if that still does not succeed, he honours the talented, thus stimulating them; if that still does not succeed, he discharges the incapable men in order to let them tremble. In this way after three years the people will be corrected. If even then there are depraved people among them who are not reformed, only then he bestows punishment on them, but then the people all will know the crime for which they are punished.

"The *Ode* says: 'The son of Heaven, him you should support, making the people not go astray.' Therefore tradition says: Let your austerity be fierce but do not apply it; let punishments be established but do not make use of them.

"But the present age is not so. Confused are their teachings, and numerous their penalties, so that the people are misled and deceived, and fall into crime; then again they try to regulate the people on top of it, and thus punishments are frequent and numerous, and yet robbery is not overcome.

"Now an obstacle of three feet high, an empty carriage cannot mount it, and why? Because it is steep. But a mountain of a hundred *jên,* a heavy load can mount it, and why? Because it slopes gently. Now that the customs of the world are gently sloping downwards, has been so for a long time, and though there be penalties and laws, could the people not pass over that slope without them?"

*Right:* Modern print of a temple picture showing Confucius surrounded by his seventy-two pupils.

*Far right:* Ancient picture of Confucius receiving a visitor.

## A Good Teacher

The Master said, "If a man keeps cherishing his old knowledge, so as continually to be acquiring new, he may be a teacher of others."

## The Scholar

The Master said, "The accomplished scholar is not a utensil." It is not consistent with the dignity of the superior man to allow himself to be used as a mere tool for the purposes of others. He is his own purpose.

## The Playing of Music

The Master instructing the Grand music-master of Lü said, "How to play music may be known. At the commencement of the piece, all the parts should sound together. As it proceeds, they should be in harmony, while severally distinct and flowing without break, and thus on to the conclusion."

## The True Spirit

The Master said, "High station filled without indulgent generosity; ceremonies performed without reverence; mourning conducted without sorrow;—wherewith should I contemplate such ways?"

## False Shame

The Master said, "A scholar, whose mind is set on truth, and who is ashamed of bad clothes and bad food, is not fit to be discoursed with."

## Men's Concerns

The Master said, "The superior man thinks of virtue; the small man thinks of comfort. The superior man thinks of the sanctions of law; the small man thinks of favors which he may receive."

## Balance and Imbalance

The Master said, "Where the solid qualities are in excess of accomplishments, we have rusticity; where the accomplishments are in excess of the solid qualities, we have the manners of a clerk. When the accomplishments and solid qualities are equally blended, we then have the man of virtue."

## A Life's Principle

The Master said, "Man is born for uprightness. If a man lose his uprightness, and yet live, his escape from death is the effect of mere good fortune."

## Poetry, Order, Music

1. The Master said, "It is by the Odes that the mind is aroused.
2. "It is by the Rules of Propriety that the character is established.
3. "It is from Music that the finish is received."

## The Secret of Learning

The Master said, "Learn as if you could not reach your object, and were always fearing also lest you should lose it."

## Winter

The Master said, "When the year becomes cold, then we know how the pine and the cypress are the last to lose their leaves."

## Three Victories

The Master said, "The wise are free from perplexities; the virtuous from anxiety; and the bold from fear."

## The Prince's Code

The Master said, "When a prince's personal conduct is correct, his government is effective without the issuing of orders. If his personal conduct is not correct, he may issue orders, but they will not be followed."

## Successful Government

The Master said, "If good men were to govern a country *in succession* for a hundred years, they would be able to transform the violently bad, and dispense with capital punishments."

## Of Friendship

Confucius said, "There are three friendships which are advantageous, and three which are injurious. Friendship with the upright; friendship with the sincere; and friendship with the man of much observation:—these are advantageous. Friendship with the man of specious airs; friendship with the insinuatingly soft; and friendship with the glib-tongued: —these are injurious."

## Words and Their Beclouding

1. The Master said, "Yū, have you heard the six words to which are attached six becloudings?" Yū replied, "I have not."
2. "Sit down, and I will tell them to you.
3. "There is the love of being benevolent without the love of learning;—the beclouding here leads to a foolish simplicity. There is the love of knowing without the love of learning;—the beclouding here leads to dissipation of mind. There is the love of being sincere without the love of learning;—the beclouding here leads to an injurious disregard of consequences. There is the love of straightforwardness without the love of learning;—the beclouding here leads to rudeness. There is the love of boldness without the love of learning;—the beclouding here leads to insubordination. There is the love of firmness without the love of learning;—the beclouding here leads to extravagant conduct."

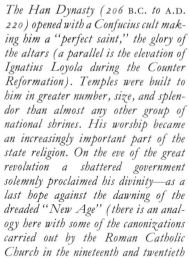

*The Han Dynasty (206 B.C. to A.D. 220) opened with a Confucius cult making him a "perfect saint," the glory of the altars (a parallel is the elevation of Ignatius Loyola during the Counter Reformation). Temples were built to him in greater number, size, and splendor than almost any other group of national shrines. His worship became an increasingly important part of the state religion. On the eve of the great revolution a shattered government solemnly proclaimed his divinity—as a last hope against the dawning of the dreaded "New Age" (there is an analogy here with some of the canonizations carried out by the Roman Catholic Church in the nineteenth and twentieth*

*centuries). The revolutionaries for their part campaigned almost continuously against Confucius, and even now Peking continues its anti-Confucian policies. These political struggles against Confucius testify among other things to the ongoing intellectual and spiritual presence of Master Kung. Key elements of his thought and of his vision of the "Great Order" of mankind continue to influence the very people who oppose him politically, not a few of whom are perhaps his most faithful spiritual heirs.*

41

# Plato's Vision of the State

Bust of Socrates.

The Greek philosopher Plato (428/7–347 B.C.) was descended on both his father's and his mother's sides from famous and wealthy families of the Athenian aristocracy. His father claimed descent from the legendary first king of Athens; his mother Perictione's family tree went back to Dropides, a friend and supporter of Solon. Plato's birth coincided with a final flowering of Athenian culture. The city and Athenian democracy, molded by Pericles in his capacity as "first man in the state," wished in view of the Persian threat to ensure first their hegemony in Hellas. This meant war with Sparta—in Hellenic terms a civil war—which Pericles duly declared in 431 B.C. It lasted until 404, and ended with severe internal upheavals within the Athenian state. It was during the war, probably around 414 B.C., that Plato first met Socrates (470–399), the man who led him into the inner realms of the mind aware of itself. Driven by his enormous anxiety concerning the collapse of the Athenian *polis,* which to him was hearth and home of all human civilization, Plato became a major political thinker. Around the middle of his life he wrote the ten books of the *Politeia* (called in English the *Republic*), and probably toward the end of his life the twelve books of the *Nomoi* (the *Laws*); these are Plato's two most comprehensive works. In the *Republic* he portrays an ideal state; the *Laws* are concerned with real possibilities as regards drawing up constitutions and passing legislation. All Plato's writings are in the form of fictitious dialogues, with various friends of his taking part in turn. Although the dialogues are not in the nature of minutes of actual exchanges, the ideas discussed were in fact current among the circle of intellectuals around Plato and Socrates. The main contributor to the discussions, including those of the *Republic*, is Socrates, a

He penetrates the depths,
more to fill them with his being
than to investigate them.
He soars to great heights in his desire
to partake once more of his origins.
Everything he expresses
relates to an eternally whole,
good, true, and beautiful,
the yearning for which
he seeks to awake in every bosom.

Johann Wolfgang von Goethe,
*History of the Theory of Color*

position he retains even in the dialogues that were written long after his death.

## THE INTELLECTUAL, VICTORIOUS IN DEFEAT

The chaotic political situation in Athens after the city's capitulation in the Peloponnesian War (404 B.C.) and the outrageous impeachment of his spiritual father and friend Socrates, followed by the latter's suicide (399 B.C.), plunged the twenty-nine-year-old Plato into an emotional crisis that was to determine the rest of his career. The very depth of his mourning, in finding affirmation, released forces that gave him fresh hope. Estranged from Athens, Plato turned to the wider Greek world that was spreading through the Mediterranean and that in southern Italy, particularly in Sicily, had created centers of Greek civilization that at times outshone Athens itself in splendor and influence. After travels that took him to other parts of Greece as well as to Egypt and Cyrenaica (present-day Libya), Plato arrived in Sicily in 389. In Syracuse, the political center of the western Hellenic world, he tried to win acceptance with its ruler Dionysius I and the latter's brother-in-law Dion as architect of a new constitution. He failed because the tyrant was not seriously prepared to let an "intellectual" tell him what to do; instead Dionysius banished him to the island of Aegina in the gulf between Athens and the Peloponnesus. On the death of Dionysius I eleven years later and the accession of his son Dionysius II, Dion, uncle of the new ruler, recalled Plato to Syracuse. Plato was now sixty years old. He proposed reforms and drew up a constitution, but they met with an unsympathetic reaction from the restless young king. The "Introduction" with which Plato prefaced his draft constitution was later incorporated in the *Laws*. It has been justly claimed that Plato's *Laws* is the earliest handbook of European jurisprudence; at the same time, since he was an old man when he wrote it, it offers an illuminating study of the repercussions of youthful romanticism in a disillusioned and melancholy old age.

At the height of his powers, shocked, hurt, and provoked by the corruption rampant in Athens and the experiences gathered on his journeys through the Greek world, Plato captured his mature vision of an ideal state in the ten books of the *Republic*. The first step toward building the new state is to educate all young people of all classes and both sexes for a period of twenty years. This is followed by further selection procedures until eventually those who pass become members of the elite class of "guardians" *(phylaces),* while those who fail become merchants, workers, peasants, and soldiers.

The guardians have all studied "divine philosophy," so all power in the state is vested in them; they must, however, remain completely propertyless. There are to be no laws. All conflicts and litigation are to be resolved by the philosopher-rulers.

The state gives all children, boys and girls, the same opportunity. No political office may be barred to women. Plato was the first and up until the mid-twentieth century the only political thinker to demand both absolute and real, active and passive equality of women in state and society.

A key passage in the *Republic* is the great saying: "There can be no end to the troubles of states, or indeed . . . of humanity itself, till philosophers become kings in this world, or till those we now call kings and rulers really and truly become philosophers" (Book V, 473). What this means is that "mind"—education, science, art, literature, and culture—cannot flourish in the absence of politics and political responsibility because they are in danger of floating aimlessly in a vacuum and becoming corrupted. Politics, on the other hand, perverts and corrupts when it rejects the counsel of the philosopher.

The great hopes that had inspired Plato to write the *Republic,* dashed by the collapse of his beloved Athens (where he had founded his own school of philosophy in the sacred grove of Heros Hecademos) both at home and abroad and by the apalling chaos he found in Sicily and Syracuse, turned to resignation. Now actively pessimistic, he conceived the model of a "closed state" to be set up in the hinterland far from the sea. Even in this hierarchically organized state Plato retained his insistence on equal rights for women.

Greek theater in Syracuse, Sicily.

## FROM "THE REPUBLIC": PORTRAIT OF A STATESMAN

### BOOK SIX

"Well, Glaucon," I [Socrates] said, "we can now see, at last, what a philosopher is

and what he is not, but we've had to go a long way round to find out."

"I doubt if we could have done it more shortly," he replied.

"I don't think we could. Though I think we could have managed better if it had been the only subject we were discussing, and we hadn't so much else to get through before we can see the difference between a just life and an unjust."

"Then where do we go from here?"

"The next question is this. If philosophers have the capacity to grasp the eternal and immutable, while those who have no such capacity are not philosophers and are lost in multiplicity and change, which of the two should be in charge of a state?"

"What would be a reasonable line to take?" he asked.

"To say that we will appoint as Guardians whichever of them seem able to guard the laws and customs of society."

School for philosophers *(below)*. Hellenistic mosaic from a villa in Pompei. It is generally believed that the mosaic depicts the Platonic Academy in Athens.

Exerpt from the oldest text of Plato's works now extant, found on the Greek island of Patmos. It comes from a manuscript that was copied in the year 895, at the order of Archbishop Aretha of Caesarea, from an original manuscript that no longer exists.

"Right."

"And isn't it obvious whether it's better for a blind man or a clear-sighted one to guard and keep an eye on anything?"

"There's not much doubt about that," he agreed.

"But surely 'blind' is just how you would describe men who have no true knowledge of reality, and no clear standard of perfection in their mind to which they can turn, as a painter turns to his model, and which they can study closely before they start laying down rules in this world about what is admirable or right or good

where such rules are needed, or maintaining, as Guardians, any that already exist."

"Yes, blind is just about what they are."

"Shall we make them Guardians then? Or shall we prefer the philosophers, who have learned to know each true reality, and have no less practical experience, and can rival them in all departments of human excellence."

"It would be absurd not to choose the philosophers, if they are not inferior in all these other respects; for in the vital quality of knowledge they are clearly superior."

"Then oughtn't we to show how knowledge can be combined with these other qualities in the same person?"

"Yes."

"As we said at the beginning of our discussion, the first thing is to find out what their natural character is. When we have agreed about that we shall, I think, be ready to agree that they can have those other qualities as well, and that they are the people to put in charge of society."

"Explain."

"One trait in the philosopher's character we can assume is his love of any branch of learning that reveals eternal reality, the realm unaffected by the vicissitudes of change and decay."

"Agreed."

"He is in love with the whole of that reality, and will not willingly be deprived even of the most insignificant fragment of it—just like the lovers and men of ambition we described earlier on."

"Yes, you are quite right."

"Then if the philosopher is to be as we described him, must he not have a further characteristic?"

"What?"

"Truthfulness. He will never willingly tolerate an untruth, but will hate it, just as he loves truth."

"That seems likely enough."

"It's not only likely," I replied, "it is an absolutely necessary characteristic of the lover that he should be devoted to everything closely connected with the object of his love."

"True."

"And is there anything more closely connected with wisdom than truth?"

"No."

"So it's hardly possible to combine in the same character a love of wisdom and a love of falsehood."

"Quite impossible."

"So the man who has a real love of learning will yearn for the whole truth from his earliest years."

"Certainly."

"But we know that if a man's desires set strongly in one direction, they are correspondingly less strong in other directions, like a stream whose water has been diverted into another channel."

"Surely."

"So when the current of a man's desires flows towards the acquisition of knowledge and similar activities, his pleasure will be in things purely of the mind, and physical pleasures will pass him by—that is if he is a genuine philosopher."

"That most certainly follows."

"And he will be self-controlled and not grasping about money. Other people are more likely to worry about the things which make men so eager to get and spend money."

"True."

"And of course, when you are distinguishing the philosophic from the unphilosophic character there is something else you must look for."

"What is that?"

"You must see it has no touch of meanness; pettiness of mind is quite incompatible with the constant attempt to grasp things divine or human as a whole and in their entirety."

"Very true."

"And if a man has greatness of mind and the breadth of vision to contemplate all time and all reality, can he regard human life as a thing of any great consequence?"

"No, he cannot."

"So he won't think death anything to be afraid of."

"No."

"And so mean and cowardly natures can't really have any dealings with true philosophy."

Bust of Plato in old age.

"No, they can't."

"And a well-balanced man, who is neither mean nor ungenerous nor boastful nor cowardly, can hardly be difficult to deal with or unjust."

"Hardly."

"So when you are looking for your philosophic character you will look to see whether it has been, from its early days, just and civilized or uncooperative and savage."

"Certainly."

"There's something else to determine."

"What is that?"

"Whether it learns easily or not. You can't expect anyone to have much love for anything which he does with pain and difficulty and little success."

"No, you can't."

"And can a man avoid being entirely without knowledge if he can't retain anything he's learnt, and has no memory at all?"

"How can he?"

"So he will labor in vain and in the end be driven to hate himself and the whole business of learning."

"Inevitably."

"So we can't include a forgetful man as one qualified for philosophy; we must demand a good memory."

"Yes, certainly."

"Again, a nature that has no taste or style will tend inevitably to lack a sense of proportion."

"It will."

"And isn't a sense of proportion nearly related to truth?"

"Yes, it is."

"So we want, in addition to everything else, a mind with a grace and sense of proportion that will naturally and easily lead it to see the form of each reality."

## INSPIRER OF UTOPIAS

*Plato's political theories are often regarded, particularly in the English-speaking world, as the core of his philosophy. It has even been said that Plato's concern was with the state and the state alone, and that he was a philosopher only against his will. Added to which, the Plato of the* Laws *is accused of having been the father of the totalitarian state, for example by Karl R. Popper in his* The Open Society and its Enemies. *Conservative thinkers have found "Platonic impulses" in the Soviet and Chinese conception of the state and in the Communist approach to the administration of cultural affairs, and education as a lifelong process. For all these possible derivations, however, let us not lose sight of the essential fact that Plato the political thinker can only be wholly understood when his political thought is seen in the context of his view of the true, the good, and the beautiful, of* eros, *of the "demon" in the soul, and of the divine. Greeks and Romans, Christians and non-Christians have seen Plato as a guide of mankind on his journey "beyond the stars."*

*Plato's ideal state inspired the utopias of Thomas More and Tommaso Campanella and served as a model for all the political thinkers from the seventeenth to the twentieth century who have ventured to draft new forms of political and social organization.*

# The Tao of Lao-tse

The ancient Chinese book of the *Tao Te Ching* is the Magna Charta of Taoism; in form and in content it is the supreme revelation of that philosophically (and religiously) based world view whose roots go back to the fourth century B.C. No author is named in the *Tao Te Ching,* but from the very earliest days it has been traditionally ascribed to a sage called Lao-tse. Historically the first mention of his name in this connection is in the celebrated *Historical Notes* of Szema Thien (163–85 B.C.).

The book consists of eighty-one short chapters, exceptionally beautifully written in a vein that might nowadays be described with fair accuracy as "contemplative lyricism." Basically it revolves round the concept of Tao, the "all-in-one." Tao is the ground of being, apprehended in a permanent dialectical cycle in which mind and matter, beginning and end eternally interpenetrate.

## A COSMIC SERENITY

Lao-tse is an "eternal" whose real historical dates are of as little concern to him and his believers as the calendar of a political system is to the cycle of the cosmos. The year of his birth is given as 1316, 1291, 786, or various dates between 606 and 585 B.C.; that of his death is given as 522 or 500. But the sources agree in citing as his place of birth the village of Khü-jen in the district of Li, Khu county, near the present county town of Lu-i ("Deer City") in eastern Honan. If the sources are to be believed, Lao-tse came of an old-established, cultured family, became an imperial archivist in the capital, retired in middle age, lived an extremely long time, and died leaving a host of grandchildren and an even bigger host of disciples.

Whereas Confucius pondered day

O lord, lord, you who dominate all things
without exercising dominion,
who give to all generations
although you possess nothing,
who have been since the beginning of time
and yet are not old,
who dwell in heaven and earth
and give all things form,
although you yourself are formless.
In you we have our roots;
from you we sprang; in you we live.

Juang-tse's prayer, the invocation of Tao

and night on man's place in the state, Lao-tse lived in the serene knowledge that man's place and being were in the bosom of the cosmos, the Tao.

Rooted in this awareness was an ultimate distance with regard to the state, politics, power, and worldly success. Hence repeated Confucian references to the Taoists as "unreliable customers" on whom there was no depending in the struggle for power. The great confrontation first became apparent in the years following 136 A.D., when Emperor Han Wuti made Confucianism, in effect, the state religion of China.

In opposition to the strong, to the men whose deeds and misdeeds make up the fabric of world history, Lao-tse invoked the female aspect, all things soft, delicate, yielding, apparently of inferior strength, childlike: "The female everlastingly vanquishes the male by its quietude, and by its quietude sojourns in the depths." This "quietude," however, can if provoked and wounded release the emotions lying dormant in its bosom and activate them in the form of indignation. Beginning as far back as the second century A.D., China has produced many political movements—especially popular uprisings—based on a messianic form of Taoism. Rebels adopted the patronymic Li, supposed to have been that of Lao-tse himself. The founders of the T'ang dynasty (618–906) claimed Lao-tse as their ancestor. Taoism gained exceptional historical influence through its association with Chinese Bud-

46

道可道非常道名可名非常名無名天地之始
有名萬物之母故常無欲以觀其妙
常有欲以觀其徼此兩者同出而異名
同謂之元元之又元眾妙之門

dhism, an association that was not without its doctrinal ups and downs. The outcome of a long process of infiltration, however, was that Buddhism absorbed numerous Taoist elements and was decisively and unmistakably colored by them. In present-day (anti-Confucian) China, Lao-tse enjoys a measure of sympathy as a counterpoise to Confucius. Mao Tse-tung's key essay "On Contradiction" contains passages that for all their "Marxist" camouflage could have been written by Lao-tse himself: "The law of the contradiction inherent in all things or the law of the unity of all opposites is the basic law of nature and of society and consequently also of thought. . . . We Chinese have a saying: 'Mutually opposed, mutually complementary.' What this means is that there is an identity between opposites." (The saying quoted here by Mao first occurred in the Taoist-inspired *Outline of the Arts,* written by the Chinese historian Ban Gu, first century A.D.)

Taoism and the Taoist interpretation and experience of the world have had an influence on Chinese (and to a great extent also on Japanese) art and literature that the non-Asian mind can probably not wholly grasp. The lyricism with which Chinese artists and poets apprehend nature and its themes, the landscape and the people living in it, is incomprehensible except in the context of Tao, the ground of all being and supreme revelation of the Godhead experienced through the phenomena of the visible world.

## TAO TE CHING

### I

The way that can be spoken of
Is not the constant way;
The name that can be named
Is not the constant name.
The nameless was the beginning of heaven and earth;
The named was the mother of the myriad creatures.
Hence always rid yourself of desires in order to observe its secrets;
But always allow yourself to have desires in order to observe its manifestations.
These two are the same
But diverge in name as they issue forth.
Being the same they are called mysteries,
Mystery upon mystery—
The gateway of the manifold secrets.

### III

Not to honor men of worth will keep the people from contention; not to value goods which are hard to come by will keep them from theft; not to display what is desirable will keep them from being unsettled of mind.
Therefore in governing the people, the sage empties their minds but fills their bellies, weakens their wills but strengthens their bones. He always keeps them innocent of knowledge and free from desire, and ensures that the clever never dare to act.
Do that which consists in taking no action, and order will prevail.

### XI

Thirty spokes
Share one hub.
Adapt the nothing therein to the purpose in hand, and you will have the use of the cart. Knead clay in order to make a vessel. Adapt the nothing therein to the purpose in hand, and you will have the use of the vessel. Cut out doors and windows in order to make a room. Adapt the nothing therein to the purpose in hand, and you will have the use of the room.
Thus what we gain is Something, yet it is by virtue of Nothing that this can be put to use.

### XVIII

When the great way falls into disuse
There are benevolence and rectitude;
When cleverness emerges
There is great hypocrisy;
When the six relations are at variance
There are filial children;
When the state is benighted
There are loyal ministers.

## XIX

Exterminate the sage, discard the wise,
And the people will benefit a hundredfold;
Exterminate benevolence, discard rectitude,
And the people will again be filial;
Exterminate ingenuity, discard profit,
And there will be no more thieves and bandits.
These three, being false adornments, are not enough
And the people must have something to which they can attach
    themselves:
Exhibit the unadorned and embrace the uncarved block,
Have little thought of self and as few desires as possible.

## XXX

One who assists the ruler of men by means of the way does not
intimidate the empire by a show of arms.

This is something which is liable to rebound.
Where troops have encamped
There will brambles grow;
In the wake of a mighty army
Bad harvests follow without fail.
One who is good aims only at bringing his campaign to a conclusion and dare not thereby intimidate. Bring it to a conclusion but
do not boast; bring it to a conclusion but do not brag; bring it to
a conclusion but do not be arrogant; bring it to a conclusion but
only when there is no choice; bring it to a conclusion but do not
intimidate.

A creature in its prime doing harm to the old
Is known as going against the way.
That which goes against the way will come to an early end.

## XXXI

(a) It is because arms are instruments of ill omen and there are
Things that detest them that one who has the way does not abide
by their use. (b) The gentleman gives precedence to the left when
at home, but to the right when he goes to war. Arms are instruments of ill omen, not the instruments of the gentleman. When
one is compelled to use them, it is best to do so without relish.
There is no glory in victory, and to glorify it despite this is to
exult in the killing of men. One who exults in the killing of men
will never have his way in the empire. (c) On occasions of rejoicing precedence is given to the left; on occasions of mourning
precedence is given to the right. A lieutenant's place is on the
left; the general's place is on the right. This means that it is
mourning rites that are observed.

## XLVI

When the way prevails in the empire, fleet-footed horses are rele-
gated to plowing the fields; when the way does not prevail in
the empire, war-horses breed on the border.
There is no crime greater than having too many desires;
There is no disaster greater than not being content;
There is no misfortune greater than being covetous.
Hence in being content, one will always have enough.

## LVII

Govern the state by being straightforward; wage war by being
crafty; but win the empire by not being meddlesome.
How do I know that it is like that? By means of this.
The more taboos there are in the empire
The poorer the people;
The more sharpened tools the people have
The more benighted the state;
The more skills the people have
The further novelties multiply;
The better known the laws and edicts
The more thieves and robbers there are.
Hence the sage says,
I take no action and the people are transformed of themselves;
I prefer stillness and the people are rectified of themselves;
I am not meddlesome and the people prosper of themselves;
I am free from desire and the people of themselves become simple
    like the uncarved block.

## LXIX

The strategists have a saying,
I dare not play the host but play the guest,
I dare not advance an inch but retreat a foot instead.
This is known as marching forward when there is no road,
Rolling up one's sleeves when there is no arm,
Dragging one's adversary by force when there is no adversary,
And taking up arms when there are no arms.

There is no disaster greater than taking on an enemy too easily. So doing nearly cost me my treasure. Thus of two sides raising arms against each other, it is the one that is sorrow-stricken that wins.

## LXXV

The people are hungry:
It is because those in authority eat up too much in taxes
That the people are hungry.
The people are difficult to govern:
It is because those in authority are too fond of action
That the people are difficult to govern.
The people treat death lightly:
It is because the people set too much store by life
That they treat death lightly.
It is just because one has no use for life that one is wiser than the man who values life.

## LXXVI

A man is supple and weak when living, but hard and stiff when dead. Grass and trees are pliant and fragile when living, but dried and shriveled when dead. Thus the hard and the strong are the comrades of death; the supple and the weak are the comrades of life.
Therefore a weapon that is strong will not vanquish;
A tree that is strong will suffer the axe.
The strong and big takes the lower position,
The supple and weak takes the higher position.

## LXXXI

Truthful words are not beautiful; beautiful words are not truthful. Good words are not persuasive; persuasive words are not good. He who knows has no wide learning; he who has wide learning does not know.
The sage does not hoard.
Having bestowed all he has on others, he has yet more;
Having given all he has to others, he is richer still.
The way of heaven benefits and does not harm; the way of the sage is bountiful and does not contend.

## INDESTRUCTIBLE RELEVANCE

*Taoism is probably history's foremost underground movement, intellectually and spiritually infiltrating the strongholds of power the whole time. To borrow a phrase of Nietzsche's, it makes revolution "on dew feet." Read today, the Tao Te Ching and other Taoist scriptures are as refreshing, dewlike, and invigorating as the day they were written. The German sinologist Wolfgang Bauer, after referring to the enormous historical dimensions of Confucianism, which "managed to dominate whole eras," goes on to say: "The hazy figure of Lao-tse, on the other hand,*

*together with his teaching, always stood outside the current of history and so in a curious way does not appear to have aged at all after all this time but rather to be bursting with genuine vitality even today. . . . Lao-tse's book will probably never lose this indestructible relevance to the present, springing as it does from a remoteness from the present."*

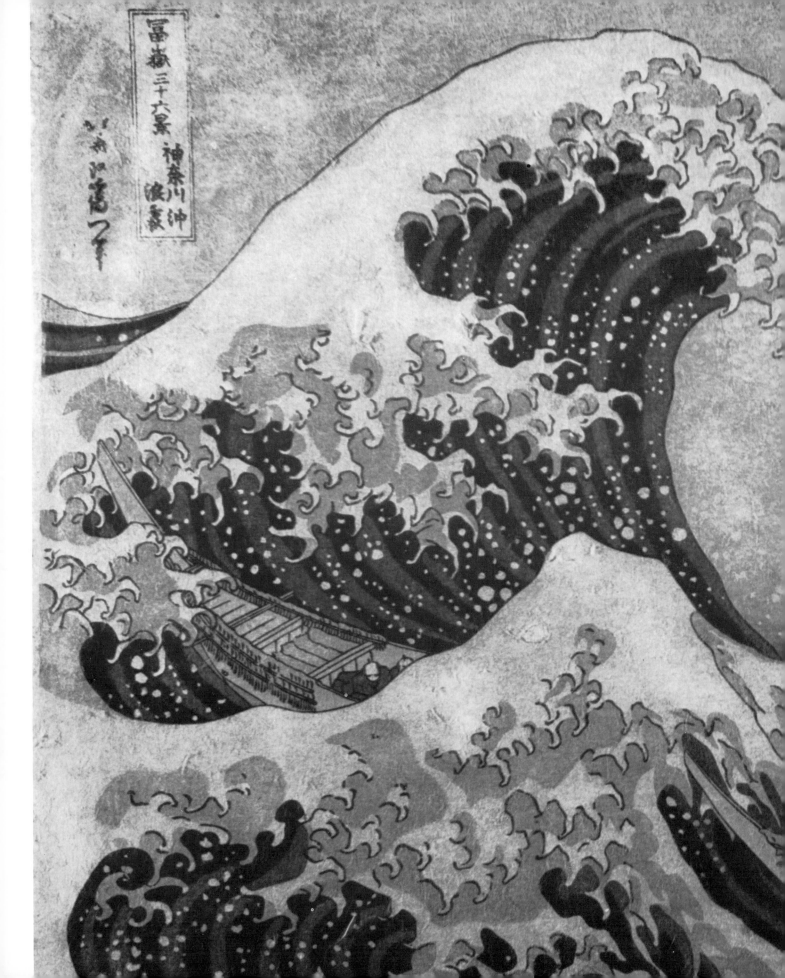

# The Sermon on the Mount

The Sermon on the Mount has come down to us through the gospels of Matthew (chapters 5–7) and Luke (6:20–49). It contains a series of ethical demands made by Jesus, presented in the form of short, memorable sayings arranged in groups. The word "gospel" first occurs in the first verse of the first chapter of Mark. It comes from an Old English rendering *(godspell)* of the Latin translation of *euaggelion,* a Greek word meaning "good news" or "joyful message." The message is that the Christ has come and the kingdom of God is at hand. The four gospels are not the outcome of an attempt to write history; their purpose is to bear witness to the proclamation of Christ in the first century. Jesus did not leave a single written document himself, nor did he take any steps to ensure that his words and teaching were passed on faithfully. Nevertheless, according to the Swiss Roman Catholic theologian Hans Küng, "there probably existed from the very beginning a simple account of Jesus's ministry, teaching, and death. The evangelists—probably . . . not direct disciples of Jesus but witnesses of the original apostolic tradition—collected it all together very much later."

In purely historical terms, all we know about Jesus is that he was a young man from Galilee (born probably in the village of Nazareth), crucified in Jerusalem under the Roman prefect Pontius Pilate around 30 A.D. No other founder of a major religion operated in so limited an area or died so young.

## THE KINGDOM OF GOD IN THIS WORLD

In the Sermon on the Mount—it was delivered at the foot of a mountain not far from the Lake of Gennesaret (Sea of Galilee)—Jesus

Christ, painted by Rembrandt in 1650.

Blessed is he who does not follow the words
    of the party,
and takes no part in its meetings,
who does not sit down at the table with
    gangsters
nor with generals in councils of war.
Blessed is he who does not spy on his
    brother
and does not denounce his schoolmates.
He shall be like a tree planted by the rivers
    of water.

Ernesto Cardenal, from the poem "Blessed Is He"

proclaims a morality without obedience. "As far as we can tell from other sources too, the word 'Obedience' never passed Jesus of Nazareth's lips," writes the theologian Ethelbert Stauffer. Jesus does not so much abrogate the "Law"—the *Torah*—as simply brush it aside. Only because the Roman Catholic Church saw itself as the heir to Israel and the "old covenant" and as a lawgiver in its own right did it make the fateful claim: "The Sermon on the Mount is the law of the new covenant." Jesus, not only in the Sermon on the Mount but in his life and ministry of love and suffering, is after something else, namely "a structurally new kind of justice" (Dorothea Sölle). Jesus's "joyful message," all too often during the two thousand years since his death, has been perverted into a threat or (as the Roman Catholic canon lawyer K. Neumann has suggested) into a conscription to drudgery; but when first spoken, this message must have shaken the disciples, shocked them with its simplicity and newness.

Jesus is no political revolutionary, no founder of a church, and no anarchist, though as the Sermon shows he does abolish all orders, powers, and rights that men have invented themselves and that bar the gate to the "kingdom of heaven" (Matthew) or the "king-

*Left:* The angel informs a shepherd of the birth of Christ. Romanesque relief from the Church of Gustorf, Germany.

The Sermon on the Mount. Fresco by Fra Angelico in the monastery of San Marco in Florence.

The Feeding of the Five Thousand *(below)* : the blessing of the loaves and fishes. Christ with an apostle. From a Roman catacomb.

## HE OPENED HIS MOUTH AND TAUGHT THEM

dom of God" (Luke). That kingdom is not for the dogmatic, the propertied (all ownership is a taking away from others), the warlike, killers and murderers, the angry, or the pious hypocrites.

Moreover, the kingdom of God or kingdom of heaven proclaimed in the Sermon on the Mount is no

fairy-tale kingdom situated in another world beyond the mountains; in fact the language of Jesus and the Bible knows no "other world." The kingdom of God is happening here and now and at every moment. It is experienced by the "poor in spirit," by all whom Jesus calls "blessed" because they are bringing about the great peace as people who "hunger and thirst after righteousness."

Jesus knew full well that his joyful message would be betrayed by the very people who called themselves his disciples: "Ye are the salt of the earth: but if the salt have lost his savor, wherewith shall it be salted? It is thenceforth good for nothing, but to be cast out, and to be trodden under foot of men" (Matthew 5:13). The history of Christianity shows just how well-founded was that fear.

And Jesus went about all Galilee, teaching in their synagogues, and preaching the gospel of the kingdom, and healing all manner of sickness and all manner of disease among the people.

And his fame went throughout all Syria: and they brought unto him all sick people that were taken with divers diseases and torments, and those which were possessed with devils, and those which were lunatick, and those that had the palsy; and he healed them.

And there followed him great multitudes of people from Galilee, and from Decapolis, and from Jerusalem, and from Judaea, and from beyond Jordan.
St. Matthew 4:23–25

And seeing the multitudes, he went up into a mountain: and when he was set, his disciples came unto him:

And he opened his mouth, and taught them, saying,

Blessed are the poor in spirit: for their's is the kingdom of heaven,

Blessed are they that mourn: for they shall be comforted.

Blessed are the meek: for they shall inherit the earth.

Blessed are they which do hunger and thirst after righteousness: for they shall be filled.

Blessed are the merciful: for they shall obtain mercy.

Blessed are the pure in heart: for they shall see God.

Blessed are the peacemakers: for they shall be called the children of God.

Blessed are they which are persecuted for righteousness' sake: for their's is the kingdom of heaven.

Blessed are ye, when men shall revile you, and persecute you, and shall say all manner of evil against you falsely, for my sake.

Rejoice, and be exceeding glad: for great is your reward in heaven: for so persecuted they the prophets which were before you.

Ye are the salt of the earth: but if the salt have lost his savor, wherewith shall it be salted? it is thenceforth good for

nothing, but to be cast out, and to be trodden under foot of men.

Ye are the light of the world. A city that is set on an hill cannot be hid.

Neither do men light a candle, and put it under a bushel, but on a candlestick; and it giveth light unto all that are in the house.

Let your light so shine before men, that they may see your good works, and glorify your Father which is in heaven.

Think not that I am come to destroy the law, or the prophets: I am not come to destroy, but to fulfill.

For verily I say unto you, Till heaven and earth pass, one jot or one tittle shall in no wise pass from the law, till all be fulfilled. Whosoever therefore shall break one of these least commandments, and shall teach men so, he shall be called the least in the kingdom of heaven; but whosoever shall do and teach them, the same shall be called great in the kingdom of heaven. For I say unto you, That except your righteousness shall exceed the righteousness of the scribes and Pharisees, ye shall in no case enter into the kingdom of heaven.

Ye have heard that it was said by them of old time, Thou shalt not kill; and whosoever shall kill shall be in danger of the judgment:

But I say unto you, That whosoever is angry with his brother without a cause shall be in danger of the judgment: and whosoever shall say to his brother, Raca, shall be in danger of the council: but whosoever shall say, Thou fool, shall be in danger of hell fire.

Therefore if thou bring thy gift to the altar, and there rememberest that thy brother hath ought against thee;

Leave there thy gift before the altar, and go thy way; first be reconciled to thy brother, and then come and offer thy gift. Agree with thine adversary quickly, whiles thou art in the way with him; lest at any time the adversary deliver thee to the judge, and the judge deliver thee to the officer, and thou be cast into prison. Verily I say unto thee, Thou shalt by no means come out thence, till thou hast paid the uttermost farthing.

Christ as a fisher of men *(right)*, a wandering preacher close to the common man. Etching by Rembrandt, 1652.

*Bottom:* The name Jesus written in the script used in Christ's lifetime.

Ye have heard that it was said by them of old time, Thou shalt not commit adultery:

But I say unto you, That whosoever looketh on a woman to lust after her hath committed adultery with her already in his heart.

And if thy right eye offend thee, pluck it out, and cast it from thee: for it is profitable for thee that one of thy members should perish, and not that thy whole body should be cast into hell.

And if thy right hand offend thee, cut if off, and cast it from thee: for it is profitable for thee that one of thy members should perish, and not that thy whole body should be cast into hell.

It hath been said, Whosoever shall put away his wife, let him give her a writing of divorcement;

But I say unto you, That whosoever shall put away his wife, saving for the cause of fornication, causeth her to commit adultery: and whosoever shall marry her that is divorced committeth adultery.

Again, ye have heard that it hath been said by them of old time, Thou shalt not forswear thyself, but shalt perform unto the Lord thine oaths:

But I say unto you, Swear not at all; neither by heaven; for it is God's throne:

Nor by the earth; for it is his footstool: neither by Jerusalem; for it is the city of the great King.

Neither shalt thou swear by thy head, because thou canst not make one hair white or black.

But let your communication be, Yea, yea; Nay, nay: for whatsoever is more than these cometh of evil.

Ye have heard that it hath been said, An eye for an eye, and a tooth for a tooth:

But I say unto you, That ye resist not evil: but whosoever shall smite thee on thy cheek, turn to him the other also.

And if any man will sue thee at the law, and take away thy coat, let him have thy cloke also.

And whosoever shall compel thee to go a mile, go with him twain.

Give to him that asketh thee, and from him that would borrow of thee turn not thou away.

Ye have heard that it hath been said, Thou shalt love thy neighbor, and hate thine enemy.

But I say unto you, Love your enemies, bless them that curse you, do good to them that hate you, and pray for them which despitefully use you, and persecute you;

That ye may be the children of your Father which is in heaven: for he maketh his sun to rise on the evil and on the good, and sendeth rain on the just and on the unjust.

For if ye love them which love you, what reward have ye? do not even the publicans the same?

And if ye salute your brethren only, what do ye more than others? do not even the publicans so?

Be ye therefore perfect, even as your Father which is in heaven is perfect.
St. Matthew 5:1–48

But when ye pray, use not vain repetitions, as the heathen do: for they think that they shall be heard for their much speaking.

Be not ye therefore like unto them: for your Father knoweth what things ye have need of, before ye ask him.

After this manner therefore pray ye: Our Father which art in heaven, Hallowed be thy name.

The Kingdom come. Thy will be done in earth, as it is in heaven.

Give us this day our daily bread.

And forgive us our debts, as we forgive our debtors.

And lead us not into temptation, but deliver us from evil: For thine is the kingdom, and the power, and the glory, for ever. Amen.
St. Matthew 6: 7–13

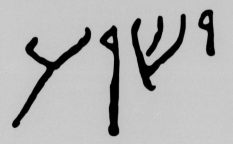

*Fired by the Sermon on the Mount, Christians have made repeated attempts to blow up the bastions of their own ecclesiastical institutions. Many died for the Sermon in the flames of the Holy Inquisition; many more were persecuted, tortured, and killed like the men, women, and children of the so-called Anabaptist movements, the sur-*

*vivors of which were able to escape to America.*

*The Sermon on the Mount was also a major source behind the Christian humanist movement that grew up around Erasmus of Rotterdam.*

*In the nineteenth and twentieth centuries the Sermon on the Mount "caught on" in various non-European, non-Christian hearts in Africa and Asia, and all over the world its message has freed people from the prison of restrictive legal traditions, saving them from spiritual suffocation. Tolstoi, Gandhi, and Albert Schweitzer all stand for this breakthrough.*

*The Christian movements of non-violent resistance that have emerged in South America and Africa (as indeed in Eastern and Western Europe) since World War II actually "practice" the Sermon in the harshest conditions.*

# The Epistle to the Romans

The Epistle to the Romans, written by Saint Paul in Corinth, Greece, in the winter of 57–58 A.D., stands apart from his other epistles. The others were written between 51 and 56 A.D. to Christian communities founded by Paul himself, whereas in his Epistle to the Romans Paul does not address friends and followers but a community of unknown heathen-Christians. Whether or not Paul intended it as a special document, the Epistle to the Romans stands out for another reason as well. It is his crowning work, the deepest expression of his theology, a theology whose substance and intrinsic value were drawn from his very own religious experiences.

This long Epistle comprises sixteen chapters, but we must restrict ourselves here to the most important statements.

## RIGHTEOUSNESS THROUGH FAITH

Paul, a saddler and tentmaker, was born in Tarsus shortly after Jesus Christ. He came from a Galilean family and, as son of a Roman subject, was named Paul. But to his family and the members of the

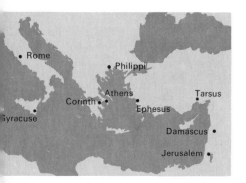

The region of the eastern Mediterranean, the area that Paul covered in his travels to preach the gospel of Christ.

This Epistle is the real heart
of the New Testament
and the purest of the Gospels,
a text truly worthy and worthwhile
not only for a Christian
to learn it by heart
but also to turn to it every day
like the soul's daily bread.
For it cannot be read too often
or too well. And the more
it is dealt with, the more
we value it and relish it.

Martin Luther, introduction to the Epistle to the Romans,
in the first edition
of his translation of the New Testament, 1522

*Above:* Saul's conversion. Relief by Benedetto Antelami on the bishop's throne in the cathedral of Parma, late twelfth century.

*Left:* Paul. Romanesque copper relief from Limoges, on the altar of the Confessio above St. Peter's tomb in the Basilica of St. Peter in Rome.

Jewish Diaspora community he was known as Saulus. Paul received a Greek education, and as pupil of the great Raw Gamaliel I in Jerusalem he obtained his religious training in Judaism. Paul became a strict and law-abiding pharisee. Around the years 34–35 A.D. a profound transformation took place in him after a mystical vision of Christ. In consequence he became Christ's follower, and as Christian missionary he worked first in Arabic Jordania, later in Syria and the western part of Turkey, which at that time was still a region of Greek culture. From there he traveled via Cyprus to Macedonia and Greece, as the first Christian missionary in Europe. After spending the winter of 55–56 in Corinth, Paul intended to return to Jerusalem in the spring with a sum of money that had been collected by Macedonian and Greek Christian communities for the original community in Jerusalem. While still in Corinth he learned of a plan to murder him at sea. He altered his route, arrived safely in Jerusalem, but was recognized at the Temple there and almost

Catacomb "dei Giordani" *(right)* in Rome, from the fourth century A.D. A stairway cut into the stone leads to the richly painted tomb of Arkosol, the vault of which shows Christ with the twelve apostles. The side walls depict Jonah escaping from the whale, and the large figure of a Christian woman kneeling in prayer.

lynched. At the very last moment he was saved by Roman guards, and the Roman commander ordered him to be brought to Caesarea. There his Jewish opponents had the opportunity to make their accusations. After the proceedings had been postponed for two years Paul, as a Roman citizen, appealed to the imperial law court and was consequently taken to Rome in the year 58. There, probably in the year 60, he was sentenced to death and executed.

In his epistles, which he addressed to various Christian communities in the Hellenic area, Paul has expressed his religious message, his "gospel." These theological documents not only establish him as the foremost theologian of the Church and Christianity but also as one of antiquity's foremost thinkers. During the first two centuries after the birth of Jesus Christ, Jews and Christians remained suspicious of him, just as in the nineteenth and twentieth centuries Nietzsche and many distressed Christians were to see him as the "inventor" of Christianity and its Church and to consider his theology an atrocious "perversion" of Jesus Christ's message. Because Christianity achieved its greatest historical impact thanks to the work of a distrusted outsider, Paul's theology was for a long time treated as an "accident."

It can be well understood that this "experience of freedom" came as a deep shock to the men of the "New Law," the Church. Paul's message is literally: "For the law of the spirit of life in Jesus Christ hath made me free from the law of sin and death." The Epistle to the Romans is the message of the *"righteousness through faith."* His question, in today's language, is: What is the sense of a human life?

The mystical mill. Saint Paul is catching the flour ground from the grain of the Old Law. High-relief capital from a pillar in the nave of the basilica of Vézelay, France.

In the language of Paul: Who or what justifies man, bears his life, makes him into what he must be and also wants to be? Paul's answer: "The righteous will live through his faith." Always in conflict with the zealous Jews around him and with the "Law" pressing heavily upon him, Paul documents in his Epistle to the Romans his breakthrough to the freedom of "the sons of God." In psychological terms, he breaks free from the fixations of his childhood, his youth, his parental traditions, because the Christ he himself has experienced makes him a free man,

a new man. He is reborn, here, today, because "whosoever believeth in him shall not be ashamed." Whoever believes is crucified with Christ and is raised up from the dead by Christ. (Paul is profoundly influenced by the Hellenic mystery religions.) Sin and death have lost their sting. Freedom from law—above all from the Torah—but also from all other laws of the world's powers! The Christian is *free,* the only human being to be really free from fear and the terror of "governing powers": For Paul human freedom begins with Christ.

FROM THE EPISTLE

### THE SUBJECT

#### 1:16-17

For I am not ashamed of the gospel of Christ: for it is the power of God unto salvation to every one that believeth; to the Jew first, and also to the Greek.
For therein is the righteousness of God revealed from faith to faith: as it is written, The just shall live by faith.

### GOD'S RIGHTEOUSNESS

#### 3:21-30

But now the righteousness of God without the law is manifested, being witnessed by the law and the prophets;
Even the righteousness of God which is by faith of Jesus Christ unto all and upon all them that believe: for there is no difference:
For all have sinned, and come short of the glory of God;
Being justified freely by his grace through the redemption that is in Christ Jesus:
Whom God hath set forth to be a propitiation through faith in his blood, to declare his righteousness for the remission of sins that are past, through the forbearance of God;
To declare, I say, at this time his righteousness: that he might be just, and the justifier of him which believeth in Jesus.
Where is boasting then? It is excluded. By what law? of works? Nay: but by the law of faith.
Therefore we conclude that a man is justified by faith without the deeds of the law.
Is he the God of the Jews only? is he not also of the Gentiles? Yes, of the Gentiles also:
Seeing it is one God, which shall justify the circumcision by faith, and uncircumcision through faith.

Epistle to the Romans. Excerpt from a scroll from Oxyrhynchos. Egypt, beginning of the fourth century.

## THE NEW MAN

### 5:1–5

Therefore being justified by faith, we have peace with God through our Lord Jesus Christ:

By whom also we have access by faith into this grace wherein we stand, and rejoice in hope of the glory of God.

And not only so, but we glory in tribulations also: knowing that tribulation worketh patience:

And patience, experience; and experience, hope:

And hope maketh not ashamed; because the love of God is shed abroad in our hearts by the Holy Ghost which is given unto us.

## THE NEW WORLD

### 5:20–21

Moreover the law entered, that the offence might abound. But where sin abounded, grace did much more abound:

That as sin hath reigned unto death, even so might grace reign through righteousness unto eternal life by Jesus Christ our Lord.

## GRACE

### 6:8–11, 20–23

Now if we be dead with Christ, we believe that we shall also live with him:

Knowing that Christ being raised from the dead dieth no more; death hath no more dominion over him.

For in that he died, he died unto sin once: but in that he liveth, he liveth unto God.

Likewise reckon ye also yourselves to be dead indeed unto sin, but alive unto God through Jesus Christ our Lord.

\*

For when ye were the servants of sin, ye were free from righteousness.

What fruit had ye then in those things whereof ye are now ashamed? for the end of those things is death.

But now being made free from sin, and become servants to God, ye have your fruit unto holiness, and the end everlasting life.

For the wages of sin is death; but the gift of God is eternal life through Jesus Christ our Lord.

## FREEDOM

### 7:1–11, 18–20

Know ye not, brethren, (for I speak to them that know the law,) how that the law hath dominion over a man as long as he liveth?

For the woman which hath an husband is bound by the law to her husband so long as he liveth; but if the husband be dead, she is loosed from the law of her husband.

So then if, while her husband liveth, she be married to another man, she shall be called an adulteress: but if her husband be dead, she is free from that law; so that she is no adulteress, though she be married to another man.

Wherefore, my brethren, ye also are become dead to the law by the body of Christ; that ye should be married to another, even to him who is raised from the dead, that we should bring forth fruit unto God.

For when we were in the flesh, the motions of sins, which were by the law, did work in our members to bring forth fruit unto death.

But now we are delivered from the law, that being dead wherein we were held; that we should serve in newness of spirit and not in the oldness of the letter.

What shall we say then? Is the law sin? God forbid. Nay, I had not known sin, but by the law: for I had not known lust, except the law had said, Thou shalt not covet.

But sin, taking occasion by the commandment, wrought in me all manner of concupiscence. For without the law sin was dead.

For I was alive without the law once: but when the commandment came, sin revived, and I died.

And the commandment, which was ordained to life, I found to be unto death.

For sin, taking occasion by the commandment, deceived me, and by it slew me.

\*

For I know that in me (that is, in my flesh) dwelleth no good thing: for to will is present with me; but how to perform that which is good I find not.

For the good that I would I do not: but the evil which I would not, that I do.

Now if I do that I would not, it is no more I that do it, but sin that dwelleth in me.

## THE DECISION

### 8:1–4, 18–25

There is therefore now no condemnation to them which are in Christ Jesus, who walk not after the flesh, but after the Spirit.

For the law of the Spirit of life in Christ Jesus hath made me free from the law of sin and death.

For what the law could not do, in that it was weak through the flesh, God sending his own Son in the likeness of sinful flesh, and for sin, condemned sin in the flesh:

That the righteousness of the law might be fulfilled in us, who walk not after the flesh, but after the Spirit.

\*

For I reckon that the sufferings of this present time are not worthy to be compared with the glory which shall be revealed in us.

For the earnest expectation of the crea-

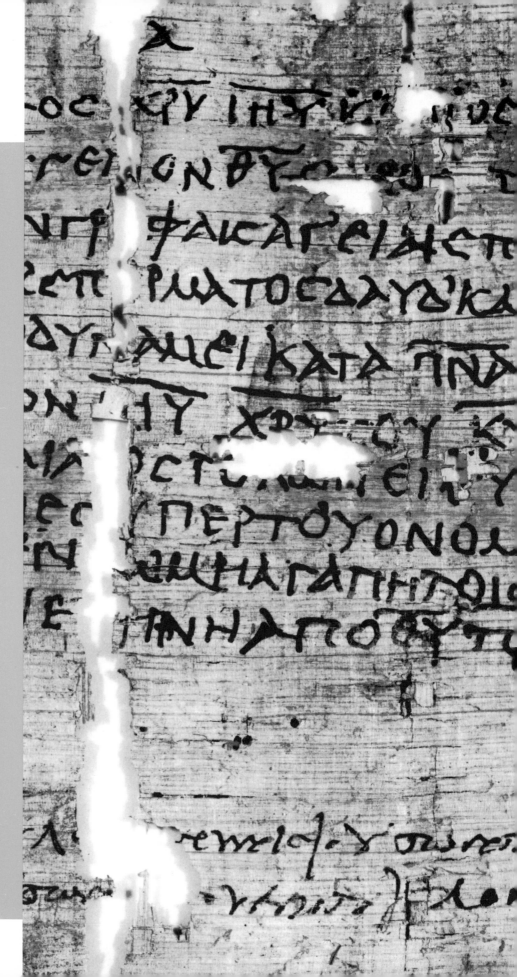

ture waiteth for the manifestation of the sons of God.

For the creature was made subject to vanity, not willingly, but by reason of him who hath subjected the same in hope.

Because the creature itself also shall be delivered from the bondage of corruption into the glorious liberty of the children of God.

For we know that the whole creation groaneth and travaileth in pain together until now.

And not only they, but ourselves also, which have the firstfruits of the Spirit, even we ourselves groan within ourselves, waiting for the adoption, to wit, the redemption of our body.

For we are saved by hope: but hope that is seen is not hope: for what a man seeth, why doth he yet hope for?

But if we hope for that we see not, then do we with patience wait for it.

## THE CALLING

### 9:24–32; 12:1–2

Even us, whom he hath called, not of the Jews only, but also of the Gentiles.

As he saith also in Osee, I will call them my people, which were not my people; and her beloved, which was not beloved.

And it shall come to pass, that in the place where it was said unto them, Ye are not my people; there shall they be called the children of the living God.

Esaias also crieth concerning Israel, Though the number of the children of Israel be as the sand of the sea, a remnant shall be saved:

For he will finish the work, and cut it short in righteousness: because a short work will the Lord make upon the earth.

And as Esaias said before, Except the Lord of Sabaoth had left us a seed, we had been as Sodoma, and been made like unto Gomorrha.

What shall we say then? That the Gentiles, which followed not after righteousness, have attained to righteousness, even the righteousness which is of faith.

But Israel, which followed after the law of righteousness, hath not attained to the law of righteousness.

*Right:* Fish figure carved into a fragment of rock crystal, from a Roman catacomb. The fish is the early Christian symbol for "Christ," derived from the Greek word for fish *ychthys.*

Wherefore? Because they sought it not by faith, but as it were by the works of the law. For they stumbled at that stumblingstone.

\*

I beseech you therefore, brethren, by the mercies of God, that ye present your bodies a living sacrifice, holy, acceptable unto God, which is your reasonable service.
And be not conformed to this world: but be ye transformed by the renewing of your mind, that ye may prove what is that good, and acceptable, and perfect, will of God.

## LOVE

### 12:9–15; 13:8–14; 14:1–4, 17–12

Let love be without dissimulation. Abhor that which is evil; cleave to that which is good.
Be kindly affectioned one to another with brotherly love; in honor preferring one another:
Not slothful in business; fervent in spirit; serving the Lord;
Rejoicing in hope; patient in tribulation; continuing instant in prayer;
Distributing to the necessity of saints; given to hospitality.
Bless them which persecute you: bless, and curse not.
Rejoice with them that do rejoice, and weep with them that weep.

\*

Owe no man any thing, but to love one another: for he that loveth another hath fulfilled the law.
For this, Thou shalt not commit adultery, Thou shalt not kill, Thou shalt not steal, Thou shalt not bear false witness, Thou shalt not covet; and if there be any other commandment, it is briefly comprehended in this saying, namely, Thou shalt love thy neighbor as thyself.
Love worketh no ill to his neighbor: therefore love is the fulfilling of the law.
And that, knowing the time, that now it is high time to awake out of sleep: for now is our salvation nearer than when we believed.
The night is far spent, the day is at hand: let us therefore cast off the works of darkness, and let us put on the armor of light.
Let us walk honestly, as in the day; not in rioting and drunkenness, not in chambering and wantonness, not in strife and envying.

But put ye on the Lord Jesus Christ, and make not provision for the flesh, to fulfill the lusts thereof.

Him that is weak in the faith receive ye, but not to doubtful disputations.
For one believeth that he may eat all things: another, who is weak, eateth herbs.
Let not him that eateth despise him that eateth not; and let not him which eateth not judge him that eateth: for God hath received him.
Who art thou that judgest another man's servant? to his own master he standeth or falleth. Yea, he shall be holden up: for God is able to make him stand.

\*

For none of us liveth to himself, and no man dieth to himself.
For whether we live, we live unto the Lord; and whether we die, we die unto the Lord: whether we live therefore, or die, we are the Lord's.
For to this end Christ both died, and rose, and revived, that he might be Lord both of the dead and living.
But why dost thou judge thy brother? or why dost thou set at nought thy brother? for we shall all stand before the judgment seat of Christ.
For it is written, As I live, saith the Lord, every knee shall bow to me, and every tongue shall confess to God.

So then every one of us shall give account of himself to God.

*The Epistle to the Romans, Paul's theological testament, elucidates even more clearly than all his previous epistles the lifework undertaken by this Jewish Saulus after his encounter with Christ: To bring to all mankind the message of the redemption through Christ, the freedom from the confinement of Judaism. This meant, at the time, to preach the Christian Gospel not only to the Jews waiting for the Messiah but also to the non-Jewish population, irrespective of their origin, race, religion, way of thinking, and culture. Paul did not organize the "Church," but he gave Christianity its spiritual "catholicism" (Greek "kata-olon" means literally "penetrating the whole, penetrating the universe"). Paul's catholicism offers sharp contrast to the constriction, the separation, the dogmatization of everything that is organized or of an ecclesiastical form of law; its aim is a comprehensive Christian ecumenicalism. So far Paul's appeals have not yet been fulfilled by Christendom, but from Luther to Karl Barth and the present, his work constitutes an explosive charge that again and again shatters the "walled-in church" (Luther adopts this description from the great church leader of the twelfth century, Bernard of Clairvaux). If, at the present time in particular, Roman Catholic theologians, as, for instance, H.U. von Balthasar, speak of "razing fortresses," then the Paul of the Epistle to the Romans is behind such statements, and very frequently he is even in the foreground of present-day discussions. Paul challenges the established churches of Christendom which forever are tempted to enforce their law as the Law of God.*
*Let us also remember what Karl Barth wrote in the preface to the first edition of his book* The Epistle to the Romans: *"Our questions are, if we understand ourselves properly, Paul's questions, and Paul's answers must, if their light shines for us, be our answers. . . . The understanding of history is a continuous, sincere, and searching dialogue between the wisdom of yesterday and the wisdom of tomorrow."*

Thy reign restores rich fruits to the
     countryside,
Augustus; brings back safe to our Capitol
Crassus's long-lost standards, ripped from
Arrogant Parthia's temple pillars;

Keeps Janus' arcade empty of warfare
     and
Shuts tight the gates there; bridles
     the runaway
Beast, Licence, strayed far off the true
     road;
Banishes vice and recalls the ancient
     rules. . . .

While Caesar stands guard, peace is assured,
     the peace
No power can break – not civil dissension
     or
Brute force or wrath, that weapon-forger,
Misery-maker for warring cities.

Horace, from Ode 15, Book 3 (translated by James Michie)

Julius Caesar Octavianus (63 B.C.–14 A.D.), adopted son
of Julius Caesar. In the year 31 he secured absolute, exclusive rule over the Roman Empire and took the name
Augustus. After a half-century of civil wars, he brought
the Roman state a period of internal peace that lasted
throughout his forty-five-year reign. Augustus was on
friendly terms with poets, especially Virgil and Horace,
who praised the emperor's peace policy in their poems.

Marcus Aurelius *(far right),* born in 121 A.D., became
emperor in 161. The most learned man of his century, he
is still celebrated as a philosopher today for his *Medita-
tions,* written in an elegant Greek. This work is the concrete representation of Stoic thought in its full development. Because Marcus Aurelius considered the human
intellect to be of divine origin, he had no doubt that all
men were equal—an idea that Stoicism and Christianity
have in common.

The reigns of these two emperors are cultural high points
in Roman history; Christians of later periods looked
back on these "civilizing" rulers as having prepared the
way for the empire's recognition of Christianity under
Constantine in the fourth century.

# The Koran of Mohammed

The Koran is Islam's Holy Book and Arabia's fundamental contribution to the documents that propagate the world's great religions. The text is based on the mystical visions experienced by the Arab Prophet Mohammed. The Prophet preached these revelations, which he had received between the years 610 and 632 A.D., to his followers and committed some of the material to writing. The Koran was given the canonical form still in use today around the year 650, twenty years after the Prophet's death. It comprises 114 Suras or chapters. The headings of these Suras derive from a key word in each text, such as "The Cow," "The Rampart," "The Earthquake." They all start, except for Sura 9 called "Remorse," with a formula called the Basmala, which reads as follows: "In the Name of God, the Compassionate, the Merciful." The Koran's Suras are not arranged in the chronological sequence in which they were revealed to Mohammed. The individual Suras, which vary greatly in

length, are ordered more or less according to their diminishing length and therefore in inverse order to their date of origin. The Suras are written in a stylized rhymed prose and are divided into Ayats—meaning literally "signs," though in European languages they are called verses by analogy with the Bible.

Arabia's Moslems believe the

Mohammed is the master of both worlds,
of both sexes,
of both nations, Arabs and foreigners.
He is our Prophet, who bids and forbids.

Sheikh El-Bousiri

Koran to be a "non-created" book that came from heaven, transmitted by the Prophet Mohammed with immaculate fidelity, and therefore a document unequaled on earth. This is why Moslems are opposed to the translation of the Koran into other languages, or at least are skeptical about such undertakings.

## ALLAH'S PROPHET

A man of medium height, athletically built, passionate and lustful, a man of violent hatred and deep love, a man who did not hesitate for a moment to kill his enemies—this was Mohammed (literally, "the praised one"), the genius of the Arab world. His full name was Abul-Kasim Mohammed ibn Abd Allah. He was born in Mecca in 570 A.D., the son of Abdullah from the old Quraish line of Hashemites and his wife Amina. Orphaned very early, he grew up in the family of his uncle Abu Talib. Around 595 he married Khadija, the wealthy widow of a merchant, whose caravan he had escorted. Now a rich merchant himself, Mohammed traveled by caravan to Syria and Palestine, where he became familiar with both Christianity and Judaism. Christians as well as Jews im-

*Far left:* The early Islamic world, which later extended to India and Indonesia and which exerts a strong influence today in Africa, America, and Europe.

*Top left:* Richly embossed binding of a copy of the Koran, from Persia, eleventh to seventeenth century. Sayings by the Prophet are copied around the margins.

*Left center:* Mohammed (at left) chooses as successor his son-in-law Ali, who is shown holding the double-pointed Sword of Islam.

*Below:* Mohammed's ascension into heaven. Persian miniature from the Safavid period, sixteenth century.

pressed him as "People of the Book" and monotheists.

As we can see in the Arabic poetry of this same period, a serious crisis had come over sensitive minds, who were filled with spiritual and emotional despair. They had lost faith in the many hundreds of gods in the Temple of the Kaaba, the holy stone. At the same time Mecca's wealthy trade aristocracy reveled in luxury and showed haughty contempt and repressive severity toward the underdogs of society, the poor, orphaned, sick, and powerless. These conditions provoked a crisis, in turn, in the forty-year-old Mohammed, who by nature was deeply religious ("God is nearer to you than the artery in your neck"). He frequently withdrew to the desert and there, when the "Tremendum" or great thrill came over him, he experienced his vision: "God commands him to preach to the Arabs the gospel of the only God." ("Allah" is the Arabic word for God.)

Mohammed became the "latter-day Prophet." "He believed with every fiber of his being that the divine judgment, God's wrath, will descend on sinful mankind. But he experienced at the same time the blissful certainty that God's mercy saves all who believe in him.

At first Mohammed's followers were harassed and persecuted. After the death of his wife and his uncle, Mohammed decided in 622 to withdraw from his native Mecca to Yathrib, an event that has come to be called the Hegira. At Yathrib, which Mohammed later named Medina ("City of the Prophet"), his prophetic self-confidence grew stronger as he also developed into an outstanding politician, organizer, and strategist. From Messina he organized the long struggle against "heathen" polytheistic Mecca. In January 630, after many battles, he returned in triumph to his native city. There he destroyed

the Kaaba's many images of gods and proclaimed: "Truth has come, error is dispersed." After Mohammed and his Moslems ("those devoted to the will of Allah") conquered Mecca, the religious and political authority of the victorious Prophet was firmly established in Arabian territories. On his order all images of gods were destroyed. On the pilgrimage to Mecca in the year 631 Mohammed and his son-in-law Ali preached the fourth Sura (verses 3 and 4), which had been revealed to him in Medina, thus permanently anathematizing polytheism. In March of the following year Mohammed, accompanied by 90,000 followers, made a pilgrimage from Medina to Mecca, to observe at the Kaaba the Islamic rites that were by then permanently established. Then he and his pilgrims marched to nearby Mount Arafa where in a sermon (his last) he implored all Arabs to stay united in the faith of Islam. He returned to Medina, fell ill, and died on 8 June 632, his head resting in the lap of his favorite wife A'isha.

Mohammed's self-revelation, his personal and historic testament, is the Koran, the essence of which can be expressed in one sentence: "There is no God but God." According to the Koran it is the heathens' aberration that they associate God with other beings, thus implying that he is not the Absolute Ruler. For Mohammed Allah is the only God, the only Necessary, the absolute Reality, the Saint and the Living, the Eternal Being, the Almighty, the Merciful, the Preserver and Protector, the Visible and the Invisible, the First and the Last, the creator of all being, to whom all being returns. With this perception of God the Koran covers the complete range of spiritual, emotional, and material forms and realities of life.

## FROM THE TEXT OF THE KORAN

### SURA I
### The Opening of the Book
### Mecca

In the Name of God, the Compassionate, the Merciful

1. Praise be to God, Lord of the worlds!
2. The compassionate, the merciful!
3. King on the day of reckoning!
4. Thee only do we worship, and to Thee do we cry for help.
5. Guide Thou us on the straight path,
6. The path of those to whom Thou hast been gracious;—
7. With whom thou art not angry, and who go not astray.

### SURA II
### The Cow
### Medina

In the Name of God, the Compassionate, the Merciful

38. O children of Israel! remember my favor wherewith I shewed favor upon you, and be true to your covenant with me; I will be true to my covenant with you; me therefore, revere me! and believe in what I have sent down confirming your Scriptures, and be not the first to disbelieve it, neither for a mean price barter my signs: me therefore, fear ye me! 39. And clothe not the truth with falsehood, and hide not the truth when ye know it: 40. And observe prayer and pay the legal impost, and bow down with those who bow. 41. Will ye enjoin what is right upon others, and forget yourselves? Yet ye read the Book: will ye not understand? 42. And seek help with patience and prayer: a hard duty indeed is this, but not to the humble, 43. Who bear in mind that they shall meet their Lord, and that unto Him shall they return. 44. O children of Israel! remember my favor wherewith I shewed favor upon you; for verily to you above all human beings have I been bounteous. 109. The East and the West is God's: therefore, whichever way ye turn, there is the face of God: Truly God is immense and knoweth all. 256. God! There is no God but He; the Living, the Eternal; Nor slumber seizeth Him, nor sleep; His, whatsoever is in the Heavens and whatsoever is in the Earth! Who is he that can intercede with Him but by His own permission? He knoweth what hath been before them and what shall be after them; yet nought of His knowledge shall they grasp, after them; yet nought of His knowledge shall they grasp, save what He willeth. His Throne reacheth over the Heavens and the Earth, and the upholding of both burdeneth Him not; and He is the High, the Great!

### SURA XXXVI—YA. SIN*
### The Heart of the Koran
### Mecca

In the name of God, the Compassionate, the Merciful

1. YA SIN. By the wise Koran! 2. Surely of the Sent Ones, Thou, 3. Upon a right path! 4. A revelation of the Mighty, the Merciful, 5. That thou shouldest warn a people whose fathers were not warned and therefore lived in heedlessness! 6. Just, now, is our sentence against most of them; therefore they shall not believe. 7. On their necks have we placed chains which reach the chin, and forced up are their heads: 8. Before them have we set a barrier and behind them a barrier, and we have shrouded them in a veil, so that they shall not see. 9. Alike is it to them if thou warn them or warn them not: they will not believe. 10. Him only shalt thou really warn, who followeth the monition and feareth the God of mercy in secret: him cheer with tidings of pardon, and of a noble recompense. 11. Verily, it is We who will quicken the dead, and write down the works which they have sent on before them, and the traces which they shall have left behind them: and everything have we set down in the clear Book of our decrees. 12. Set forth to them the instance of the people of the city when the Sent Ones came to it. 13. When

---

* Ya. Sin: The 28th and 312th character of the Arabian alphabet.

*Left:* Excerpt from a Koran manuscript from Iraq or Persia (fifth to eleventh century) in eastern Kufic script. It contains verses 1 to 9 of Sura LXXXVI ("The Morning Star").

we sent two unto them and they charged them both with imposture—therefore with a third we strengthened them: and they said, "Verily we are the Sent unto you of God." 14. They said, "Ye are only men like us: Nought hath the God of Mercy sent down. Ye do nothing but lie." 15. They said, "Our Lord knoweth that we are surely sent unto you; 16. To proclaim a clear message is our only duty." 17. They said, "Of a truth we augur ill from you: if ye desist not we will surely stone you, and a grievous punishment will surely befall you from us." 18. They said, "Your augury of ill is with yourselves. Will ye be warned? Nay, ye are an erring people." 19. Then from the end of the city a man came running: He said, "O my people! follow the Sent Ones; 20. Follow those who ask not of you a recompense, and who are rightly guided. 21. And why should I not worship Him who made me, and to whom ye shall be brought back? 22. Shall I take gods beside Him? If the God of Mercy be pleased to afflict me, their intercession will not avert from me aught, nor will they deliver: 23. Truly then should I be in a manifest error. 24. Verily, in your Lord have I believed; therefore hear me." 25. It was said to him, "Enter thou into Paradise:" And he said, "Oh that my people knew; 26. How gracious God hath been to me, and that He hath made me one of His honoured ones." 27. But no army sent we down out of heaven after his death, nor were we then sending down our angels—28. There was but one shout from Gabriel, and lo! they were extinct. 29. Oh! the misery that rests upon my servants! No apostle cometh to them but they laugh him to scorn. 30. See they not how many generations we have destroyed before them? 31. Not to false gods is it that they shall be brought back, 32. But all, gathered together, shall be set before Us. 33. Moreover, the dead earth is a sign to them: we quicken it and bring forth the grain from it, and they eat thereof: 34. And we make in it gardens of the date and vine; and we cause springs to gush forth in it; 35. That they may eat of its fruits and of the labor of their hands. Will they not therefore be thankful? 36. Glory be to Him, who hath created all the sexual pairs of such things as Earth produceth, and of mankind themselves; and of things beyond their ken! 37. A sign to them also is the Night. We withdraw the day from it, and lo! they are plunged in darkness; 38. And the Sun hasteneth to her place of rest. This, the ordinance of the Mighty, the Knowing! 39. And as for the Moon, We have decreed stations for it, till it change like an old and crooked palm branch. 40. To the Sun it is not given to overtake the Moon, nor doth the night outstrip the day; but each in its own sphere doth journey on. 41. It is also a sign to them that we bare their posterity in the full-laden Ark; 42. And that we have made for them vessels like it on which they embark; And if we please, we drown them, and there is none to help them, and they are not rescued, 44. Unless through our mercy, and that they may enjoy themselves for yet awhile. 45. And when it is said to them, Fear what is before you and what is behind you, that ye may obtain mercy. . . . 46. Aye, not one sign from among the signs of their Lord dost thou bring them, but they turn away from it! 47. And when it is said to them, Give alms of what God hath bestowed on you, they who believe not say to the believers, "Shall we feed him whom God can feed if He will? Truly ye are in no other than a plain error." 48. And they say, "When will this promise be fulfilled, if what ye say be true?" 49. They await but a single blast: as they are wrangling shall it assail them: 50. And not a bequest shall they be able to make, nor to their families shall they return. 51. And the trumpet shall be blown, and, lo! they shall speed out of their sepulchers to their Lord: 52. They shall say, "Oh! woe to us! who hath roused us from our sleeping place? 'Tis what the God of Mercy promised; and the Apostles spake the truth." 53. But one blast shall there be, and, lo! they shall be assembled before us, all together. 54. And on that day shall no soul be wronged in the least: neither shall ye be rewarded but as ye shall have wrought.

The seven circles of heaven. Nineteenth century. Indian manuscript.

*Below:* The mosque of Cordoba, Spain.

55. But joyous on that day shall be the inmates of Paradise, in their employ; 56. In shades, on bridal couches reclining, they and their spouses: 57. Therein shall they have fruits and shall have whatever they require— 58. "Peace!" shall be the word on the part of a merciful Lord. 59. "But be ye separated this day, O ye sinners! 60. Did I not enjoin on you, O sons of Adam, 'Worship not Satan, for that he is your declared foe,' 61. But 'Worship Me: this is a right path'? 62. But now hath he led a vast host of you astray. Did ye not then comprehend? 63. This is Hell with which ye were threatened: 64. Endure its heat this day, for that ye believed not." 65. On that day will we set a seal upon their mouths; yet shall their hands

speak unto us, and their feet shall bear witness of that which they shall have done. 66. And, if we pleased, we would surely put out their eyes: yet even then would they speed on with rivalry in their path: but how should they see? 67. And, if we pleased, we would surely transform them as they stand, and they would not be able to move onward, or to return. 68. Him cause we to stoop through age whose days we lengthen. Will they not understand? 69. We have not taught him (Mohammed) poetry, nor would it beseem him. This Book is no other than a warning and a clear Koran, 70. To warn whoever liveth; and, that against the Infidels sentence may be justly given. 71. See they not that we have created for them among the things which our hands have wrought, the animals of which they are masters? 72. And that we have subjected them unto them? And on some they ride, and of others they eat; 73. And they find in them profitable uses and beverages: 74. Yet have they taken other gods beside God that they might be helpful to them. 75. No power have they to succor them: yet are their votaries an army at their service. 76. Let not their speech grieve thee: We know what they hide and what they bring to light. 77. Doth not man perceive that we have created him of the moist germs of life? Yet lo! is he an open caviller. 78. And he meeteth us with arguments, and forgetteth his creation: "Who," saith he, "shall give life to bones when they are rotten?" 79. Say: He shall give life to them who gave them being at first, for in all creation is he skilled: 80. Who even out of the green tree hath given you fire, and lo! ye kindle flame from it. . . . 83. So glory be to Him in whose hand is sway over all things! And to Him shall ye be brought back.

### SURA CIX
### Unbelievers
### Mecca

In the name of God, the Compassionate, the Merciful
1. Say: O ye Unbelievers!

2. I worship not that which ye worship,
3. And ye do not worship that which I worship;
4. I shall never worship that which ye worship,
5. Neither will ye worship that which I worship.
6. To you be your religion; to me my religion.

### SURA CXII
#### The Unity
#### Mecca

In the Name of God, the Compassionate, the Merciful
1. Say: He is God alone:
2. God the eternal!
3. He begetteth not, and He is not begotten;
4. And there is none like unto Him.

### SURA CXIII
#### The Daybreak
#### Mecca or Medina

In the Name of God, the Compassionate, the Merciful
1. Say: I betake me for refuge to the Lord of the Daybreak
2. Against the mischiefs of his creation;
3. And against the mischief of the night when it overtaketh me;
4. And against the mischief of weird women;
5. And against the mischief of the envier when he envieth.

### SURA CXIV
#### Men
#### Mecca or Medina

In the Name of God, the Compassionate, the Merciful
1. Say: I betake me for refuge to the Lord of Men,
2. The King of Men,
3. The God of men,
4. Against the mischief of the stealthily withdrawing whisperer,
5. Who whispereth in man's breast—
6. Against djinn and men.

*Below:* In the mosque of Mecca several thousand pilgrims surround the Kaaba, the holy stone that constitutes the physical center of the Moslem world.

*Bottom:* Pilgrim camp site in Mecca. The Koran prescribes that every Moslem, at least once in his lifetime, must make a pilgrimage to the Kaaba in Mecca.

## AN HISTORICAL DIALECTIC

*In his Koran, Mohammed, both prophet and politician, first established the identification of Arabhood with Islam. He thus laid the groundwork for the political rise of the Arabians, which in turn was to ensure the historic impact of Islam. Only one hundred years after Mohammed's death, Arabs advanced westward via North Africa and Spain as far as Tours and Poitiers in France and founded strongholds in southern Italy and in Provence. In the East they reached Samarkand via Persia, and converted all these regions.*

*The confrontation between Islam and Western Christianity was a dialectic of major historical import. Crusades lasting for centuries, and "Holy Wars" —both in religious disguise although motivated by power politics— characterized the unfortunate, bloody struggle of the world's two leading monotheistic religions. An encounter on a spiritual and religious level did not take place until the late eighteenth century. Two isolated events shed a ray of hope in the darkness of this long period: In 1219, in the middle of the Crusades, Francis of Assisi visited the Sultan of Babylonia and they became good friends. And in the fall of 1453, after the conquest of Constantinople by Moslem Turks, the Roman cardinal Nicholas of Cusa wrote the essay* De Pace Fidei *(Concerning Concord in Religious Belief), which was withheld from Christians until the Second Vatican Council. In this document Nicholas summons all representatives of the world's religions to Jerusalem to prove the underlying spiritual unity of all religions by making peace in God's name. At this council of churches the Islamic religion was to be represented by the "Arab" and "Persian" delegations. The statements that Nicholas attributes to them fictitiously, express a depth of understanding that has never since been reached in encounters between Islam and Christianity. What mankind today is beginning slowly to realize was already understood by Nicholas of Cusa: namely that Islam is one of the*

*world's great religions, one that has an intimate link with Christianity. Nicholas's Christology anticipated the positions of today's theology.*

*In the nineteenth century, when the political strongholds of the Turkish Empire fell, Christian Europe began at last to respect the religious and cultural achievements of Islam and Mos-*

*lem Arabia which had long since been appreciated by freethinkers of the eighteenth and nineteenth centuries. The West recognized its great indebtedness to the Arabs for their transmission of Greek philosophy and for their immense influence on poetry, particularly medieval love poetry, on the sciences, especially medicine, and on Gothic architecture.*

Magna Charta Libertatum, "The Great Charter of Liberties," is a document which King John of England, nicknamed John Lackland, signed on 19 June 1215, reluctantly yielding to the demands of the rebellious barons and prelates of North England. In sixty-three clauses, King John reconfirmed "ancient rights" of his feudal barons with binding effect. It was the first time in the Middle Ages that the Crown's relations with a group of its subjects were laid down as a matter of law. Put in modern terms, the powers of the executive were limited by contract. Still highly topical today, both legally and politically, is clause 29, providing in principle that no "freeman" shall be imprisoned without a judge's warrant.

Yet the king had only signed Magna Charta under the pressure of circumstances: When Stephen Langton was appointed Archbishop of Canterbury in 1207, King John, who disapproved, quarreled with the politically most gifted Pope of the Middle Ages, Innocent III. In 1209 the Pope excommunicated the king; in 1213 he declared him "deposed" and offered the English crown to King Philip II Augustus of France. In 1214 the French king won a complete victory over King John's forces at Bovines. To save his crown, King John then agreed to negotiate with the rebellious English barons at Runnymede near Windsor. And so the barons submitted their demands in sixty-three clauses on 15 June 1215. After three days of negotiating, the text of Magna Charta was signed by the king. This document marks the beginning of the gradual development of English, and European, democracy. What it means to the British people may be gathered from the fact that in World War II one of the original manuscripts of 1215 was sent in a battleship to the United States for safekeeping.

# The Magna Charta

Seal of Cardinal Stephen Langton, Archbishop of Canterbury.

King John Lackland, 1167–1216.

## FREEDOM FOR THE BARONS

Magna Charta is not a charter granting the rights of freedom to all Englishmen; rather it is a document intended to protect the rights of the barons, and was conceived as a bulwark of the feudal system. The "freemen" mentioned in clause 29 are in fact the barons, and the "laws of the land" mean feudal law. It is for the benefit of these barons that the king's power is to be limited by law, arbitrary taxation abolished and made subject to the consent of the peers. All these and other rights and freedoms laid down in Magna Charta relate almost entirely to the lords temporal and spiritual. It must not be forgotten, however, that the struggle for freedom in Europe, spanning the period between the eleventh and the twentieth century, was fought out in stages, first by one group of the population, then by other groups. And because Magna Charta also granted privileges to the cities, it constituted a decisive opening for future democratic and constitutional developments. This is also true of the provisions that require the king to keep his officers of state strictly to the law and to give indemnity for any unlawful acts.

Without the preceding political struggle between Pope and king, Magna Charta would not have come into being. This process has a symbolic significance inasmuch as it shows that England's attainment of all its freedoms in State, Church, and society proceeded in a struggle with papal Rome that continued from the twelfth to the eighteenth century.

Magna Charta, though confirmed thirty-eight times by the English kings until the close of the Middle Ages, gradually fell into oblivion, until it was revived in 1534. The English lawyer George Ferrers translated Magna Charta from Latin into English, with the object of bringing it into the debates then raging on constitutional law. His translation, slightly simplified and "modernized" on the original, gained quite a new significance as a

Count Lotario di Segni as Pope Innocent III (1198–1216). The conflict among King John, Cardinal Langton, and Pope Innocent III was a decisive factor in the creation of the Magna Charta of 1215.

weapon against the absolutism of the Stuarts, and influenced the shaping of the House of Commons. Ferrers reduced the length of the original document from sixty-three to thirty-seven clauses; we present here a more modern translation of the passages he retained from the original.

1. We have, in the first place, granted to God, and by this Our present Charter confirmed for Us and Our heirs forever—That the English Church shall be free and enjoy her rights in their integrity and her liberties untouched. . . . We have also granted to all the free men of Our kingdom, for Us and Our heirs forever, all the liberties underwritten, to have and to hold to them and their heirs of Us and Our heirs.

2. If any of Our earls, barons, or others who hold of Us in chief by knight's service shall die, and at the time of his death his heir shall be of full age and owe a relief, he shall have his inheritance by ancient relief; to wit, the heir or heirs of an earl of an entire earl's barony, £100; the heir or heirs of a baron of an entire barony, £100; the heir or heirs of a knight of an entire knight's fee, 100s. at the most; and he that owes less shall give less, according to the ancient custom of fees.

3. If, however, any such heir shall be under age and in ward, he shall, when he comes of age, have his inheritance without relief or fine.

4. The guardian of the land of any heir thus under age shall take therefrom only reasonable issues, customs, and services, without destruction or waste of men or property; and if We shall have committed the wardship of any such land to the sheriff or any other person answerable to Us for the issues thereof, and he commit destruction or waste, We will take an amends from him, and the land shall be committed to two lawful and discreet men of that fee, who shall be answerable for the issues to Us or to whomsoever We shall have assigned them. And if We shall give or sell the wardship of any such land to anyone, and he commit destruction or waste upon it, he shall lose the wardship, which shall be committed to two lawful and discreet men of that fee, who shall, in like manner, be answerable unto Us as has been aforesaid.

5. The guardian, so long as he shall have the custody of the land, shall keep up and maintain the houses, parks, fishponds, pools, mills, and other things pertaining thereto, out of the issues of the same, and shall restore the whole to the heir when he comes of age, stocked with plows and tillage, according as the season may require and the issue of the land can reasonably bear.

6. Heirs shall be married without loss of station, and the marriage shall be made known to the heir's nearest of kin before it be contracted.

7. A widow, after the death of her husband, shall immediately and without difficulty have her marriage portion and inheritance. She shall not give anything for her marriage portion, dower, or inheritance which she and her husband held on the day of his death, and she may remain in her husband's house for forty days after his death, within which time her dower shall be assigned to her.

No widow shall be compelled to marry so long as she has a mind to live without a husband, provided,

An original handwritten manuscript of the
Magna Charta, 1215, from the British Library,
London.

that she give security that she will not
marry without Our assent, if she holds
of Us, or that of the lord of whom
she holds, if she holds of another.

8. Neither We nor Our bailiffs shall
seize any land or rent for any debt so
long as the debtor's chattels are
sufficient to discharge the same; nor
shall the debtor's sureties be distrained so long as the debtor is able to
pay the debt. If the debtor fails to pay,
not having the means to pay, then the
sureties shall answer the debt, and, if
they desire, they shall hold the debt-
or's lands and rents until they have
received satisfaction of the debt which
they have paid for him, unless the
debtor can show that he has discharged
his obligation to them.

9. The City of London shall have all
her ancient liberties and free customs,
both by land and water. Moreover,
We will and grant that all other cities,
boroughs, towns, and ports shall have
all their liberties and free customs.

10. No man shall be compelled to perform more service for a knight's fee or
other free tenement than is due therefrom.

11. Common Pleas shall not follow
Our Court, but shall be held in some
certain place.

12. Recognizances of novel disseisin,
mort d'ancestor, and darrein present-
ment shall be taken only in their
proper counties, and in this manner:
We or, if We be absent from the realm,
Our Chief Justiciary shall send two
justiciaries through each county four

times a year, and they, together with four knights elected out of each county by the people thereof, shall hold the said assizes in the county court, on the day and in the place where that court meets.

13. If the said assizes cannot be held on the day appointed, so many of the knights and freeholders as shall have been present on that day shall remain as will be sufficient for the administration of justice, according as the business to be done be greater or less.

14. A free man shall be amerced for a small fault only according to the measure thereof, and for a great crime according to its magnitude, saving his position; and in like manner a merchant saving his trade, and a villein saving his tillage, if they should fall under Our mercy. None of these amercements shall be imposed except by the oath of honest men of the neighborhood.

15. Earls and barons shall be amerced only by their peers, and only in proportion to the measure of the offense.

16. No amercement shall be imposed upon a clerk's lay property, except after the manner of the other persons aforesaid, and without regard to the value of his ecclesiastical benefice.

17. No village or person shall be compelled to build bridges over rivers except those bound by ancient custom and law to do so.
No sheriff, constable, coroners, or other of Our bailiffs shall hold pleas of Our Crown.

The English kings Henry III and Edward I, who acknowledged the Magna Charta's validity in the thirteenth and fourteenth centuries.

18. If anyone holding a lay fee of Us shall die, and the sheriff or Our bailiff show Our letters patent of summons touching the debt due to Us from the deceased, it shall be lawful for such sheriff or bailiff to attach and catalogue the chattels of the deceased found in the lay fee to the value of that debt, as assessed by lawful men. Nothing shall be removed therefrom until Our whole debt be paid; then the residue shall be given up to the executors to carry out the will of the deceased. If there be no debt due from him to Us, all his chattels shall remain the property of the deceased, saving to his wife and children their reasonable shares.

19. No constable or other of Our bailiffs shall take corn or other chattels of any man without immediate payment, unless the seller voluntarily consents to postponement of payment.

20. No constable shall compel any knight to give money in lieu of castle-guard when the knight is willing to perform it in person or (if reasonable cause prevents him from performing it himself) by some other fit man. Further, if We lead or send him into military service, he shall be quit of castle-guard for the time he shall remain in service by Our command.

21. No sheriff or other of Our bailiffs, or any other man, shall take the horses or carts of any free man for carriage without the owner's consent.
Neither We nor Our bailiffs will take another man's wood for Our castles or for any other purpose without the owner's consent.

22. We will retain the lands of persons convicted of felony for only a year and a day, after which they shall be restored to the lords of the fees.

23. All fishweirs shall be entirely removed from the Thames and Medway, and throughout England, except upon the seacoast.

24. The writ called "praecipe" shall not in the future issue to anyone respecting any tenement if thereby a free man may not be tried in his lord's court.

25. There shall be one measure of wine throughout Our kingdom, and one of ale, and one measure of corn, to wit, the London quarter, and one breadth of dyed cloth, russets, and haberjets, to wit, two ells within the selvages. As with measures so shall it also be with weights.

26. Henceforth nothing shall be given or taken for a writ of inquisition upon life or limbs, but it shall be granted gratis and not be denied.

27. If anyone holds of Us by fee farm, socage, or burgage, and also holds land of another by knight's service, We will not by reason of that fee farm, socage, or burgage have the wardship of his heir, or the land which belongs to another man's fee; nor will We have the wardship of such fee farm, socage, or burgage unless such fee farm owe knight's service. We will not have the wardship of any man's heir, or the land which he holds of another by knight's service, by reason of any petty serjeanty which he holds of Us by service of rendering Us daggers, arrows, or the like.

28. In the future no bailiff shall upon his own unsupported accusation put any man to trial without producing credible witnesses to the truth of the accusation.

29. No free man shall be taken, imprisoned, disseised, outlawed, banished, or in any way destroyed, nor will We proceed against or prosecute him, except by the lawful judgment of his peers and by the law of the land.
To no one will We sell, to none will We deny or delay, right or justice.

30. All merchants shall have safe conduct to go and come out of and into England, and to stay in and travel through England by land and water for purposes of buying and selling, free of illegal tolls, in accordance with ancient and just customs, except, in

*Below:* Excerpt from the original text of the
Magna Charta Libertatum of 1534, showing
Articles 12 to 14.

time of war, such merchants as are of a country at war with Us. If any such be found in Our dominion at the outbreak of war, they shall be attached, without injury to their persons or goods, until it be known to Us or Our Chief Justiciary how Our merchants are being treated in the country at war with Us, and if Our merchants be safe there, then theirs shall be safe with Us.

31. If anyone die holding of any escheat, such as the honor of Wallingford, Nottingham, Boulogne, Lancaster, or other escheats which are in Our hands and are baronies, his heir shall not give any relief or do any service to Us other than he would owe to the baron, if such barony had been in the hands of a baron, and We will hold the escheat in the same manner in which the baron held it.

32. Persons dwelling outside the forest need not in the future come before Our justiciaries of the forest in answer to a general summons unless they be impleaded or are sureties for any person or persons attached for breach of forest laws.

33. All barons who have founded abbeys, evidenced by charters of English kings or ancient tenure, shall, as is their due, have the wardship of the same when vacant.
All forests which have been created in Our time shall forthwith be disafforested. So shall it be done with regard to rivers which have been placed in fence in Our time.

34. No one shall be arrested or imprisoned upon a woman's appeal for the death of any person other than her husband.

35. If We have disseised or deprived the Welsh of lands, liberties, or other things, without legal judgment of their peers, in England or Wales, they shall immediately be restored to them, and if a dispute shall arise thereon, the question shall be determined in the Marches by judgment of their peers according to the law of England as to English tenements, the law of Wales as to Welsh tenements, and the law of the Marches as to tenements in the Marches. The same shall the Welsh do to Us and Ours.

36. All the customs and liberties aforesaid, which We have granted to be enjoyed, as far as in Us lies, by Our people throughout Our kingdom, let all Our subjects, whether clerks or laymen, observe, as far as in them lies, toward their dependents.

37. Wherefore We will, and firmly charge, that the English Church shall be free, and that all men in Our kingdom shall have and hold all the aforesaid liberties, rights, and concessions, well and peaceably, freely, quietly, fully, and wholly, to them and their heirs, of Us and Our heirs, in all things and places forever, as is aforesaid. It is moreover sworn, as well on Our part as on the part of the barons, that all these matters aforesaid shall be kept in good faith and without deceit. Witness the abovenamed and many others. Given by Our hand in the meadow which is called Runnymede, between Windsor and Staines, on the fifteenth day of June in the seventeenth year of Our reign.

*Magna Charta can be considered the founding charter of European democracy because it established a revolutionary precedent from which in the course of time the democratic constitutions of Europe (and their non-European derivatives) developed. The small number of peers, both temporal and spiritual, who in 1215 compelled their king to grant them "freedoms" (or, more correctly, feudal privileges) realized that they needed support from elsewhere, and found it first in the free citizens of the cities. This resulted in the legal protection of the citizen from arbitrary acts by the king. In European history, this precedent was to be repeated over and over again. By charters, treaties, and alliances, groups, cities and small states, and similar entities obtained "freedoms" and "rights" of the most varied kinds. A prominent instance in the century of Magna Charta is the Swiss defense league of 1291, by which the Swiss secured self-government under Imperial suzerainty. Such local precedents were infectious, both politically and socially. Accordingly, the political rights and social privileges that the citizenry gained through the French Revolution did not remain confined to a single class, but eventually sparked the political awareness of the proletariat, which also successfully struggled for social equality. Wherever we see people fighting for the free self-realization of the human being as against the encroaching power of the State, we can, historically speaking, detect the spirit of Magna Charta. Again, the stipulation of clause 30 of Magna Charta is highly topical, in that it grants every merchant the right "to leave or to enter" the territory of a state; while clause 14 stipulates that a freeman shall be punished according to the gravity of his crime, but not on political considerations. Yet in 1976, according to Amnesty International, at least 500,000 people in this world were being held in prisons and concentration camps as political prisoners, often without trial or judgment by a court of law.*

# St. Francis: Canticle of the Sun

"Hymn of Brother Sun" *(Cantum fratris Solis)* is the name St. Francis himself gave to that hymn which he had composed, in the shadow of death, between the autumn of 1224 and the autumn of 1226 in the garden of the house of San Damiano in which his pupil and sister in spirit, Clara, and her companions lived. The "Canticle to the Sun," known soon after St. Francis' death as "Hymn of Creation," is a poem of nine stanzas reflecting a cosmic view of the world. Enthroned in the center is the "Good Lord" in the splendor of His universal power. The universe and every creature is by its very nature attuned to Him, pervaded and inspired by Him: The longing of the creatures is for God, and man sees God's omnipresence in nature and in the creatures, revealing to man the continual praise of God.

St. Francis composed this hymn at a time when, having seen his life's work destroyed, he was living through dark hours of doubt and despair. The divine eros which pervades the entire poem lives by that love which linked St. Francis and Clara, and to which she stayed true until the end of her days.

The "Sun Hymn" or "Canticle of the Sun" was not written in one draft. When St. Francis, nearly blind, was lying sick in San Damiano, civil war once again threatened Assisi. St. Francis added a new stanza (the last but one), the Stanza of Peace, to his hymn, and sent his brethren to sing this sermon of peace to the warring parties. Hearing the message, the parties sought mutual conciliation, and for more than a generation Assisi was to enjoy political peace.

When St. Francis felt death approaching in September 1226, he dictated to his brethren the stanza on Brother Death, the last of the "Sun Hymn." Dying, he directed that he should be carried to Porziuncola and there laid on the bare earth. With his left hand on the

Earliest portrait of Francis of Assisi, Subiaco, probably painted during his lifetime.

When the Lord gave me brothers,
no one showed me
what I must do,
but the Almighty himself
made it clear
that I should live
by the word of the Holy Gospel.

Testament of Francis of Assisi

stigma at his side, he said to his companions: "I have done my share. What you must do—may Christ show you." Then he asked his brethren to sing him the "Sun Hymn." After sunset on 3 October 1226, he was released from his misery by Brother Death—or Sister Death, "Sorella Morte," as the Italian language has it.

### The Radical

There is no saint, no great figure in all Christianity whose image has until our own day been so distorted, sentimentalized, and prettified as has the figure of St. Francis of Assisi, who was worshiped for a time by radical disciples as "Old Christ," as a second Christ.

St. Francis was born in 1181 or 1182, son of the rich cloth merchant Pietro Bernardone and of Donna Johanna Pica, daughter of a noble family of Picardy. In his father's absence, he was christened Giovanni. When his father returned from southern France, he gave his son a new name —Francesco, meaning "Little Frenchman"—in honor of his beloved wife. At twenty, Francesco was taken prisoner in a feud between Assisi and Perugia. Captivity and sickness set free his "genius," his ability to see everything in a new light, in relation to

God. This meant, as the first obligation, serene detachment from all that engenders war, hatred, and envy. In an Italy rent by continual civil war, St. Francis received an insight which might well apply to all Europe: He who desires peace must renounce all "worldly" power, all possessions of this world. And so he parted with his father first—and with all the masters of money and war: "Listen all, and understand it well: Until now I have called Pietro Bernardone my father; but now that I am resolved to serve the Lord, I shall give back to may father the money over which he has made so much ado, besides all clothes that I have from his hand; and henceforth I shall say: Our Father who art in heaven. And I shall say no more; My father Pietro Bernardone."

It is here that St. Francis' radical way begins: Trust only in God! Heeding the words in Matthew 10:5-16, he decided in 1209 to take up a life of complete poverty, in absolute imitation of Christ. The layman Francis did not intend founding an order. With his brethren he went praying, working, and preaching through Italy, southern France, and, probably, Spain. This was the first great confraternity movement that attained to historical significance in Christian Europe. Around himself and his brethren gathered many others—"heretics," Waldenses and Cathari, whom the established Church persecuted to destruction.

Hoping to save his own much suspected brethren, St. Francis, with a heavy heart, accepted the advice of Cardinal Ugolino of Ostia: that his confraternity needed papal approval or a rule if it was to escape destruction. The "Friars Minor," as they had been called since 1216, became a monastic order in 1219–1220. St. Francis, sick and handicapped by an eye disease, had to lay down the direction of the Order as early as 1220. For the Second Order, he sought in vain to establish the principles of poverty, itinerant preaching, and physical work. In 1223 Pope Honorius III, while sanctioning the rule of the Order *(Regula bullata),* struck out the critical poverty clause. Complete poverty was only applicable to the individual and therefore a private matter. The principle of itinerant preaching also was dropped.

The last years of St. Francis are the restless wandering years of a man crucified, one who is well aware that his work has been destroyed, his work as a radical peace movement which, by the flame of love, freedom, and poverty, sought to abolish the old law of the day. Man is wolf unto man. St. Francis introduced the wolf as man's brother to the city of Gubbio (that is the meaning of this great teaching legend). Penetrating ever more deeply into Christ's passion, he received the stigmata of the five wounds of Christ while praying on Monte Alverno. Frightened, he concealed them until his death.

The only two manuscripts by his hand still extant are addressed to the friar Leo, one of the few followers who stayed with him until the end: a letter, a blessing for Friar Leo. Here, on the reverse of the "blessing", are the words written by his hand which are St. Francis's own comment on his "Sun Hymn":

"You are the holy and one Lord and God who works miracles. You are strong, you are great, you, the All-high, are almighty; you are the holy Father, King of Heaven and Earth. You are Three and One, the King of Kings. You are love, wisdom, humility, patience, beauty; you are the haven, peace, joy. You are our hope, you are justice and fairness, you are wealth and sufficiency. You are our shelter and strength; you are the boundless, great, and adorable kindness."

Painting by Bonaventura Berlinghieri, 1235, from the Church of St. Francis in Pescia. St. Francis is flanked by scenes showing events from his life.

Most high, omnipotent, good Lord,
Praise, glory and honor and benediction all, are
Thine.
To Thee alone do they belong, most High,
And there is no man fit to mention Thee.

Praise be to Thee, my Lord, with all Thy crea-
tures,
Especially to my worshipful brother sun,
The which lights up the day, and through him dost
Thou brightness give;
And beautiful is he and radiant with splendor
great;
Of Thee, most High, signification gives.

Praised be my Lord, for sister moon and for the
stars,
In heaven Thou hast formed them clear and precious and fair.

Praised be my Lord for brother wind
And for the air and clouds and fair and every kind
of weather,
By the which Thou givest to Thy creatures nour-
ishment.
Praised be my Lord for sister water,
The which is greatly helpful and humble and pre-
cious and pure.

Praised be my Lord for brother fire,
By the which Thou lightest up the dark.
And fair is he and gay and mighty and strong.

Praised be my Lord for our sister, mother earth,
The which sustains and keeps us
And brings forth diverse fruits with grass and
flowers bright.

Praised be my Lord for those who for Thy love
forgive
And weakness bear and tribulation.
Blessed those who shall in peace endure,
For by Thee, most High, shall they be crowned.

Praised be my Lord for our sister, the bodily death,
From the which no living man can flee.
Woe to them who die in mortal sin;
Blessed those who shall find themselves in Thy
most holy will,
For the second death shall do them no ill.

Praise ye and bless ye my Lord, and give Him
thanks,
And be subject unto Him with great humility.

## NATURE FREE FROM SIN

*It might not be idle to draw attention to the two greatest antecedents of the "Sun Hymn" of St. Francis: the "Sun Hymn" of the heretical Pharaoh Ikhnaton (reigned 1364–1347 B.C.) who, a revolutionary, sought to oust the gods of ancient Egypt by a universal monotheistic creed. This again has an antecedent in the "Sun Liturgy" addressed to the god Ra, composed at the court of Amenophis I (r. 1527–1506 B.C.).*

*After the death of St. Francis, the Order of Franciscans was repeatedly split up over the next centuries, first in the "poverty dispute." Radical Franciscans still uphold the founder's vow of poverty. The "joyful message" of St. Francis—a very personal combination of an archaic faith in the ultimate goodness of all life with his experience of the*

*In the twentieth century, we find credible witnesses reporting that the dying Lenin concerned himself with St. Francis. More important is this: Youth movements, far beyond the circles of Hippies and Yippies, experience a St. Francis who lived a message of freedom, joy, and peace. Religious and political protest-song movements invoke the "Great Halleluiah" and the image of St. Francis's brethren going out with sermon and song in the Italian civil wars.*

*The brotherliness of St. Francis belongs to the invaluable legacy of a mankind that is at pains still to learn brotherliness—not as a private matter, but rather as a cause that concerns all, the whole family of man.*

*Another significant aspect is that the "Sun Hymn" is the first modern poetical document in which nature is felt to be free from sin. Thus the poem basically anticipates an idea that was to*

The Chapel and Monastery of St. Damian in Assisi, which epitomize in architectural terms the simple way of life espoused by Francis of Assisi.

*Cross—proceeded in Europe's modern age to filter past the control posts of the churches and confessions and gradually permeated Europe's religious underground, which gave rise to the Enlightenment as well as to religious movements. In the nineteenth century, St. Francis came to be admired by poets, romantics, and nature enthusiasts.*

*preoccupy the minds of the Renaissance. Striking are the basic affinities of the Franciscan "Sun Hymn" with the ideas of the twentieth-century Jesuit Teilhard de Chardin, still suspected of heresy, whose work suggests the same Christian-accented pantheism as that we find in the "Sun Hymn."*

79

# Nicholas of Cusa: De Pace Fidei

Shortly after the capture of Constantinople by the Turks in 1453, the Roman Cardinal and Bishop of Brixen, Nicholas of Cusa, wrote an essay in the form of a dramatic dialogue: *De Pace Fidei (Concerning Concord in Religious Belief)*. In this work Nicholas imagines the representatives of the world's religions meeting in Jerusalem in a kind of council appointed to agree on a universal religion which might unite all men and nations of the world in the service of the one and only true God, yet without overriding the traditional conflicting religious customs and rites. Until our very day, opinion is divided as to whether this plea for religious tolerance constitutes "enlightenment before the Age of Enlightenment," or whether we have here a dialectically expert late Scholastic who is seeking by tricks of philosophical theology to "bag" the world's religions for Christianity and the Catholic Church.

Birthplace of the Humanist Nikolaus Krebs, who is remembered in intellectual history as Nicholas of Cusa, Nicolaus de Cusa, or Cusanus.

What is certain is that *De Pace Fidei* expresses the idea of religious tolerance in a form and with a consistency such as had never before been applied in the Christian West

*Below:* Nicholas of Cusa. Relief portrait from his tombstone in the Church of St. Peter in Chains, Rome.

Where everything is One, there can be
no particular names.
Since God is the totality of all things,
he can have no name.
Therefore his name must be expressed as:
One and All,
or better, All in Oneness.

Nicholas of Cusa,
*De Docta Ignorantia (On Learned Ignorance)*

within organized Christianity, and which was not to be applied again until the Second Vatican Council in 1962–1963.

## NON-CONFORMIST CARDINAL

Nicholas of Cusa (hence called Cusanus) was born in 1401 the son of the well-to-do Mosel skipper Johannes Krebs (pronounced, and often spelled, "Cryffz" in the Moselle dialect). At sixteen he went up to Heidelberg University, where he became acquainted with the traditional late medieval school wisdom. From 1417 to 1423 he was enrolled at Padua University, Europe's most modern university of the time, where he studied civil and ecclesiastic law, the natural sciences, mathematics, and philosophy. He completed his philosophical and theological studies at Cologne. In 1427 he was appointed deacon of St. Florin's in Coblenz, and in 1432 attended the Council of Basel. He did not take holy orders until some time between 1436 and 1440.

The Council of Basel clashed with Pope Eugenius IV, because it postulated the basic superiority of the Councils over the Pope. Nicholas of Cusa justified this near-revolutionary stand against papal primacy in an essay that made him famous overnight: *De Concordantia Catholica (On Catholic Concordance)*. In 1437, however, he changed sides to join the papal party, and thus began a brilliant career. In 1438 he headed an embassy sent by the Pope to Constantinople to negotiate an ecclesiastic union, which proved short-lived.

After the death of Pope Eugenius IV on 23 February 1447, Cusanus also received votes in the conclave convened to elect the new Pope. The conclave elected the Italian Tommaso Parentucelli, who as-

Enea Silvio de' Piccolomini. A friend and backer of Cusanus, he became Pope Pius II (1458–1464), the first Humanist to ascend the papal throne.

cended the papal throne as Nicholas V on 6 March 1447. He appointed Cusanus cardinal on 20 December 1448, and continually entrusted him with embassies and visits. In 1450, moreover, Cusanus became Bishop of Brixen. When, in 1458, the great humanist Enea Silvio Piccolomini was elected Pope Pius II, he called his friend Cusanus from Brixen to Rome, so that he might not waste his energies "in the snow and in dark vales." Cusanus became papal Vicar-General, worked for the reform of the Roman clergy, and exercised an important influence on all papal decisions. He died on 11 August 1464, in the small Umbrian town of Todi.

Remarkable is the compass of his writings, which he managed to produce despite the demands of his uninterrupted representative functions. Not less remarkable is the fact that the philosopher Cusanus was "suppressed" in the Christian traditions, and that it is only recently that a Cusanus "revival" has begun.

Cusanus's treatise, which is presented here in extracts, belongs to the great intellectual achievements of the fifteenth century. The tolerance advocated appears in bright contrast to the Christian practice of a century in which the Spanish Inquisition held its bloody sway and in which the preacher Savonarola was burned at the stake in Florence. Even more important than the document itself is the intellectual foundation on which it is compellingly based, namely, Cusanus's conception of God. This is set

forth in his fascinating treatise *De Docta Ignorantia (On Learned Ignorance)*. What is meant here is not the realization of a judicious individual who, precisely through his great knowledge, comes to realize how little he really knows. What Cusanus means is that human science is not capable of knowing anything about God. This, because God is absolutely infinite in which everything, all opposites, all contradictions, the maximum and the minimum, unite and therefore coincide. That is why God is the union of opposites.

On this philosophical basis rests the work *De Pace Fidei*. As God is the union of opposites, the phenomena of life and, accordingly, the different religions are not absolute opposites. They are justified by God. "You, God, who give life and being, are he who is variously sought and variously named in the different religions, because you in your true being remain hidden and inexpressible to all. For you, the infinite creative power, are nothing of anything that you have created, and no creature can comprehend your infinity, because no relation exists between the finite and the infinite. Yet you, Almighty God, who are incomprehensible to all reason, can reveal yourself recognizably to anyone in the manner you deem fit."

Cusanus's great achievement, unsurpassed in his century, is that he admits all religions as holding a measure of truth coming from God, and thereby presents tolerance as an ethical duty demanded by God. The fact that he especially advocates the Christian religion as a vehicle for the general agreement of all religions yet to be achieved, need not surprise us, for no man can fully elude the spirit of his age. But the postulate of peace among the religions, and the logical argumentation given in support, is one of the great achievements of the Renaissance.

## CONCERNING CONCORD IN RELIGIOUS BELIEF

Due to the news of the atrocities which had recently been reported to have taken place in a most cruel fashion at Constantinople, at the hand of the king of the Turks, a certain individual, fired with the love of God, and since he had visited the aforementioned region, prayed with much weeping and besought the Creator of all that He might, out of compassion, alleviate the persecution that was raging there because of a difference of religious rites. It happened, perchance, from a long and serious meditation on this problem, that a vision appeared to this same zealous man. In this visitation it was made clear, by reason of the experience of a number of select individuals versed in the matter of religious pluralism throughout the world, how concord might be discovered and, through it, how lasting peace based on agreeable and truthful means might be established. Hence it is, so that this vision of those who were present might be made known, the author, in so far as he recalls, has clearly set it forth below. After, he was lifted up to a certain intellectual height where, as though in the company of those who had already departed from life, a discussion of this matter was held in the presence of these distinguished individuals, with the Almighty presiding. The King of Heaven and Earth then related that His messengers had brought news of the groans of those oppressed in the kingdom of this world, and that many, because of religion, were warring with one another, and that they were violently forcing others to either reject the faith to which they had so long adhered, or accept death. There were many reporters of these lamentations throughout the world, and these the King ordered to report to the entire assembly of the elect. Moreover, there were also seen here all of those whom the King Himself had, at the very beginning of the world, set in charge of all the provinces and sects of the earth. Their appearance was not anthropomorphic, but they appeared rather as intellectual agents.

Then one of the prominent individuals representing all of those assembled posed this query: "O Lord, King of the Universe, what does anyone possess that you have not bestowed upon him? It has pleased you to inspire the body of man, formed out of the slime of the earth, with a rational soul, so that in him the image of your ineffable excellence may shine forth. From one person a vast multitude has been increased so that it now inhabits the entire surface of the earth. And even though that spirit of the intellect, planted in the earth and hidden in the shadows, does not perceive the light and the beginning of its origin, nonetheless, everything else that you have created is a means by which, once being perceived by his senses, he is able from time to time to lift the eyes of his mind to you, the Creator of all things. He is thereby able to be reunited with you in sublime charity, and finally to return to his source with accomplishment.

"But you are aware, O Lord, that such a vast multitude cannot exist without a great deal of diversity, and that a large portion of this multitude is forced to live a life laden with woes and misery. They live, in many cases, subject to servility and umbrage to those who rule them. As a result, it happens that very few have sufficient leisure to enable them to proceed to a knowledge of themselves by using their own freedom of judgment. Burdened and preoccupied with the cares of the body they cannot seek you, the hidden God. It is because of this that you have provided certain leaders and overseers, whom we call prophets, for your people. A number of these, acting as your vicars and legates, have in your name formulated laws and divine cults, and instructed the uneducated in their meaning and practice. These regulations they have accepted just as if it was You yourself Who personally dictated them, and their credence was in you rather than in them. At various times you have sent various prophets and teachers, now to this nation, now to that nation. Yet human nature has this weakness, that after a long passage of time certain customs are gradually accepted and defended as immutable truths. Thus it happens that not a few dissensions grow out of the fact that some communities prefer their particular beliefs to those of other groups.

"Since you alone are all powerful, come to our aid in this matter. This rivalry comes about simply because each group seems to worship you in all that they appear to adore. No one really wants as his way of worship something that is common practice for all. To want what everyone else wants is imitation. In all those things that man seeks after, that alone is really sought which is the good, and that is You Yourself. What does the person who sees seek other than to see? He who exists, does he not endeavor to continue existing? You, therefore, who are the giver of life and of being, are that one who seems to be sought in the different rites, and who are designated with different names. For since you are Yourself an infinite power, you are something of those things that you have created, nor is any created being able to comprehend the idea of your infinity, since between the finite and the infinite there is no proportion. You can, however, O powerful God, even though you are invisible to all minds, show Yourself in any visible manner you want. Therefore, please do not conceal Yourself any longer. Be kind to us and reveal your face, and all people will be saved, who will desire all the more the artery of life, with a little foretaste of its sweetness. For no one really removes himself from you unless he is ignorant of you.

"If you would only deign to do this then the sword of envy and hatred would cease along with all other evils, and all would recognize that there is, in spite of màny varieties of rites, but one religion. If, perchance, this diversity cannot be done away with, or its reduction would not be advisable, since in many cases a particular religion would actually be more vigilant in guarding what it considers to be the noblest way of manifesting its devotion to you as its Kind, at least just as you are God alone, so also let there be in the same manner one religion and one cult of divine worship. Therefore, O Lord, since your very anger is piety itself and your justice is mercy, be pleased with this suggestion and spare your weak creatures. We, therefore, who are your commissaries, whom you have made the custodians of your people, and, as you already know this situation, we humbly pray and beseech your majesty in the best way we know."

. . . The Word of God spoke to them in this way: "The Lord of Heaven and Earth has heard the groans of those who have been slaughtered and imprisoned and reduced to slavery, and who suffer because of diversity of religion. And because all of these, who either are the

Seal of Cardinal Nicholas of Cusa.

It was not until the Second Vatican Council *(right)*, 1962–1963, that the Church officially accepted Cusanus's ideas on tolerance and the divine unity of all religions.

Everyone answered simultaneously that there was no doubt of this.

The Word then added: "There cannot be but one wisdom. If it were possible to have several wisdoms these would have to be from one; for before there is any plurality there must be a unity." . . .

*The discussion continues, joined by an Italian, an Arab, an Indian, a Chaldean, a Jew, a Scythian, a Frenchman, a Persian, a Syrian, a Spaniard, a Turk, a German, a Tatar, an Armenian, an Englishman, with the continuing participation of St. Peter and St. Paul. On the conclusion of this "Council," Nicholas of Cusa goes on in these words:*

After some time, when these matters had been duly considered by the wise men of the various nations, a number of books were produced, culled from among those who wrote on the observances of the ancients. These works were from among the most excellent authors, as for example Marcus Varro representing the Latins, and Eusebius representing the Greeks, who gathered together the varieties of religion. After an examination of these and many others it was ascertained that this diversity was reducible to the worship of one God. It was discovered that from the very beginning there had been but one cult which was everywhere and continually observed in the veneration of the divine. Yet it happened that quite often, due to the simplicity of the people, they were led astray by the power of the Prince of Darkness, and were not aware of what they were doing.

Therefore, it was concluded from reason that in heaven a harmony is somehow permitted. And the King of Kings commanded that these wise men return, and that they lead the various nations to the unity of the true cult; and that in this endeavor they be led and assisted by the spiritual administrators, and finally, that with plenipotentiary power over all they assemble in Jerusalem, as in a common center, and that they accept in the name of all one common faith, and thus secure everlasting peace for themselves, so that the Creator of all men might be praised in peace and blessed for all ages.      Amen

agents of this persecution or suffer the persecution, are motivated in no other way but that they believe that this is necessary for salvation and pleasing to the Creator, He is moved with pity toward His people and will try to reduce all diversity of religion to one that in the opinion of everyone is inviolable in its greater harmony. This task He has given to you chosen individuals by giving you, as assistants, angelic administrators from His own court who will guard you and direct you, and He has pointed out that Jerusalem should be the place most suitable for this."

At this, one who is a little older than the others and, as it appeared, a Greek, making proper adoration, answered: "We give praise to our God whose mercy is above all His works, Who alone is able to bring it about that diversity of religion can be found in one concordant peace, Whose command we His creatures are not able to disobey. We beseech you that you instruct us how this unity of religion may be introduced by us, for a faith other than that which some nations have defended with their very blood will, as we see it, be accepted only with difficulty."

The Word answered: "You will find that it is not another faith but the very same faith which is everywhere presupposed. You who are now present, among those who speak your own language, are called wise, or at least philosophers or the lovers of wisdom."

"This is true," said the Greek, "If everyone loves wisdom, do they not presuppose the same wisdom?"

## BETRAYAL AND RESTITUTION

*De Pace Fidei, written about sixty years before Luther published his Theses, was not only ignored by Christianity, but thoroughly betrayed for centuries; suffice it here to mention the religious wars and the aggressive aspects of the Counter Reformation. This betrayal also showed in many forms of religiously motivated and church-sanctioned anti-Semitism. Often enough Christian "missionizing" implied the disparaging and reviling of other religions. And even the internal application of the Index and the practice of excommunicating inconvenient thinkers amounted to the flouting of the De Pace Fidei. It was left for the Second Vatican Council to integrate in the doctrine of the Church the views of Cusanus on tolerance and the identity of the godhead worshiped in all religions.*

# Martin Luther's Protest

The German Reformation, initiated by the Augustinian friar Martin Luther, is an historical and cultural event whose effects and forces are still felt on a worldwide scale today. These forces have shaped our present attitudes toward civilization, culture, and humanity.

The Reformation was sparked off by the Ninety-five Theses, or propositions, which Martin Luther sent to the Archbishop of Magdeburg-Mainz, Albrecht von Brandenburg, on 31 October 1517, along with a covering letter which is still extant. In these Theses, Luther pointed out to the Archbishop that many preachers of the time, by the sale of indulgences, were making a mockery of penance.

Only a few weeks after Luther had sent his Latin Theses to the archbishop, there were copies in circulation, and the rumor went around that Luther himself had nailed his Theses to the north entrance door of All Saints Church in Wittenberg, at noon on 31 October 1517.

JOHANNES TECELIUS PIRNENSIS
Dominicanus, Nundinator Romani Pontificis, anno
1517. à summo Luthero territus & in fugam versus,
uti reliquæ effigies videtur in templo Pirnensi.

The object of the Ninety-five Theses, often referred to as "indulgence theses," was to cleanse the idea of penance of all the travesties practiced by the indulgence preachers, and to expound the true meaning of penance in the spirit of the gospel and the valid doctrine of

Martin Luther. Portrait by his friend Lukas Cranach.

Luther was not a reformer.
Luther set out to change the
spiritual foundation of the Christian Church.
He began, full of joy and confidence,
in the knowledge
that God was with him and in him,
so that he might rediscover
the lost springs that did not flow
—or had ceased to flow—
in the councils of the Church
or in the cloisters of monasteries.

Lucien Febvre,
*Martin Luther: Religion as Destiny,* 1928

the Church. They constitute, so to speak, the Magna Charta of the Reformation, not so much for their wording as for the religious spirit that lies at their root.

## THE INDULGENCE CONTROVERSY

The background: On 30 August 1513, the Marquis Albrecht von Brandenburg, then twenty-three, was appointed Archbishop of Magdeburg and Bishop of Halberstadt. On 9 March 1514, the diocesan chapter of Mainz elected him Archbishop of Mainz in the hope that he might pay the pallium money (payable to the Pope for the archiepiscopal insignia), because the chapter was deep in debt through the rapid changes in office (three archbishops had died within a few years). For this purchase of office, prohibited by the canon law, Albrecht was to pay 23,379 ducats to Rome. The Fugger family of bankers finally advanced the sum required, and Rome granted him full papal absolution for eight years. By a secret arrangement, half the expected profit was allotted to Albrecht, while officially the total amount raised by the sale of indulgences was to be used for the building of St. Peter's in Rome.

The sale of these indulgences had been put into the hands of the Dominican Johann Tetzel, a ruthless demagogue, who falsely, but without incurring any rebuke from Rome, explained the sale of indulgences to his hearers as follows: He who pays now—for himself or for anyone else—can buy his way out of Purgatory and Hell. Thus, we read in Mykonius, commenting on Tetzel: "It is unbelievable what this insolent monk was allowed to preach. He gave sealed writing to the effect that even sins which a man might later commit would be forgiven; that the Pope held more

*Below, far left:* Satirical woodcut showing Tetzel, the seller of indulgences, riding a donkey.

*Below:* Anonymous painting showing Luther and the other Reformers writing the Ninety-five Theses on the door of All Saints Church in Wittenberg with a gigantic quill.

power than all the Apostles, all Angels and Saints, even more than the Virgin Mary; for these all were inferior to Christ, but the Pope was equal to Christ; and he claimed that, after the Ascension, even Christ himself now had no more to say in the Church until the Day of Judgment, but had entrusted all to the Pope as his deputy."

The Augustinian friar Martin Luther (born in Eisleben on 10 November 1483, deceased there on 18 February 1546), professor at the University of Wittenberg (where he graduated in theology on 19 October 1512), knew that he had written those Ninety-five Theses as a devout Catholic, a passionate defender of Church and Papacy. He was still emphatic about this in 1545, a year before his death: He said that in 1517 he had been "a monk and a quite raving papist, filled, almost intoxicated, with the Pope's doctrines." Luther had not masterminded the Reformation in anything like the same way as Zwingli and the Scots and English reformers; he was in fact carried away by it, "like a horse whose eyes have been put out," he was later to say in his vigorous style. It was with all due humility that he sent the Ninety-five Theses to Albrecht of Mainz on 31 October 1517. Similarly, in June 1518 he sent Pope Leo X his resolution on the Ninety-five Theses: "Bring to life, kill, revoke, approve, disapprove as you please: I shall hear in your voice the voice of Christ ruling and speaking through you." Rome declined this invitation to a dialogue within the Church, feeling itself unequal to the occasion. Instead, Rome declared with finality that, in the matter of indulgences, anyone claiming that the Church was not authorized to do what it was in fact doing, was a heretic. On 15 June 1520, Rome issued a bull threatening Luther with excommunication. Luther reacted with vehemence.

On 10 December 1520, Luther publicly burned the books of the canon law and the papal bull at the Elster gate. That was the signal for open war with Rome. Then, on 3 January 1521 he was excommunicated. In his three great polemics of 1520 (the most important being "On the Babylonian Captivity of the Church"), Luther became the spokesman of the German nation. The Ninety-five Theses are Luther's first great manifesto of his "joyful message," which he had gained in a hard spiritual struggle with St. Paul's Epistle to the Romans. Put in the language of his Sixty-second Thesis: "The true treasure of the Church is the Holy

Gospel of the glory and grace of God." And the last two Theses: "Christians should be exhorted to strive to follow Christ their head through pains, deaths, and hells" (94), "And thus to enter heaven through many tribulations, rather than in the security of peace" (95).

1. Our Lord and Master Jesus Christ in saying "Repent ye," etc., intended that the whole life of believers should be penitence.

2. This word cannot be understood of sacramental penance (that is, of the confession and satisfaction which are performed under the ministry of priests).

3. It does not, however, refer solely to inward penitence; nay, such inward penitence is naught, unless it outwardly produces various mortifications of the flesh.

4. The penalty thus continues as long as the hatred of self (that is, true inward penitence); namely, till our entrance into the kingdom of heaven.

5. The Pope has neither the will nor the power to remit any penalties, except

The Hohenzollern prince Albrecht von Brandenburg *(right)*, who as Archbishop of Mainz favored the selling of indulgences. Detail from a painting of the crucifixion by Lukas Cranach.

Coin with the portrait of Giovanni de Medici *(left)*, who sat on the papal throne from 1513 to 1521 and who excommunicated Luther.

those which he has imposed by his own authority, or by that of the canons.

6. The Pope has no power to remit any guilt, except by declaring and warranting it to have been remitted by God; or at most by remitting cases reserved for himself; in which cases, if his power were to be despised, guilt would certainly remain.

7. Certainly God remits no man's guilt, without at the same time subjecting him, humbled in all things, to the authority of his representative the priest.

8. The penitential canons are imposed only on the living, and no burden ought to be imposed on the dying, according to them.

9. Hence, the Holy Spirit acting in the Pope does well for us, in that, in his decrees, he always makes exception of the article of death and of necessity.

10. Those priests act unlearnedly and wrongly, who, in the case of the dying, reserve the canonical penances for purgatory.

11. Those tares about changing of the canonical penalty into the penalty of purgatory seem surely to have been sown while the bishops were asleep.

12. Formerly the canonical penalties were imposed not after, but before absolution, as tests of true contrition.

13. The dying pay all penalties by death, and are already dead to the canon laws, and are by right relieved from them.

14. The imperfect vigor or love of a dying person necessarily brings with it great fear, and the less it is, the greater the fear it brings.

15. This fear and horror is sufficient by itself, to say nothing of other things, to constitute the pains of purgatory, since it is very near to the horror of despair.

16. Hell, purgatory, and heaven appear to differ as despair, almost despair, and peace of mind differ.

17. With souls in purgatory it seems that it must needs be that, as horror diminishes, so love increases.

18. Nor does it seem to be proved by any reasoning or any Scriptures, that they are outside of the state of merit or of the increase of love.

19. Nor does this appear to be proved, that they are sure and confident of their own blessedness, at least all of them, though we may be very sure of it.

20. Therefore the Pope, when he speaks of the plenary remission of all penalties, does not mean really of all, but only of those imposed by himself.

21. Thus those preachers of indulgences are in error who say that, by the indulgences of the Pope, a man is loosed and saved from all punishment.

22. For in fact he remits to souls in purgatory no penalty which they would have had to pay in this life according to the canons.

23. If any entire remission of all penalties can be granted to any one, it is certain that it is granted to none but the most perfect, that is to very few.

24. Hence, the greater part of the people must needs be deceived by this indiscriminate and high-sounding promise.

25. Such power as the Pope has over purgatory in general, such has every bishop in his own diocese, and every curate in his own parish, in particular.

26. The Pope acts most rightly in granting remission to souls, not by the power of the keys (which is of no avail in this case) but by the way of intercession.

27. They preach man, who say that the soul flies out of purgatory as soon as the money thrown into the chest rattles.

28. It is certain that, when the money rattles in the chest, avarice and gain may be increased, but the effect of the intercession of the Church depends on the will of God alone.

29. Who knows whether all the souls in purgatory desire to be redeemed from it, according to the story told of Saints Severinus and Paschal.

30. No man is sure of the reality of his own contrition, much less of the attainment of plenary remission.

31. Rare as is a true penitent, so rare is one who truly buys indulgences—that is to say, most rare.

32. Those who believe that, through letters of pardon, they are made sure of their own salvation, will be eternally damned along with their teachers.

33. We must especially beware of those who say that these pardons from the Pope are that inestimable gift of God—namely, divine grace—by which man is reconciled to God.

34. For the grace conveyed by these pardons has respect only to the penalties of sacramental satisfaction, which are of human appointment.

35. They preach no Christian doctrine, who teach that contrition is not necessary for those who buy souls out of purgatory or buy confessional licenses.

36. Every Christian who feels true compunction has of right plenary remission of punishment and guilt even without letters of pardon.

37. Every true Christian, whether living or dead, has a share in all the benefits of Christ and of the Church, given him by God, even without letters of pardon.

38. The remission, however, imparted by the Pope is by no means to be despised, since it is, as I have said, a declaration of the Divine remission.

39. It is a most difficult thing, even for the most learned theologians, to exalt at the same time in the eyes of the people the ample effect of pardons and the necessity of true contrition.

40. True contrition seeks and loves punishment; while the ampleness of pardons relaxes it, and causes men to hate it, or at least gives occasion for them to do so.

41. Apostolical pardons ought to be proclaimed with caution, lest the people should falsely suppose that they are placed before other good works of charity.

42. Christians should be taught that it is not the wish of the Pope that the buying of pardons is to be in any way compared to works of mercy.

43. Christians should be taught that he who gives to a poor man, or lends to a needy man, does better than if he bought pardons.

44. Because by a work of charity, charity increases, and the man becomes better; while by means of pardons, he does not become better, but only freer from punishment.

45. Christians should be taught that he who sees any one in need, and, passing him by, gives money for pardons, is not purchasing for himself the indulgences of the Pope, but the anger of God.

46. Christians should be taught that, unless they have superfluous wealth, they are bound to keep what is necessary for the use of their own households, and by no means to lavish it on pardons.

47. Christians should be taught that, while they are free to buy pardons, they are not commanded to do so.

48. Christians should be taught that the Pope, in granting pardons, has both more need and more desire that devout prayer should be made for him, than that money should be readily paid.

49. Christians should be taught that the Pope's pardons are useful, if they do not put their trust in them, but most hurtful, if through them they lose the fear of God.

50. Christians should be taught that, if the Pope were acquainted with the exactions of the Preachers of pardons, he would prefer that the Basilica of St. Peter should be burnt to ashes, than that it should be built up with the skin, flesh, and bones of his sheep.

51. Christians should be taught that, as it would be the duty, so it would be the wish of the Pope even to sell, if necessary, the Basilica of St. Peter, and to give of his own money to very many of those from whom the preachers of pardons extract money.

52. Vain is the hope of salvation through letters of pardon, even if a commissary—nay the Pope himself—were to pledge his own soul for them.

53. They are enemies of Christ and of the Pope, who, in order that pardons may be preached, condemn the word of God to utter silence in other churches.

54. Wrong is done to the Word of God when, in the same sermon, an equal or longer time is spent on pardons than on it.

55. The mind of the Pope necessarily is that, if pardons, which are a very small matter, are celebrated with single bells, single processions, and single ceremonies, the Gospel, which is a very great matter, should be preached with a hundred bells, a hundred processions, and a hundred ceremonies.

56. The treasures of the Church, whence the Pope grants indulgences, are neither sufficiently named nor known among the people of Christ.

57. It is clear that they are at least not temporal treasures, for these are not so readily lavished, but only accumulated, by many of the preachers.

58. Nor are they the merits of Christ and of the saints, for these, independently of the Pope, are always working grace to the inner man, and the cross, death, and hell to the outer man.

59. St. Lawrence said that the treasures of the Church are the poor of the Church, but he spoke according to the use of the word in his time.

60. We are not speaking rashly when we say that the keys of the Church, bestowed through Christ, are that treasure.

61. For it is clear that the power of the Pope is sufficient of itself for the remission of all penalties and of reserved cases.

62. The true treasure of the Church is the Holy Gospel of the glory and grace of God.

63. This treasure, however, is deservedly most hateful, because it makes the first to be last.

64. While the treasure of indulgences is deservedly most acceptable, because it makes the last to be first.

65. Hence the treasures of the Gospel are nets, wherewith of old they fished for the men of riches.

66. The treasures of indulgences are nets, wherewith they now fish for the riches of men.

67. Those indulgences, which the preachers loudly proclaim to be the greatest of all possible graces, are seen to be truly such as regards the promotion of gain.

68. Yet they are in reality in no degree to be compared to the grace of God and the piety of the cross.

69. Bishops and curates are bound to receive the commissaries of apostolical pardons with all reverence.

70. But they are still more bound to see to it with all their eyes, and take heed with all their ears, that these men do not preach their own dreams in place of the Pope's commission.

71. He who speaks against the truth of apostolical pardons, let him be anathema and accursed.

72. But he, on the other hand, who exerts himself against the wantonness and licence of speech of the preachers of pardons, let him be blessed.

73. As the Pope justly thunders against those who use any kind of contrivance to the injury of the traffic in pardons.

74. Much more is it his intention to thunder against those who, under the pretext of pardons, use contrivances to the injury of holy charity and of truth.

75. To think that papal pardons have such power that they could absolve a man even if—by an impossibility—he had violated the Mother of God, is madness.

76. We affirm on the contrary that papal pardons cannot take away even the least of venial sins, as regards its guilt.

77. The saying that, even if St. Peter were now Pope, he could grant no greater graces, is blasphemy against St. Peter and the Pope.

78. We affirm on the contrary that both he and any other Pope has greater graces to grant, namely, the Gospel, powers, gifts of healing, etc. (1 Cor. xii. 9.)

79. To say that the cross set up among the insignia of the papal arms is of equal power with the cross of Christ, is blasphemy.

80. Those bishops, curates and theologians, who allow such discourses to have currency among the people, will have to render an account.

81. This licence in the preaching of pardons makes it no easy thing, even for learned men, to protect the reverence due to the Pope against the calumnies, or, at all events, the questionings of the laity.

82. As for instance: Why does not the Pope empty purgatory for the sake of most holy charity and of the supreme necessity of souls—this being the most just of all reasons—if he redeems an infinite number of souls for the sake of that most fatal thing, money, to be spent on building a basilica—this being a very slight reason?

83. Again; why do funeral masses and anniversary masses for the deceased continue, and why does not the Pope return, or permit the withdrawal of the funds bequeathed for this purpose, since it is a wrong to pray for those who are already redeemed?

84. Again; what is this new kindness of God and the Pope, in that, for money's sake, they permit an impious man and an enemy of God to redeem a pious soul which loves God, and yet do not redeem that same pious and beloved soul out of free charity, on account of its own need?

85. Again; why is it that the penitential canons, long since abrogated and dead in themselves in very fact and not only by usage, are yet still redeemed with money, through the granting of indulgences, as if they were full of life?

86. Again; why does not the Pope, whose riches are at this day more ample than those of the wealthiest of the wealthy, build the one Basilica of St. Peter with his own money, rather than with that of poor believers?

87. Again; what does the Pope remit or impart to those, who through perfect contrition, have a right to plenary remission and participation?

88. Again; what greater good could the Church receive than if the Pope, instead

of once, as he does now, were to bestow these remissions and participations a hundred times a day on any one of the faithful?

89. Since it is the salvation of souls, rather than money, that the Pope seeks by his pardons, why does he suspend the letters and pardons granted long ago, since they are equally efficacious?

90. To repress these scruples and arguments of the laity by force alone, and not to solve them by giving reasons, is to expose the Church and the Pope to the ridicule of their enemies, and to make Christian men unhappy.

91. If then pardons were preached according to the spirit and mind of the Pope, all these questions would be resolved with ease; nay, would not exist.

*Right:* Title page of the first edition of Luther's complete translation of the Bible, published in 1534 (his New Testament had already appeared in print).

*Far right:* Contemporary representation of a scene from the civil-religious war of 1524–1525.

92. Away then with all those prophets who say to the people of Christ: "Peace, peace," and there is no peace.

93. Blessed be all those prophets who say to the people of Christ: "The cross, the cross," and there is no cross.

94. Christians should be exhorted to strive to follow Christ their head through pains, deaths, and hells.

95. And thus trust to enter heaven through many tribulations, rather than in the security of peace.

## Our Debt to Luther

*The immediate effects of Luther's endeavor to reform the degenerate religious attitudes are known: Pope Leo X, a friendly epicure of the house of Medici, was incapable of understanding Luther's motives. He decided to settle the "monkish quarrel" by his bull of 3 January 1521, which excommunicated Luther. This gesture put the Reformation outside the Catholic Church. Luther's translation of the Bible (the New Testament appearing in print in 1522, the complete Bible in 1534) began to take religious and political ef-*

*fect. The German Peasant War and the Anabaptist movement under Thomas Münzer shook the established feudal system.*
*In the course of the sixteenth century, the Reformation spread throughout Europe in many variant forms, some successfully, others not so. The Thirty Years' War (1618–1648) resulted in "consolidating" the religious spheres of influence. The cultural effects of the Reformation in Europe are most prominent in the French and Anglo-Saxon era of the Enlightenment and in German classical literature and philosophy. These are "daughters of Evangelical theology." It is significant to hear what Goethe, almost prophetically, told Eckermann on 11 March 1832:*
*"We do not realize fully what in general we owe Luther and the Reformation. We have become free from the fetters of narrow-mindedness; through our steadily growing culture we have become capable of returning to the source and seeing Christianity in its purity. We have regained the courage to stand on God's earth with firm feet and to experience ourselves in our God-given human nature. Let the culture of the mind now advance; let the natural sciences grow ever wider and deeper; let the human intellect broaden out as it may. . . .*
*"And the more ably we Protestants go ahead in noble development, the more rapidly the Catholics will follow. Once they feel themselves drawn by the ever widening circles of the great enlightenment of our age, they must follow up, however much they may resist, and eventually the stage will be reached where at long last all will be one.*
*"And so also will cease the tiresome Protestant sectarianism, along with the hatred and enmity between father and son, between brother and sister. For once the pure teaching and love of Christ in its simplicity is understood and lived, we shall feel great and free as human beings and no longer attach undue importance to this way or that in the form of worship.*
*"And so we shall all gradually grow through a Christianity of word and faith into a Christianity of attitude and deed."*

# Grotius on International Order

The Dutch theologian, lawyer, and statesman Hugo Grotius is the founder of international law and the science of international law. A refugee in Paris, living on a small pension granted by King Louis XIII, he wrote in Latin his great work on international law *De Iure Belli ac Pacis libri tres (On the Law of War and Peace, in Three Books),* in 1623–1624. It was published in Paris in March 1625. Grotius had already written the nucleus of this fundamental work in 1605 or 1606, but did not publish it, except for the chapter *Mare Librum* ("The Free Sea"), which appeared in 1609. The occasion for publishing this chapter was the tension between Portugal and the Dutch East India Company, which, with the slogan "Freedom of the Seas," claimed the right of the Dutch to free navigation and unhindered trade with East India. In his standard work *De Iure Belli ac Pacis,* Grotius goes far beyond the ephemeral politics of Dutch interests and also refrains from tak-

Two of Grotius's intellectual fathers: Aristotle *(left),* and Francisco Suarèz (1548–1617), Spanish Jesuit, whose work on legal philosophy, *De Legibus,* influenced Grotius.

ing sides in the Thirty Years' War (1618–1648). His objective is ultimately to put an end to all war; in

The origin of the state
—which Grotius sees in natural law—
is the *appetitus socialis,* the need for
an orderly, peaceful community;
consequently, injustice is anything that
troubles or impedes this community,
and justice is whatever keeps it
in motion in accordance with its
original concept. This ideal justice
is clearly bourgeois-democratic . . .
above all in its exalted demand
for a uniform validity of laws for all.

Ernst Bloch, *The Principle of Hope,* Chapter 36

this, he derived the principles of international law from the generally valid natural law: "Natural law is so unalterable that even God cannot alter it." He was the first to coin the term *ius gentium* ("law of nations"), implying as an axiom of natural law that the nations should live under the protection of the law.

## To Put an End to War

Hugo Grotius (Latinized from Huigh de Groot), born in Delft, Holland, in 1583, deceased in 1645 while traveling from Sweden to Paris, came of a noted family of lawyers. Maturing early, a university graduate at fifteen, he was attached to a Dutch mission to Paris, where he was presented to King Henry IV personally as "Le miracle de la Hollande." At seventeen he opened a law office in Holland, and was appointed state attorney in 1607. In the spring of 1613, he was appointed "pensionary," or chief officer, of Rotterdam. As such he became involved in the ecclesiastic dispute between the "liberal" Arminians, to whom he felt pledged, and the reactionary Gomarians, and was arrested in August 1618 together with the great statesman J. van Oldenbarnevelt, the latter being executed in 1619. Grotius himself was sentenced to life imprisonment and sequestration. His gallant wife, Maria of Reigersberch, smuggled him out of the fortress of Loevestein on 22 May 1621, using a wooden case which had served him to exchange the books allowed to him. Grotius then took refuge in Paris.

Grotius's chief work is divided into three books, the first of which treats the nature of war and law. In the second book he investigates the causes of war and the associated problems of law. The third book sets forth rules of natural law

to determine what is acceptable and what is unlawful in war.

Briefly, Grotius may be said to teach that natural law is a dictate of reason, and beside natural law he sets *ius voluntarium,* or the law laid down by deliberate act, which he also calls *ius gentium,* or "law of nations." He declares that natural law contains injunctions only, but no norms; the latter are set by the states in the form of treaties. In the practice of the law, the statute law of nations, rooted in natural law, takes precedence over this natural law.

In his argumentation, Grotius draws on the great thinkers of antiquity, such as Aristotle, Livy, Seneca, Tacitus, Virgil, Socrates, Plutarch, Thucydides, and Xenophon, all of whom he cites as extensively as he does the Scriptures and St. Augustine. He further draws on the Catholic law philosophers of Spain, such as Franciscus de Victoria and Balthasar Ayala, and on the political philosophy of the Jesuit Francisco Suarèz. It is worth remembering the religious background of *De Iure Belli,* for it was Grotius's lifelong concern to reconcile the factions of Christianity. This enlightened Erasmian Calvinist wrote a treatise in 1640 to refute the Protestant view that the Pope was the Antichrist mentioned in the New Testament. His ecumenical book *On the Truth of the Christian Religion* was published in 110 editions and was even translated into Arabic. To Grotius, peace gained in the religious sphere goes hand in hand with political peace.

## ON THE LAW OF WAR AND PEACE

### CHAPTER I
### WHAT IS WAR? WHAT IS LAW?

I.    Scope of the treatise

Controversies among those who are not held together by a common bond of municipal law are related either to times of war or to times of peace. Such controversies may arise among those who have not yet united to form a nation, and those who belong to different nations, both private persons and kings; also those who have the same body of rights that kings have, whether members of a ruling aristocracy, or free peoples.

War, however, is undertaken in order to secure peace, and there is no controversy which may not give rise to war. In undertaking to treat the law of war, therefore, it will be in order to treat such controversies, of any and every kind, as are likely to arise. War itself will finally conduct us to peace as its ultimate goal.

II.    Definition of war, and origin of the word

Cicero defined war as a contending by force. A usage has gained currency, however, which designates by the word not a contest but a condition; thus war is the condition of those contending by force, viewed simply as such. This general definition includes all the classes of wars which it will hereafter be necessary to discuss. For I do not exclude private war, since in fact it is more ancient than public war and has, incontestably, the same nature as public war; wherefore both should be designated by one and the same term.

III.    Law is considered as a rule of action, and divided into rectorial law and equatorial law

1. In giving to our treatise the title "The Law of War," we mean first of all, as already stated, to inquire whether any war can be just, and then, what is just in war. For law in our use of the term here means nothing else than what is just, and that, too, rather in a negative than in an affirmative sense, that being lawful which is not unjust.

Now that is unjust which is in conflict with the nature of society of beings endowed with reason. Thus Cicero declares that to take away from another in order to gain an advantage for oneself is contrary to nature; and in proof he adduces the argument that, if this should happen, human society and the common good would of necessity be destroyed. Florentinus shows that it is wrong for a man to set a snare for a fellow man, because nature has established a kind of blood-relationship among us.

2. Moreover, just as there is one form of social relationship without inequality, as that between brothers, or citizens, or friends, or allies; another with inequality—the "paramount" type, in the view of Aristotle—as that between father and children, master and slave, king and subjects, God and men; so there is one type of that which is lawful applying to those who live on an equality, and another type applying to him who rules and him who is ruled, in their relative positions. The latter type, if I mistake not, we shall properly call rectorial law; the former, equatorial law.

X.    Definition of the law of nature, division, and distinction from things which are not properly so called

1. The law of nature is a dictate of right reason, which points out that an act, according as it is or is not in conformity with rational nature, has in it a quality of moral baseness or moral necessity; and that, in consequence, such an act is either forbidden or enjoined by the author of nature, God.

2. The acts in regard to which such a dictate exists are, in themselves, either obligatory or not permissible, and so it is understood that necessarily they are enjoined or forbidden by God. In this characteristic the law of nature differs not

only from human law, but also from volitional divine law; for volitional divine law does not enjoin or forbid those things which in themselves and by their own nature are obligatory or not permissible, but by forbidding things it makes them unlawful, and by commanding things it makes them obligatory.

3. For the understanding of the law of nature, again, we must note that certain things are said to be according to this law not in a proper sense but—as the Schoolmen love to say—by reduction, the law of nature not being in conflict with them; just as we said above that things are called just which are free from injustice. Sometimes, also, by misuse of the term, things which reason declares are honorable, or better than their opposites, are said to be according to the law of nature, although not obligatory.

4. It is necessary to understand, further, that the law of nature deals not only with things which are outside the domain of the human will, but with many things also which result from an act of the human will. Thus ownership, such as now obtains, was introduced by the will of man; but, once introduced, the law of nature points out that it is wrong for me, against your will, to take away that which is subject to your ownership. Wherefore Paul the jurist said that theft is prohibited by the law of nature; Ulpian, that it is by nature base; and Euripides declares that it is displeasing to God.

5. The law of nature, again, is unchangeable—even in the sense that it cannot be changed by God. Measureless as is the power of God, nevertheless it can be said that there are certain things over which that power does not extend; for things of which this is said are spoken only, having no sense corresponding with reality and being mutually contradictory. Just as even God, then, cannot cause that two times two should not make four, so He

cannot cause that that which is intrinsically evil be not evil.

This is what Aristotle means when he says: "Some things are thought of as bad the moment they are named." For just as the being of things, from the time that they begin to exist, and in the manner in which they exist, is not dependent on anything else, so also the properties, which of necessity characterize that being; such a property is the badness of certain acts, when judged by the standard of a nature endowed with sound reason.

## Chapter III
## Distinction Between Public and Private War; Explanation of Sovereignty

I. Division of war into public and private

1. A public war is that which is waged by him who has lawful authority to wage it; a private war, that which is waged by one who has not the lawful authority; and a mixed war is that which is on one side public, on the other side private. Let us deal first with private war, as the more ancient.

2. That private wars in some cases may be waged lawfully, so far as the law of nature is concerned, is, I think, sufficiently clear from what was said above, when we showed that the use of force to ward off injury is not in conflict with the law of nature. But possibly some may think that after public tribunals had been established private wars were not permissible. For although public tribunals are the creation not of nature but of man, it is, nevertheless, much more consistent with moral standards, and more conducive to the peace of individuals, that a matter be judicially investigated by one who has no personal interest in it, than that individ-

uals, too often having only their own interests in view, should seek by their own hands to obtain that which they consider right; wherefore equity and reason given to us by nature declare that so praiseworthy an institution should have the fullest support. Says Paul the jurist, "Individuals must not be permitted to do that which the magistrate can do in the name of the state, in order that there may be no occasion for raising a greater disturbance." "The reason," King Theodoric said, "why laws were clothed with a reverential regard, was that nothing might be done by one's own hand, nothing on individual impulse. For what difference is there between tranquil peace and the hurly-burly of war, if controversies between individuals are settled by the use of force?"

The laws term it a use of force "when an individual tries to enforce his claim to what he thinks is due him without having recourse to a judge."

II. The proposition, that according to the law of nature not all private war is unpermissible since the establishment of courts, is defended, illustrations being added

1. It is surely beyond doubt that the licence which was prevalent before the establishment of courts has been greatly restricted. Nevertheless there are circumstances under which such licence even now holds good, that is, undoubtedly, where judicial procedure ceases to be available. For the law which forbids a man to seek to recover his own otherwise than through judicial process is ordinarily understood as applicable only where judicial process has been possible.

Now judicial procedure ceases to be available either temporarily or continuously. It ceases to be available temporarily when one cannot wait to refer a

The port of Amsterdam in the seventeenth century. At center, the Admiralty House. This was also the seat of the Dutch East India Company, founded by the great statesman Oldenbarnevelt (a friend of Grotius). The company's territorial conquests in the Malaysian Archipelago laid the foundation for Holland's colonial empire in the seventeenth century. Grotius's *Freedom of the Seas* favored the company's commercial interests.

matter to a judge without certain danger or loss. It ceases to be available continuously either in law or in fact: in law, if one finds himself in places without inhabitants, as on the sea, in a wilderness, or on vacant islands, or in any other places where there is no state; in fact, if those who are subject to jurisdiction do not heed the judge, or if the judge has openly refused to take cognizance.

2. What we said, that even after the establishment of courts not all private wars were in conflict with the law of nature, can be supported also from the law which was given to the Jews; for therein through the agency of Moses God said (*Exodus*, xxii. 2): "If the thief be found breaking in, and be smitten so that he dieth, there shall be no bloodguiltiness for him. If the sun be risen upon him, there shall be bloodguiltiness for him." It seems clear that this ordinance, which makes so careful a distinction, not only assures impunity but also explains the law of nature, and that it is not founded upon a special divine mandate, but grounded in common equity. Hence, we see, other nations also followed it. Well known is the provision of the Twelve Tables, undoubtedly taken from the ancient Attic law: "If a theft has been committed at night, and any one has killed the thief, be it that the thief was rightly slain." Thus by the laws of all peoples known to us the person who in peril of his life has by means of arms defended himself against an assailant is adjudged innocent. An agreement so manifest furnishes in itself the proof that in it there is nothing in conflict with the law of nature.

III. The proposition is defended that private war in some cases is permissible even according to the law of the Gospel, objections being met

1. In the case of the volitional divine law in its more perfect form, that is, the law of the Gospel, a greater difficulty presents itself. I do not doubt that God, Who has over our lives a more absolute right than we ourselves, might have required of us so great a degree of forbearance that, as individuals, when confronted with danger, it would be our duty to allow ourselves to be killed rather than to kill. But did God purpose to bind us in so extreme a fashion? That is the point which we are to investigate.

On the affirmative side, two passages are commonly brought forward to which, in the discussion of the general question, we have already referred. They are: "But I say unto you, Resist not him that is evil" (*Matthew*, v. 39); and "Avenge not yourselves, beloved" (*Romans*, xii. 19), where the Latin translation has "Defend not yourselves, beloved."

2. Among the early Christians there was no lack of those who did not indeed disapprove of public war, but who thought that in the case of an individual self-defense was forbidden. The passages of Ambrose favorable to war we quoted above. Familiar to all are the statements of Augustine, which are even more numerous and more clear. But the same Ambrose says: "And perchance He said to Peter, who offered him two swords, 'It is enough,' as if He had said that the use of the sword in self-defense was permissible up to the time of the Gospel; with the implication that the teaching of the law stressed equity, while the teaching of the Gospel stressed truth." And in another passage he adds: "The Christian, even if he fall in the way of an armed brigand, cannot strike in turn one who strikes him, from fear that, while defending his safety, he mar his piety."

"I find no fault," says Augustine, "with the law which permits the slaying of such people" (brigands and others who assault with violence), "but I do not see how to justify those who put them to death."

## Chapter III
### On War That Is Lawful or Public According to the Law of Nations; on the Declaration of War

I.   A public war according to the law of nations is a war between different peoples

1. In a previous passage we began to say that by authors of repute a war is often called lawful not from the cause from which it arises, nor, as is done in other cases, from the importance of its exploits, but because of certain peculiar legal consequences. Of what sort a lawful war is, however, will best be perceived from the definition of enemies given by the Roman jurists.

"Enemies are those who in the name of the state declare war upon us, or upon whom we in the name of the state declare war; others are brigands and robbers," says Pomponius.

2. It needs only to be noted further that we may understand that any one who has the supreme authority in a state may take the place of the Roman people in our illustration. "An enemy," says Cicero, "is the one that has a state, a senate, a treasury, the agreement and concord of the citizens, and the power, if the course of events leads thereto, to conclude peace and an alliance."

## Chapter XXV
### Conclusion, with Admonitions on Behalf of Good Faith and Peace

I.   Admonitions to preserve peace

At this point I think that I can bring my work to an end, not because all has been said that could be said, but because sufficient has been said to lay the foundations. Whoever may wish to build on these foundations a more imposing structure will not only find me free from envy, but will have my sincere gratitude.

Yet before I dismiss the reader I shall add a few admonitions which may be of value in war, and after war, for the preservation of good faith and of peace; just as in treating of the commencement of war I added certain admonitions regarding the avoidance of wars, so far as this can be accomplished.

And good faith should be preserved, not only for other reasons but also in order that the hope of peace may not be done away with. For not only is every state sustained by good faith, as Cicero declares, but also that greater society of states. Aristotle truly says that, if good faith has been taken away, "all intercourse among men ceases to exist." Rightly the same Cicero says that "it is an impious act to destroy the good faith which holds life together." To use Seneca's phrase, it is "the most exalted good of the human heart." And this good faith the supreme rulers of men ought so much the more earnestly than others to maintain as they violate it with greater impunity; if good faith shall be done away with, they will be like wild beasts, whose violence all men fear. Justice, it is true, in its other aspects often contains elements of obscurity; but the bond of good faith is in itself plain to see, nay more, it is brought into use to so great an extent that it removes all obscurity from business transactions.

II.   In war peace should always be kept in view

Again, during the entire period of administration of a war the soul cannot be kept serene and trusting in God unless it is always looking forward to peace. Sallust most truly said, "The wise wage war for the sake of peace." With this the opinion of Augustine agrees: "Peace is not sought that war may be followed, but war is waged that peace may be secured." Aristotle himself more than once condemns those nations which made warlike pursuits, as it were, their end and aim.

III.   And peace should also be accepted even at a loss, especially by Christians

If, then, it is possible to have peace with sufficient safety, it is well established by condonation of offences, damages, and expenses; this holds especially among Christians, on whom the Lord has bestowed His peace. And His best interpreter wishes us, so far as it is possible within our power, to seek peace with all men. It is characteristic of a good man, as we read in Sallust, to be unwilling to begin war, not gladly to pursue it to the bitter end.

HVGONIS GROTII
DE IVRE BELLI
AC PACIS
LIBRI TRES.

In quibus ius naturæ & Gentium : item iuris publici præcipua explicantur.

PARISIIS;

Apud NICOLAVM BVON, in via Iacobæa, sub S. Claudij, & Hominis Siluestris.

M. DC. XXV.
CVM PRIVILEGIO REGIS.

Niccolò Machiavelli *(above)*. Portrait by Santi di Tito in the Palazzo Vecchio, Florence. Machiavelli (1469–1527) pleaded for a legal system that would ensure Italy's internal peace; this was an idea that Grotius formulated in universal terms.

*Below:* On the basis of specific principles enunciated in the constitution of the League of Nations, a group of Foreign Ministers from several countries assembled in Lugano, Switzerland, in 1928 to confer on peace measures from the 1925 Locarno Pact. *From left to right:* Zaleski, Poland; Adatei, Japan; Chamberlain, Great Britain; Stresemann, Germany; Scialoja, Italy; and Briand, France.

#### IV. The consideration stated is useful to the conquered

This one consideration ought to be sufficient. However, human advantage also often draws in the same direction, first, those who are weaker, because a long contest with a stronger opponent is dangerous, and, just as on a ship, greater misfortune must be avoided at some loss, with complete disregard of anger and hope which, as Livy has rightly said, are deceitful advisers.

#### V. The consideration stated is also useful to the conqueror

Again, human advantage draws in the same direction also the stronger. The reason is, as the same Livy no less truly says, that peace is bounteous and creditable to those who grant it while their affairs are prosperous; and it is better and safer than a victory that is hoped for. It must be kept in mind that Mars is on both sides. As Aristotle says, "In war men ought to consider how many and how unexpected changes are wont to occur."

#### VI. The consideration stated is useful likewise to those whose fortunes are in doubt

But, if both sides seem to be equal to each other, this in truth, as Caesar says, is the best time to treat of peace, while each has confidence in himself.

#### VII. Peace, when made, must be kept with the utmost scruple

Moreover peace, whatever the terms on which it is made, ought to be preserved absolutely, on account of the sacredness of good faith, which I have mentioned; and not only should treachery be anxiously avoided, but everything else that may arouse anger. What Cicero said about private friendships you may apply to public friendships no less correctly: not only should all friendships be safeguarded with the greatest devotion and good faith, but especially those which have been restored to goodwill after enmity.

*The work of Grotius is enjoying a revival in the twentieth century. In 1915, the Grotius Society was founded in London. The League of Nations and later the United Nations have invoked Grotius. At the Nuremberg trials, he played the part of the crown witness whose authority is undisputed. The rules Grotius set forth for the interpretation of treaties reappeared in the Vienna Convention on treaty law, 1969. The Viennese international lawyer Karl Zemanek has said: "While his views are now only partly identical with present international law, his basic ideas have conditioned the world's attitudes." It is relevant here to draw attention to another great European political thinker whose work is usually seen in the wrong light: Niccolò Machiavelli (1469–1527). A high-ranking official and ambassador of the Florentine Republic, he wrote, after the fall of the republic and the return of the Medici, his* Il Principe, *which has since become identified with his name. It was published in 1532. In this work Machiavelli developed his political ideas against the background of Italy's political distress generally and the catastro-*

*phe of the Florentine Republic in particular, and in acute awareness of the rapid disintegration of Europe as "Christendom." His object is to rescue the people and the nations from their frenzy of self-destruction, called "world history," which is foreseeable by means of political science.*

*Machiavelli is as controversial today as he was in his own time. His realistic*

*approach (enriched with mythical elements), which outspokenly exposes the brutality, the terror, and the subtlety practiced by those in power, was, and still is, thrown in his face. Yet Machiavelli is not the devil's advocate, but rather an incorruptible critic resolved to help human beings, though first and foremost the "poor devils," his own sorely tried Italian countrymen.*

# 1776

# The Virginia Declaration of Rights

This declaration of human rights, which provided the model for the American Bill of Rights, contains sixteen briefly formulated articles in which the basic American concepts of the freedom of the individual and the sovereignty of the people were laid down just one month before the formal United States Declaration of Independence. The draft of the Virginia Declaration of Rights was presented and adopted on 12 June 1776 whereas the U.S. independence was proclaimed on 4 July that year. George Mason, who, like George Washington, Thomas Jefferson, and Richard Henry Lee, came from Virginia, the oldest and most populous of the English Colonies, is chiefly credited with having formulated and edited the text. Ultimately, this declaration is rooted in the ideas developed by the Euro-

First page of the draft of the British Bill of Rights of 1688. The original 1688 document is in the Record Office of the House of Lords, London.

George Mason, 1725–1792.

We hold these Truths to be self-evident, that all Men are created equal, that they are endowed by their Creator with certain unalienable Rights, that among these are Life, Liberty, and the Pursuit of Happiness— That to secure these Rights, Governments are instituted among Men, deriving their just Powers from the Consent of the Governed, that when any Form of Government becomes destructive of these Ends, it is the Right of the People to alter or to abolish it. . . .

Declaration of Independence of the United States, 1776

pean Enlightenment. Directly, it continues the political traditions of the motherland, England.

## FORERUNNERS OF THE BILL OF RIGHTS

The background of this declaration was that in 1775 the American Continental Congress of Philadelphia had requested the then Colonies to form new governments. New constitutions were drafted within a few months. These constitutions, however, had been preceded by the Virginia declaration, laying down the human rights as the basic ideology. It was modeled on the traditional rights established in the English motherland, from which the English-Americans broke away with great reluctance, hardly realizing it themselves. These English model rights are chiefly found in the Bill of Rights of William of Orange, 1689, and in the Habeas Corpus Act of 1679, which had been integrated with the Common Law of England's American Colonies. The Habeas Corpus Act of 1679, adopted to protect the citizen from wrongful imprisonment, was the result of a long development dating back to the twelfth century, to the time preceding Magna Charta. It reflects the phases of the English struggle for freedom, which reached a certain conclusion with the Bill of Rights on 13 February 1689. The bloody Restoration of the Stuarts which arose with the accession of James II on 6 February 1685 brought death to 330 notables, and more than 800 were deported to America. Against the Catholic Stuarts, the Anglican opposition called William of Orange, the Protestant son-in-law of James II, to intervene "to save the liberties of England." William landed at Torbay on 15 November 1688, the masts of his vessels em-

End of the colonial period: The Declaration of Independence.

*Right:* Revolutionary patriots tear down the statue of King George III, New York, 1776.

*Far right:* The committee delegated to draft the Declaration of Independence consisted of Thomas Jefferson, John Adams, Benjamin Franklin, Roger Sherman, and Robert Livingston. The picture shows the committee presenting the draft, on 28 June 1776, to the Philadelphia congress.

*Below:* Philadelphia. Engraving of 1790.

blazoned with the motto: "The Protestant Religion and the Freedom of England."

The "Glorious Revolution" won its cause without bloodshed when John Churchill, the later Duke of Marlborough, went over to William. William III and his consort Mary Stuart, before being crowned in Westminster Abbey, solemnly signed the "Bill of Rights" settling the rights of Parliament, banning

gle for human rights with the rights and liberties gained since the colonization of America, to produce something new. Here in Virginia we have men who, on their own responsibility and of their own free will, give laws to themselves, as clearly expressed in Article 6. Quite remarkable, and important for the future, is Article 12, which concerns freedom of the press. The spirit, forever topical,

## VIRGINIA'S BILL OF RIGHTS

1. That all men are by nature equally free and independent, and have certain inherent rights, of which, when they enter into a state of society, they cannot, by any compact, deprive or divest their posterity; namely, the enjoyment of life and liberty, with the means of acquiring and possessing property, and pursuing and obtaining happiness and safety.

arbitrary taxation, and confirming the freedom of speech and that of elections.

On these English models, the Virginia Declaration of Rights fuses England's experience in its strug-

behind the Virginia Declaration is impressively revealed in its last clause: "It is the mutual duty of all to practise Christian forbearance, love, and charity towards each other."

2. That all power is vested in, and consequently derived from, the people; that magistrates are their trustees and servants, and at all times amenable to the people.

3. That government is, or ought to be, instituted for the common benefit, protection, and security of the people, nation, or community; of all the various modes and forms of government that is best which is capable of producing the greatest degree of happiness and safety, and is most effectually secured against the danger of maladministration; and that when any government shall be found inadequate or contrary to these purposes, a majority of the community hath an indubitable, unalienable, and indefeasible right, to reform, alter or abolish it, in such manner as shall be judged most conducive to the public weal.

4. That no man, or set of men, are entitled to exclusive or separate emoluments or privileges from the community, but in consideration of publick services; which, not being descendible, neither ought the offices of magistrate, legislator, or judge to be hereditary.

5. That the legislative and executive powers of the state should be separate and distinct from the judiciary; and that the members of the two first may be restrained from oppression, by feeling and participating the burthens of the people, they should, at fixed periods, be reduced to a private station, return into that body from which they were originally taken, and the vacancies be supplied by frequent, certain, and regular elections, in which all, or any part of the former members, to be again eligible, or ineligible, as the laws shall direct.

6. That elections of members to serve as representatives of the people in assembly, ought to be free; and that all men having sufficient evidence of permanent common interest with, and attachment to, the community, have the right of suffrage, and cannot be taxed or deprived of their property for publick uses, without their own consent, or that of their representatives so elected, nor bound by any law to which they have not, in like manner, assented for the public good.

7. That all power of suspending laws, or the execution of laws, by any authority without consent of the representatives of the people, is injurious to their rights, and ought not to be exercised.

8. That in all capital or criminal prosecutions a man hath a right to demand the cause and nature of his accusation, to be confronted with the accusers and witnesses, to call for evidence in his favour, and to a speedy trial by an impartial jury of his vicinage, without whose unanimous consent he cannot be found guilty; nor can he be compelled to give evidence against himself; that no man be deprived of his liberty, except by the law of the land or the judgment of his peers.

9. That excessive bail ought not to be required, nor excessive fines imposed, nor cruel and unusual punishments inflicted.

10. That general warrants, whereby an officer or messenger may be commanded to search suspected places without evidence of a fact committed, or to seize any person or persons not named, or whose offence is not particularly described and supported by evidence, are grievous and oppressive, and ought not to be granted.

11. That in controversies respecting property, and in suits between man and man, the ancient trial by jury is preferable to any other, and ought to be held sacred.

12. That the freedom of the press is one of the great bulwarks of liberty, and can

## SOURCE OF MORAL STRENGTH

*This Virginia Declaration served as the model for "The Unanimous Declaration of the Thirteen United States of America," which has gone down in history as the American Declaration of Independence. This great act was, incidentally, to have yet another consequence: The French Marquis Marie Joseph de Lafayette, who had taken part as a general in the American War of Independence, affixed two boards to the wall of his study. On one was the text of the Virginia Declaration of Rights; the other board, however, was left blank, except for the heading: "The Human Rights of the French." In 1789, as Deputy in the French National Assembly, he championed the adoption of the human rights in the French constitution. And so, in the French Revolution, the Virginia Declaration returned to its spiritual home, Europe.*

*In the United States, the Virginia Declaration has throughout the country's history remained the standard which the nation's political conscience, despite many slips, has constantly invoked. Today more than ever, it is the source of moral strength from which the American nation draws its ideals and its hopes for the future.*

never be restrained but by despotick governments.

13. That a well-regulated militia, composed of the body of the people trained to arms, is the proper, natural and safe defence of a free state; that standing armies in time of peace, should be avoided, as dangerous to liberty; and that in all cases the military should be under strict subordination to, and governed by, the civil power.

14. That the people have a right to uniform government; and, therefore, that no government separate from, or independent of, the government of Virginia, ought to be erected or established within the limits thereof.

15. That no free government, or the blessing of liberty, can be preserved to any people but by a firm adherence to justice, moderation, temperance, frugality and virtue, and by frequent recurrence to fundamental principles.

16. That religion, or the duty which we owe to our CREATOR, and the manner of discharging it, can be directed only by reason and conviction, not by force or violence, and therefore all men are equally entitled to the free exercise of religion, according to the dictates of conscience; and that it is the mutual duty of all to practise Christian forbearance, love, and charity towards each other.

*Right:* The Watergate building complex. Site of the offices of the Democratic party's National Committee. During the presidential election campaign of 1972 these offices were burglarized in an attempt to steal documents. Two reporters from *The Washington Post,* Robert Woodward and Carl Bernstein, after a meticulous investigation of this scandal, discovered that President Richard Nixon was involved. In order to avoid impeachment the President agreed to resign from office. The revelation of the Watergate scandal was a triumph for the principle of freedom of the press, a right that is guaranteed in the second amendment to the Constitution and was proclaimed in the Virginia Declaration as "one of the great bulwarks of liberty."

# The United States Constitution

The American Declaration of Independence was unanimously enacted by the thirteen United States in Congress on 4 July 1776. (New York State soon followed suit, signing on 9 July, and in Congress on 15 July.) The official separation of the English Colonies from the mother country began with a decision of North Carolina on 12 April. The decisive initiative then came from Virginia, resolving "that these united colonies are and of right ought to be free and independent states." A committee con-

American Declaration of Independence, foundation of the United States Constitution.

sisting of Thomas Jefferson, John Adams, Benjamin Franklin, Roger Sherman, and Robert R. Livingston finally commissioned Jefferson with the drafting of the Declaration of Independence. During the American Revolution of 1776–1787, eleven of the thirteen United States gave themselves new constitutions. It fell to the Continental Congress to bring them all into alignment. It therefore called a second Convention, which assembled in Philadelphia on 25 May 1787 with the state representatives.

George Washington, first president of the United States.
Painting by Edward Savage, 1787.

Free government shall prove
its superiority with qualities
that win the goodwill
of its citizens
and the respect of the whole world.

George Washington,
Inaugural Address of 30 April 1789 in New York City,
the first capital of the new government

*Above:* Thomas Jefferson. Painting by Charles Willson Peale. Jefferson (1743–1826) was the principal author of the 1776 Declaration of Independence.

## FROM THE DECLARATION OF INDEPENDENCE TO THE CONSTITUTION

The Declaration of Independence breathes the spirit and political ethos of Jefferson, who believed that the United States would only succeed if it saw its future as a continual educational process—self-education is the basis for any open democracy—and as a kind of permanent revolution.

The need at this point was to translate the moral and ethical substance of the Declaration of Independence into political, economic, social, and legal practice by framing a constitution. The framers' guiding principle was to avoid as far as possible any discrepancy between formal legality and the diversified facts of real life.

The Constitution of the United States was formulated at a Convention, chaired by George Washington, in which there were at first two opposing parties. The Virginia plan championed the interests of the "large" (populous) states. It proposed a Congress comprising two houses, with the central government having control of everything. For the "small" states, which lived in fear of being swallowed up by the "large" ones, Pat-

George Washington presided at the last session of the Convention of 1787 (*below*), which ratified the United States Constitution.

terson presented the New Jersey plan, with greater emphasis on the federal aspect. The Constitution of the United States has been a living charter, growing by amendments in the historical process of the development and national awareness of the United States. It has been a center of stability, the standard for all subsequent legislation, yet it has also generated a restless dispute over its interpretation. The struggle for the final ratification of the Constitution by all the

states lasted until 1789. After its ratification, Washington was elected President by all sixty-nine electoral votes on 6 April 1789. Washington has by his example set the basic style of the President's office for the future. He was a master of compromise. His parting charge was: "Be united, be Americans." He confined himself to two terms as President (1789–1793 and 1793–1797). This became a tradition and was finally laid down in an amendment to the Constitution. In his cabinet, opposing interests were represented by Alexander Hamilton and Thomas Jefferson, forerunners of the two big parties.

## WE THE PEOPLE

We the People of the United States, in Order to form a more perfect Union, establish Justice, insure domestic Tranquility, provide for the common defense, promote the general Welfare, and secure the Blessings of Liberty to ourselves and our Posterity, do ordain and establish this Constitution for the United States of America.

### ARTICLE ONE

#### Section One

All legislative powers herein granted shall be vested in a Congress of the United States, which shall consist of a Senate and House of Representatives.

#### Section Two

1. The House of Representatives shall be composed of members chosen every second year by the people of the several States, and the Electors in each State shall have the qualifications requisite for Electors of the most numerous branch of the State Legislature.

2. No person shall be a Representative who shall not have attained to the age of twenty-five years, and been seven years a citizen of the United States, and who shall not, when elected, be an inhabitant of that State in which he shall be chosen.

#### Section Three

1. The Senate of the United States shall be composed of two Senators from each State, chosen by the Legislature thereof, for six years; and each Senator shall have one vote. . . .

3. No Person shall be a Senator who shall not have attained to the age of thirty years, and been nine years a citizen of the United States, and who shall not, when elected, be an inhabitant of that State for which he shall be chosen.

4. The Vice-President of the United States shall be President of the Senate, but shall have no vote, unless they be equally divided. . . .

6. The Senate shall have the sole power to try all impeachments. When sitting for that purpose, they shall be on oath or affirmation. When the President of the United States is tried, the Chief Justice shall preside: And no person shall be convicted without the concurrence of two-thirds of the members present.

7. Judgment in cases of impeachment shall not extend further than to removal from office, and disqualification to hold and enjoy any office of honor, trust, or profit under the United States: but the party convicted shall nevertheless be liable and subject to indictment, trial, judgment, and punishment, according to law.

#### Section Four

1. The times, places, and manner of holding elections for Senators and Representatives shall be prescribed in each State by the Legislature thereof; but the Congress may at any time by law make or alter such regulations, except as to the places of choosing Senators. . . .

#### Section Seven

1. All bills for raising revenue shall originate in the House of Representatives, but the Senate may propose or concur with amendments, as on other bills.

2. Every bill which shall have passed the House of Representatives and the Senate shall, before it becomes a law, be presented to the President of the United States; if he approve, he shall sign it, but if not, he shall return it, with his objections, to that House in which it shall have originated, who shall enter the objections at large on their journal, and proceed to reconsider it. If after reconsideration two-thirds of that House shall agree to pass the bill, it shall be sent, together with the objections, to the other House, by which it shall likewise be reconsid-

ered, and if approved by two-thirds of that House, it shall become a law. But in all such cases the votes of both Houses shall be determined by yeas and nays, and the names of the persons voting for and against the bill shall be entered on the journal of each House respectively. If any bill shall not be returned by the President within ten days (Sundays excepted) after it shall have been presented to him, the same shall be a law in like manner as if he had signed it, unless the Congress by their adjournment prevent its return, in which case it shall not be a law.

### Section Eight

1. The Congress shall have power: To lay and collect taxes, duties, imposts, and excises, to pay the debts and provide for the common defense and general welfare of the United States; but all duties, imposts, and excises shall be uniform throughout the United States;

2. To borrow money on the credit of the United States;

3. To regulate commerce with foreign nations, and among the several States, and with the Indian tribes;

4. To establish a uniform rule of naturalization, and uniform laws on the subject of bankruptcies throughout the United States;

5. To coin money, regulate the value thereof, and of foreign coin, and fix the standard of weights and measures;

6. To provide for the punishment of counterfeiting the securities and current coin of the United States;

7. To establish Post Offices and Post Roads;

8. To promote the progress of science and useful arts, by securing for limited times to authors and inventors the exclusive right to their respective writings and discoveries;

9. To constitute tribunals inferior to the Supreme Court;

10. To define and punish piracies and fel-

onies committed on the high seas, and offenses against the law of nations;

11. To declare war, grant letters of marque and reprisal, and make rules concerning captures on land and water;

12. To raise and support armies, but no appropriation of money to that use shall be for a longer term than two years;

13. To provide and maintain a navy;

14. To make rules for the government and regulation of the land and naval forces;

15. To provide for calling forth the militia to execute the laws of the Union, suppress insurrections and repel invasions;

16. To provide for organizing, arming, and disciplining the militia, and for governing such part of them as may be employed in the service of the United States, reserving to the States respectively, the appointment of the officers, and the authority of training the militia according to the discipline prescribed by Congress; . . .

18. To make all laws which shall be necessary and proper for carrying into execution the foregoing powers, and all other powers vested by this Constitution in the Government of the United States, or in any department or officer thereof.

### Section Nine

2. The privilege of the Writ of Habeas Corpus shall not be suspended, unless when in the cases of rebellion or invasion the public safety may require it.

3. No Bill of Attainder or *ex post facto* law shall be passed. . . .

### Section Ten

1. No State shall enter into any treaty, alliance, or confederation, grant letters of marque and reprisal, coin money, emit bills of credit, make anything but gold and silver coin a tender in payment of debts, pass any Bill of Attainder, *ex post facto* law, or law impairing the obligation of contracts, or grant any title of nobility.

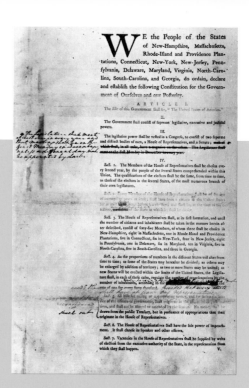

2. No State shall, without the consent of the Congress, lay any impost or duties on imports or exports. . . .

## ARTICLE TWO

### Section One

1. The Executive power shall be vested in a President of the United States of America. He shall hold his office during the term of four years, and, together with the Vice-President, chosen for the same term, be elected, as follows:

2. Each State shall appoint, in such manner as the Legislature thereof may direct, a number of Electors, equal to the whole number of Senators and Representatives to which the State may be entitled in the Congress. . . .

3. The Congress may determine the time of choosing the Electors, and the day on which they shall give their votes; which day shall be the same throughout the United States.

4. No person except a natural born citizen, or a citizen of the United States at the time of the adoption of this Constitution, shall be eligible to the office of the President; neither shall any person be eligible to that office who shall not have attained to the age of thirty-five years, and been fourteen years a resident within the United States. . . .

# We the People

of the United States, in order to form a more perfect Union, establish Justice, insure domestic Tranquility, provide for the common defence, promote the general Welfare, and secure the Blessings of Liberty to ourselves and our Posterity, do ordain and establish this Constitution for the United States of America.

## Article. I.

Section. 1. All legislative Powers herein granted shall be vested in a Congress of the United States, which shall consist of a Senate and House of Representatives.

Section. 2. The House of Representatives shall be composed of Members chosen every second Year by the People of the several States, and the Electors in each State shall have the Qualifications requisite for Electors of the most numerous Branch of the State Legislature.

No Person shall be a Representative who shall not have attained to the Age of twenty five Years, and been seven Years a Citizen of the United States, and who shall not, when elected, be an Inhabitant of that State in which he shall be chosen.

Representatives and direct Taxes shall be apportioned among the several States which may be included within this Union, according to their respective Numbers, which shall be determined by adding to the whole Number of free Persons, including those bound to Service for a Term of Years, and excluding Indians not taxed, three fifths of all other Persons. The actual Enumeration shall be made within three Years after the first Meeting of the Congress of the United States, and within every subsequent Term of ten Years, in such Manner as they shall by Law direct. The Number of Representatives shall not exceed one for every thirty Thousand, but each State shall have at Least one Representative; and until such enumeration shall be made, the State of New Hampshire shall be entitled to chuse three, Massachusetts eight, Rhode Island and Providence Plantations one, Connecticut five, New York six, New Jersey four, Pennsylvania eight, Delaware one, Maryland six, Virginia ten, North Carolina five, South Carolina five, and Georgia three.

When vacancies happen in the Representation from any State, the Executive Authority thereof shall issue Writs of Election to fill such Vacancies.

Section. 3. The Senate of the United States shall be composed of two Senators from each State, chosen by the Legislature thereof, for six Years; and each Senator shall have one Vote.

Immediately after they shall be assembled in Consequence of the first Election, they shall be divided as equally as may be into three Classes. The Seats of the Senators of the first Class shall be vacated at the Expiration of the second Year, of the second Class at the Expiration of the fourth Year, and of the third Class at the Expiration of the sixth Year, so that one third may be chosen every second Year; and if Vacancies happen by Resignation, or otherwise, during the Recess of the Legislature of any State, the Executive thereof may make temporary Appointments until the next Meeting of the Legislature, which shall then fill such Vacancies.

No Person shall be a Senator who shall not have attained to the Age of thirty Years, and been nine Years a Citizen of the United States, and who shall not, when elected, be an Inhabitant of that State for which he shall be chosen.

The Vice President of the United States shall be President of the Senate, but shall have no Vote, unless they be equally divided.

The Senate shall chuse their other Officers, and also a President pro tempore, in the Absence of the Vice President, or when he shall exercise the Office of President of the United States.

The Senators and Representatives before mentioned, and the Members of the several State Legislatures, and all executive and judicial Officers, both of the United States and of the several States, shall be bound by Oath or Affirmation, to support this Constitution; but no religious Test shall ever be required as a Qualification to any Office or public Trust under the United States.

## Article. VII.

The Ratification of the Conventions of nine States, shall be sufficient for the Establishment of this Constitution between the States so ratifying the Same.

done in Convention by the Unanimous Consent of the States present the Seventeenth Day of September in the Year of our Lord one thousand seven hundred and Eighty seven and of the Independence of the United States of America the Twelfth In witness whereof We have hereunto subscribed our Names,

Attest William Jackson Secretary

G°. Washington—Presidt and deputy from Virginia

Delaware { Geo: Read / Gunning Bedford jun / John Dickinson / Richard Bassett / Jaco: Broom

Maryland { James McHenry / Dan of St Thos. Jenifer / Danl Carroll

Virginia { John Blair— / James Madison Jr.

North Carolina { Wm. Blount / Richd. Dobbs Spaight. / Hu Williamson

South Carolina { J. Rutledge / Charles Cotesworth Pinckney / Charles Pinckney / Pierce Butler

Georgia { William Few / Abr Baldwin

New Hampshire { John Langdon / Nicholas Gilman

Massachusetts { Nathaniel Gorham / Rufus King

Connecticut { Wm. Saml. Johnson / Roger Sherman

New York { Alexander Hamilton

New Jersey { Wil: Livingston / David Brearley. / Wm. Paterson. / Jona: Dayton

Pennsylvania { B Franklin / Thomas Mifflin / Robt. Morris / Geo. Clymer / Thos. FitzSimons / Jared Ingersoll / James Wilson / Gouv Morris

---

7. Before he enter on the execution of his office, he shall take the following oath or affirmation:—"I do solemnly swear (or affirm) that I will faithfully execute the Office of President of the United States, and will, to the best of my ability, preserve, protect, and defend the Constitution of the United States."

### Section Two

1. The President shall be Commander-in-Chief of the Army and Navy of the United States, and of the militia of the several States, when called into the actual service of the United States; he may require the opinion, in writing, of the principal officer in each of the Executive Departments upon any subject relating to the duties of their respective offices, and he shall have power to grant reprieves and pardons for offenses against the United States, except in cases of impeachment.

### Section Three

He shall from time to time give to the Congress information of the State of the Union, and recommend to their consideration such measures as he shall judge necessary and expedient.

### Section Four

The President, Vice-President, and all civil officers of the United States, shall be removed from office on impeachment for, and conviction of, treason, bribery, or other high crimes and misdemeanors.

## ARTICLE THREE

### Section One

The judicial power of the United States shall be vested in one Supreme Court, and in such inferior courts as the Congress may from time to time ordain and establish. The Judges, both of the Supreme and inferior courts, shall hold their offices during good behavior. . . .

A DISPLAY of the UNITED STATES of AMERICA

*Left:* "Contemporary Display of the newly United States of America." In the center, the portrait of George Washington surrounded by the coats of arms of the original thirteen states, crowned with the seal of the new nation.

### Section Two

1. The judicial power shall extend to all cases, in law and equity, arising under this Constitution, the laws of the United States, and treaties made, or which shall be made, under their authority. . . .

### Section Three

1. Treason against the United States shall consist only in levying war against them, or in adhering to their enemies, giving them aid and comfort. . . .

## ARTICLE FOUR

### Section Three

1. New States may be admitted by the Congress into this Union; but no new State shall be formed or erected within the jurisdiction of any other State; nor any State be formed by the junction of two or more States, or parts of States, without the consent of the Legislatures of the States concerned as well as of the Congress.

### Section Four

The United States shall guarantee to every State in this Union a Republican form of government, and shall protect each of them against invasion; and on application of the Legislature, or of the Executive (when the Legislature cannot be convened) against domestic violence.

## ARTICLE FIVE

The Congress, whenever two-thirds of both Houses shall deem it necessary, shall propose amendments to this Constitution, or, on the application of the legislatures of two-thirds of the several States, shall call a convention for proposing amendments, which, in either case, shall be valid to all intents and purposes, as part of this Constitution, when ratified by the Legislatures of three-fourths of the several States, or by conventions in three-fourths thereof, as the one or the other mode of ratification may be proposed by the Congress.

## ARTICLE SIX

2. This Constitution, and the laws of the United States which shall be made in pursuance thereof; and all treaties made, or

*Right:* Seal of the United States. The shield (in blue) is a symbol of the Congress, the highest governmental authority, which is supported by thirteen vertical bars (alternating between red and white) symbolizing the original states. The olive branch and arrows gripped by the eagle represent Congress's power to make decisions of peace and war.

which shall be made, under the authority of the United States, shall be the supreme law of the land; and the Judges in every State shall be bound thereby, anything in the Constitution or laws of any State to the contrary notwithstanding.

3. The Senators and Representatives before mentioned, and the members of the several State Legislatures, and all Executive and Judicial Officers, both of the United States and of the several States, shall be bound by oath or affirmation, to support this Constitution; but no religious test shall ever be required as a qualification to any office or public trust under the United States.

## ARTICLE SEVEN

The ratification of the Conventions of nine States, shall be sufficient for the establishment of this Constitution between the States so ratifying the same.

In the twentieth century, parts of the U.S. Constitution were copied in form by the "young democracies" emerging in Africa and South America. In Europe, as early as 1776, the constitutions of the individual American states were published first in Paris, then in other countries. It was chiefly the constitutions of Massachusetts, Pennsylvania, and Virginia that influenced political ideas.

They had their greatest impact in France, in the decade following 1789, with the watchwords freedom and equality, civic rights without ecclesiastic ties, freedom of the press, authority vested in the people, and control of political power by representatives of the people. Benjamin Franklin asked the Duke de La Rochefoucauld in Paris to make a new and complete translation of the U.S. Constitution, and handed out copies to all foreign ambassadors in Paris, with the support of the royal French government.

The American Declaration of Independence and the Constitution based upon it also affected Latin America in the nineteenth century, resulting in the liberation of that continent from Spanish and Portuguese colonial rule. The objective of the great "Liberator" Simón Bolívar, to create the United Latin American States on the North American model, failed to materialize, however. After World War II, the United States model acted as a catalyst in Asia and Africa.

# Declaration of the Rights of Man

Marie Joseph de Lafayette, who had taken part as a general in the American War of Independence, presented a bill in the French National Assembly on 11 July 1789, calling for the passage, concurrently with the future constitution, of a declaration of the rights of man. Three days later, the Bastille was stormed, and the ongoing debate in the National Assembly over the contents of the future constitution received fresh incentive. In the sessions between 20 and 26 August 1789, the National Assembly decided to integrate the Declaration of the Rights of Man and of Citizens in the constitution. The Declaration was formally adopted on 26 August and it received the assent of King Louis XVI on 5 October. It comprises a preamble and seventeen principles, and was added by way of introduction to the new French Constitution, ratified on 3 September 1791 as the *Constitution française*.

*Above:* Louis XVI, toasting the Revolution, wearing Jacobin cockade and hat.

## FRUIT OF THE ENLIGHTENMENT

Seldom in history have the supranational links been so tangible as in the creation of the French declaration of human rights. Lafayette, in close communication with his American friends Washington, Franklin, Adams, and Jefferson, asked Thomas Jefferson, who had succeeded Franklin as ambassador in Paris, to go over his first draft. At the same time, there were more than fifty different drafts under debate. The American model, the Virginia Declaration of Rights, which repeatedly comes through in the wording of the French Declaration of 1789, was an invaluable help to the men around Lafayette. Yet he knew only too well that the concerns in Paris were different from those in Virginia. The Declaration of the Rights of Man and of Citizens is inspired by the spirit of revolt against the ancien régime. It is therefore more polemical, more aggressive, more pointed, as well as specifically revolutionary and specifically liberal. It is focused on freedom from the State, establishment of a demarcation line protecting free and equal men.

Virginia Declaration of Rights, American human rights manifesto of 1776.

*Right:* Marie Joseph de Lafayette. Painting by Joseph Désiré Court.

Behind the Declaration of the Rights of Man and of Citizens stands the credo of the French En-

ceptance for a declaration of the *duties* of man and citizen as a counterpart to his rights. This reflects a

lightenment at its zenith: Freedom, Equality, Fraternity. Claude de Saint-Martin, the "elegant theosopher," stationed between Voltaire and the Romantics, had first proclaimed this "sacrament of the holy ternary," this new "trinity," on the eve of the Revolution, in the *salon* of Mathilde d'Orléans, Duchess of Bourbon, with whom he was living. This new sacred trinity was to supersede the old Trinity of the Father, the Son, and the Holy Ghost, in whose names all great treaties of Old Europe had been sanctioned.

In the stormy debates over the seventeen principles of the declaration of human rights in the French National Assembly, the representatives of the clergy failed to win ac-

certain lack of balance which has often been held against the French declaration of rights and which is specially formulated in the fourth principle: "Political Liberty consists in the power of doing whatever does not injure another." Also disappointing to some deputies was the fact that the freedom of worship was not included. It was only after prolonged debate that the National Assembly established the freedom of faith, though not that of worship, in the tenth principle, albeit with reservations which left the door wide open for future intervention. States which have since adopted the principles of the French Revolution take full advantage of this loophole in their constitutions.

## CRUSADE FOR FREEDOM

*It is virtually impossible to give an exact translation of the French word* citoyen *by which the French Declaration of the Rights of Man and Citizens designates a new "species" born in the Revolution, and which is therefore not fully identical with the English "citizen." The* citoyen *of the French Revolution and the French human rights declaration is the "new" citizen of the "new" nation, which sees itself as a society of salvation with the mission of carrying the blessings of the Revolution and the human rights declaration to all corners of the world. It embarks on a crusade for freedom. Revolutionary France believed itself authorized to assist the liberation of the "oppressed nations" in all Europe and to promote the Revolution everywhere, a task in which Bonaparte was for a time successful. Remarkably, it was Maximilien de Robespierre who opposed this revolutionary missioning zeal in a prophetic comment: "The most foolish idea for which a politician might fall would be to believe that a nation need only invade another with force of arms to induce that nation to adopt its laws and constitution. No one loves armed missionaries!" The warrior-missionary Napoleon finally failed because of belief in arms, although, seen historically, he did indeed promote the acceptance and adoption of human rights by all Europe.*

Contemporary chart of the Declaration
of the Rights of Man and of Citizens.

# Declaration of the Rights of Man and of Citizens

## By the National Assembly of France

The representatives of the people of France, formed into a National
Assembly, considering that ignorance, neglect, or contempt of human
rights, are the sole causes of public misfortunes and corruptions of
Government, have resolved to set forth in a solemn declaration, these
natural, imprescriptible, and inalienable rights; that this declaration
being constantly present to the minds of the members of the body
social, they may be ever kept attentive to their rights and their duties;
that the acts of the legislative and executive powers of Government,
being capable of being every moment compared with the end of political institutions, may be more respected; and also, that the future
claims of the citizens, being directed by simple and incontestable principles, may always tend to the maintenance of the Constitution, and
the general happiness.
For these reasons the National Assembly doth recognize and declare, in
the presence of the Supreme Being, and with the hope of his blessing and favor, the following *sacred* rights of men and of citizens:

I. Men are born, and always continue, free and equal in respect of
their rights. Civil distinctions, therefore, can be founded only on public utility.

II. The end of all political associations is the preservation of the
natural and imprescriptible rights of man; and these rights are Liberty, Property, Security, and Resistance of Oppression.

III. The Nation is essentially the source of all sovereignty; nor can
any individual, or any body of men, be entitled to any authority which
is not expressly derived from it.

IV. Political Liberty consists in the power of doing whatever does
not injure another. The exercise of the natural rights of every man, has
no other limits than those which are necessary to secure to every *other*
man the free exercise of the same rights; and these limits are determin-
able only by the law.

V. The law ought to prohibit only actions hurtful to society. What is
not prohibited by the law should not be hindered; nor should any one
be compelled to that which the law does not require.

VI. The law is an expression of the will of the community. All citizens
have a right to concur, either personally or by their representatives, in
its formation. It should be the same to all, whether it protects or
punishes; and all being equal in its sight, are equally eligible to all
honors, places, and employments, according to their different abilities, without any other distinction than that created by their virtues
and talents.

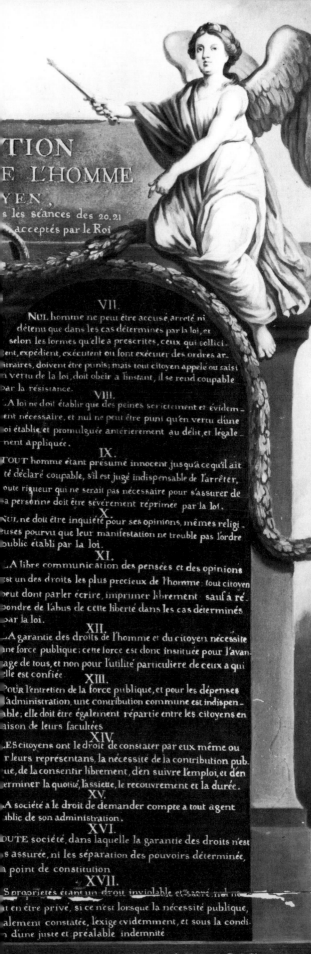

VII. No man should be accused, arrested, or held in confinement, except in cases determined by the law, and according to the forms which it has prescribed. All who promote, solicit, execute, or cause to be executed, arbitrary orders, ought to be punished, and every citizen called upon, or apprehended by virtue of the law, ought immediately to obey, and renders himself culpable by resistance.

VIII. The law ought to impose no other penalties but such as are absolutely and evidently necessary; and no one ought to be punished, but in virtue of a law promulgated before the offense, and legally applied.

IX. Every man being presumed innocent till he has been convicted, whenever his detention becomes indispensable, all rigor to him, more than is necessary to secure his person, ought to be provided against by the law.

X. No man ought to be molested on account of his opinions, not even on account of is religious opinions, provided his avowal of them does not disturb the public order established by the law.

XI. The unrestrained communication of thoughts and opinions being one of the most precious Rights of Man, every citizen may speak, write, and publish freely, provided he is responsible for the abuse of this liberty, in cases determined by the law.

XII. A public force being necessary to give security to the Rights of Men and of citizens, that force is instituted for the benefit of the community and not for the particular benefit of the persons with whom it is intrusted.

XIII. A common contribution being necessary for the support of the public force, and for defraying the other expenses of Government, it ought to be divided equally among the members of the community, according to their abilities.

XIV. Every citizen has a right, either by himself or his representative, to a free voice in determining the necessity of public contributions, the appropriation of them, and their amount, mode of assessment, and duration.

XV. Every community has a right to demand of all its agents an account of their conduct.

XVI. Every community in which a separation of powers and a security of rights is not provided for, wants a Constitution.

XVII. The right to property being inviolable and sacred, no one ought to be deprived of it, except in cases of evident public necessity, legally ascertained, and on condition of a previous just indemnity.

# Kant's Peace Manifesto

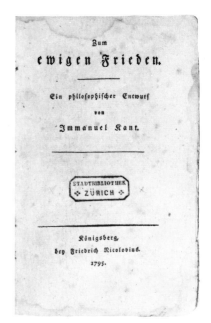

On the morning of 13 August 1795, Immanuel Kant, a philosophy professor at the University of Königsberg in Prussia, and already famous all over Europe, hurried over to his neighbor, the publisher Friedrich Nicolovius, with a manuscript 100 pages long: *Perpetual Peace: A Philosophical Essay.* On that very same morning author and publisher came to an agreement on the publication of this essay. In record time it was set and printed so that it could be ready for Michaelismass, the Leipzig book fair that traditionally opened on the last Sunday in August.

This essay is essentially a peace treaty, whose individual tenets are analyzed and clarified at length. Kant maintains that "perpetual peace"—an irrevocable human right—can be achieved by stripping politics of all untruth and by practicing "harmony" of law, morality, and politics. Man can thus work steadily toward a constitutional and international law based on ethics, the condition of perpetual peace.

We must forget the stereotyped inhuman image of Kant pent up in his bachelor's den, critically reflecting on the theory of knowledge and the process of perception. He was in fact a universal scholar, open to life and striving in his philosophy to form and transform the reality of life. He followed all the major political events of this day with unflagging attention. He sympathized with the Americans in their struggle for independence and with the French in their revolution. In 1794 his conflict with Prussia's reactionary censorship, after smoldering for three years, came to a head. A "special order" charged Kant with misusing his philosophy to the "distortion and depreciation of many leading and fundamental doctrines of holy writ and Christianity." Professors in Königsberg were forbidden to teach his theological philosophy.

I have had the good luck
to know a philosopher who was also my teacher. . . .
In the same spirit as he studied Leibniz,
Wolff, Baumgarter, Crusius, Hume and examined
the laws of nature as developed by
the physicists Newton and Kepler, he also
absorbed the works by Rousseau that appeared
at the time, his *Emile* and *Héloise,* as well
as any scientific discoveries that he heard about,
appreciating them fully and always
stressing unprejudiced knowledge of nature
and the value of man. He always encouraged me,
and in his gentle manner compelled me,
to think on my own; despotism was alien to his nature.
This man, of whom I think with
utmost gratitude and respect, is Immanuel Kant.

Johann Gottfried Herder
*Letters for the Advancement of Humanity,* No. 49

This defamation no doubt lent speed to the writing of his peace treatise and must have inspired the accusations against despotism that it contained. Kant's *Perpetual Peace* is the first comprehensive peace manifesto in the history of German-speaking countries. The date of its appearance was no accident: The writing of this treatise in the summer of 1795 and its hurried publication must be viewed in the light of a political event welcomed at the time by progressive intellectuals and the people alike—the ratification of the peace treaty by France and Prussia in Basel on 5 April 1795. The common longing for peace, a peace which was to last only a year, made Kant's treatise a "bestseller" until 1797.

## KANT AND THE FRENCH REVOLUTION

Immanuel Kant, a teacher at the University of Königsberg (today Kaliningrad), was born there in 1724 the son of a saddler, and he died in the same town in 1804. His father probably descended from Scottish immigrants who came to East Prussia in the early seventeenth century.

Kant's claims for peace have their roots in the three volumes of a French œuvre by Abbé Charles

*Left:* Title page of the first edition of *Perpetual Peace,* which Friedrich Nicolovius published hurriedly in Königsberg in 1795 so that it could be available at the Leipzig book fair.

Irenée Castel de Saint-Pierre which appeared between 1712 and 1716, called *Projet de la paix perpétuelle.* We can assume that Kant was not familiar with the original Saint-Pierre work but merely with the excerpt by Rousseau. Kant took up Saint-Pierre's reasonings and, motivated by the French Revolution, elaborated and completed them. The theologian Heinz Gollwitzer is right in saying, "What Kant actually has in mind since the beginning of the French Revolution when, in his capacity as political philosopher, he sets forth his conception of a European state based on reason and peace, is the French nation, a constituted republic since 1792. Kant's essay *Perpetual Peace* is a democratic declaration in disguise which must be viewed in historical relationship with left-wing opposition, and with Prussia's pro-French political party. His foreign policy objective is a European entente with revolutionary France as cornerstone." Many of the theses and propositions contained in *Perpetual Peace* have not lost their significance; e.g.: "Standing armies shall be abolished. . . . they are always threatening other states with war by appearing to be in constant readiness to fight." Kant explained that of the three prerequisites for war—"the power of arms, the power of alliance, and the power of money"—the last can be considered the "most reliable instrument of war," and he maintained that interference in the internal affairs of another state is the main cause. Kant condemned all wars: "punitive war" and "war of extermination," as well as crusades and missionary wars, and also colonial wars. Peace is not a "natural state," says Kant; "thus the state of peace must be *established.*" Perpetual peace is no "empty idea, but rather a problem which gradually works out its own solution," so that "we approach ever nearer to this goal."

*Left:* Memorial to Kant in the Paradeplatz in his native city of Königsberg (now Kaliningrad in the USSR). Statue by Christian Rauch.

## PERPETUAL PEACE

### FIRST SECTION

CONTAINING THE PRELIMINARY ARTICLES OF PERPETUAL PEACE BETWEEN STATES

1. "No treaty of peace shall be regarded as valid, if made with the secret reservation of material for a future war."

For then it would be a mere truce, a mere suspension of hostilities, not peace.

2. "No state having an independent existence—whether it be great or small—shall be acquired by another through inheritance, exchange, purchase or donation."

For a state is not a property *(patrimonium),* as may be the ground on which its people are settled. It is a society of human beings over whom no one but itself has the right to rule and to dispose. Like the trunk of a tree, it has its own roots, and to graft it on to another state is to do away with its existence as a moral person, and to make of it a thing. Hence it is in contradiction to the idea of the original contract without which no right over a people is thinkable.

3. "Standing armies *(miles perpetuus)* shall be abolished in course of time."

For they are always threatening other states with war by appearing to be in constant readiness to fight. They incite the various states to outrival one another in the number of their soldiers, and to this number no limit can be set. Now, since owing to the sums devoted to this purpose, peace at last becomes even more oppressive than a short war, these standing armies are themselves the cause of wars of aggression, undertaken in order to get rid of this burden. To which we must add that the practice of hiring men to kill or to be killed seems to imply a use of them as mere machines and instruments in the hand of another (namely, the state) which cannot easily be reconciled with the right of humanity in our own person.

4. "No national debts shall be contracted in connection with the external affairs of the state."

This source of help is above suspicion, where assitance is sought outside or within the state, on behalf of the economic administration of the country (for instance, the improvement of the roads, the settlement and support of new colonies, the establishment of granaries to provide against seasons of scarcity, and so on). But, as a common weapon used by the Powers against one another, a credit system under which debts go on indefinitely increasing and are yet always assured against immediate claims (because all the creditors do not put in their claim at once) is a dangerous money power.

5. "No state shall violently interfere with the constitution and administration of another."

For what can justify it in so doing? The scandal which is here presented to the subjects of another state? The erring state can much more serve as a warning by exemplifying the great evils which a nation draws down on itself through its own lawlessness. Moreover, the bad example which one free person gives another (as *scandalum acceptum*) does no injury to the latter.

6. "No state at war with another shall countenance such modes of hostility as would make mutual confidence impossible in a subsequent state of peace: such are the employment of assassins *(percussores)* or of poisoners *(venefici)*, breaches of capitulation, the instigating and making use of treachery *(perduellio)* in the hostile state."

These are dishonorable stratagems. For some kind of confidence in the disposition of the enemy must exist even in the midst of war, as otherwise peace could not be concluded, and the hostilities

would pass into a war of extermination *(bellum internecinum)*. War, however, is only our wretched expedient of asserting a right by force, an expedient adopted in the state of nature, where no court of justice exists which could settle the matter in dispute. In circumstances like these, neither of the two parties can be called an unjust enemy, because this form of speech presupposes a legal decision: the issue of the conflict—just as in the case of the so-called judgments of God—decides on which side right is. Between states, however, no punitive war *(bellum punitivum)* is thinkable, because between them a relation of superior and inferior does not exist. Whence it follows that a war of extermination, where the process of annihilation would strike both parties at once and all right as well, would bring about perpetual peace only in the great graveyard of the human race. Such a war then, and therefore also the use of all means which lead to it, must be absolutely forbidden.

## SECOND SECTION

### CONTAINING THE DEFINITIVE ARTICLES OF A PERPETUAL PEACE BETWEEN STATES

A state of peace among men who live side by side is not the natural state *(status naturalis)*, which is rather to be described as a state of war: that is to say, although there is not perhaps always actual open hostility, yet there is a constant threatening that an outbreak may occur. Thus the state of peace must be *established*.

### FIRST DEFINITIVE ARTICLE OF PERPETUAL PEACE

I. "The civil constitution of each state shall be republican."

The only constitution which has its origin in the idea of the original contract, upon which the lawful legislation of every nation must be based, is the republican. It is a constitution, in the first place, founded in accordance with the principle of the freedom of the members of society as human beings: secondly, in accordance with the principle of the dependence of all, as subjects, on a common legislation: and, thirdly, in accordance with the law of the equality of the members as citizens. It is then, looking at the question of right, the only constitution whose fundamental principles lie at the basis of every form of civil constitution. And the only question for us now is, whether it is also the one constitution which can lead to perpetual peace.

Now the republican constitution apart from the soundness of its origin, since it arose from the pure source of the concept of right, has also the prospect of attaining the desired result, namely, perpetual peace. And the reason is this. If, as must be so under this constitution, the consent of the subjects is required to determine whether there shall be war or not, nothing is more natural than that they should weigh the matter well, before undertaking such a bad business. For in decreeing war, they would of necessity be resolving to bring down the miseries of war upon their country. This implies: they must fight themselves; they must hand over the costs of the war out of their own property; they must do their poor best to make good the devastation which it leaves behind; and finally, as a crowning ill, they have to accept a burden of debt which will embitter even peace itself, and which they can never pay off on account of the new wars which are always impending. On the other hand, in a government where the subject is not a citizen holding a vote (i.e., in a constitution which is not republican), the plunging into war is the least serious thing in the world.

### Second Definitive Article of Perpetual Peace

II. "The law of nations shall be founded on a federation of free states."

Nations, as states, may be judged like individuals who, living in the natural state of society—that is to say, uncontrolled by external law—injure one another through their very proximity. Every state, for the sake of its own security, may—and ought to—demand that its neighbor should submit itself to conditions, similar to those of the civil society where the right of every individual is guaranteed. This would give rise to a federation of nations which, however, would not have to be a State of nations. The method by which states prosecute their rights can never be by process of law—as it is where there is an external tribunal—but only by war.

Hence there must be an alliance of a particular kind which we may call a covenant of peace (foedus pacificum), which would differ from a treaty of peace (pactum pacis) in this respect, that the latter merely puts an end to one war, while the former would seek to put an end to war forever. This alliance does not aim at the gain of any power whatsoever of the state, but merely at the preservation and security of the freedom of the state for itself and of other allied states at the same time. The latter do not, however, require, for this reason, to submit themselves like individuals in the state of nature to public laws and coercion.

There is no intelligible meaning in the idea of the law of nations as giving a right to make war; for that must be a right to decide what is just, not in accordance with universal, external laws limiting the freedom of each individual, but by means of one-sided maxims applied by force. We must then understand by this that men of such ways of thinking are quite justly served, when they destroy one another, and thus find perpetual peace in the wide grave which covers all the abominations of acts of violence as well as the authors of such deeds. For states, in their relation to one another, there can be, according to reason, no other way of advancing from that lawless condition which unceasing war implies, than by giving up their savage lawless freedom, just as individual men have done, and yielding to the coercion of public laws. Thus they can form a State of nations (civitas gentium), one, too, which will be ever increasing and would finally embrace all the peoples of the earth.

### Third Definitive Article of Perpetual Peace

III. "The rights of men, as citizens of the world, shall be limited to the conditions of universal hospitality."

We are speaking here, as in the previous articles, not of philanthropy, but of right; and in this sphere hospitality signifies the claim of a stranger entering foreign territory to be treated by its owner without hostility. The latter may send him away again, if this can be done without causing his death; but, so long as he conducts himself peaceably, he must not be treated as an enemy. It is not a right to be treated as a guest to which the stranger can lay claim—a special friendly compact on his behalf would be required to make him for a given time an actual inmate—but he has a right of visitation. This right to present themselves to society belongs to all mankind in virtue of our common right of possession on the surface of the earth.

### FIRST SUPPLEMENT

#### Concerning the Guarantee of Perpetual Peace

This guarantee is given by no less a power than the great artist nature (natura dædala rerum) in whose mechanical course is clearly exhibited a predetermined design to make harmony spring from human discord, even against the will of man. Now this design, although called Fate when looked upon as the compelling force of a cause, the laws of whose operation are unknown to us, is, when considered as the purpose manifested in the course of nature, called Providence, as the deep lying wisdom of a Higher Cause, directing itself toward the ultimate practical end of the human race and predetermining the course of things with a view to its realization. This Providence we do not, it is true, perceive in the cunning contrivances of nature; nor can we even conclude from the fact of their existence that it is there; but, as in every relation between the form of things and their final cause, we can, and must, supply the thought of a Higher Wisdom, in order that we may be able to form an idea of the possible existence of these products after the analogy of human works of art. The representation to ourselves of the relation and agreement of these formations of nature to the moral purpose for which they were made and which reason directly prescribes to us, is an Idea, it is true, which is in theory superfluous; but in practice it is dogmatic, and its objective reality is well established. Thus we see, for example, with regard to the ideal of perpetual peace, that it is our duty to make use of the mechanism of nature for the realization of that end.

Kant's handwriting *(below)*. Final sentence of the original manuscript of *Perpetual Peace*.

*Right:* Jean-Jacques Rousseau (1712–1778). Kant was influenced by his ideas on political freedom and his demystification of the concept of the State.

## SECOND SUPPLEMENT

### A SECRET ARTICLE FOR PERPETUAL PEACE

A secret article in negotiations concerning public right is, when looked at objectively or with regard to the meaning of the term, a contradiction. When we view it, however, from the subjective standpoint, with regard to the character and condition of the person who dictates it, we see that it might quite well involve some private consideration, so that he would regard it as hazardous to his dignity to acknowledge such an article as originating from him.

The only article of this kind is contained in the following proposition: "The opinions of philosophers, of a public peace, shall be taken into consideration by states armed for war."

It seems, however, to be derogatory to the dignity of the legislative authority of a state—to which we must of course attribute all wisdom—to ask advice from subjects (among whom stand philosophers) about the rules of its behavior to

That kings should philosophize, or philosophers become kings, is not to be expected. But neither is it to be desired; for the possession of power is inevitably fatal to the free exercise of reason. But it is absolutely indispensable, for their enlightenment as to the full significance of their vocations, that both kings and sovereign nations, which rule themselves in accordance with laws of equality, should not allow the class of philosophers to disappear, nor forbid the expression of their opinions, but should allow them to speak openly.

## APPENDIX I

### ON THE DISAGREEMENT BETWEEN MORALS AND POLITICS WITH REFERENCE TO PERPETUAL PEACE

Politics says, "Be wise as serpents"; morals adds the limiting condition, "and guileless as doves." If these precepts cannot stand together in one command, then there is a real quarrel between politics and morals. But if they can be completely

than any policy," is exalted high above every possible objection, is indeed the necessary condition of all politics.

The practical man, however, for whom morals is mere theory, even while admitting that what ought to be can be, bases his dreary verdict against our well-meant hopes really on this: he pretends that he can foresee from his observation of human nature, that men will never be willing to do what is required in order to bring about the wished-for results leading to perpetual peace.

Any ruler who has once got the power in his hands will not let the people dictate laws for him. A state which enjoys an independence of the control of external law will not submit to the judgment of the tribunals of other states, when it has to consider how to obtain its rights against them. And even a continent, when it feels its superiority to another, whether this be in its way or not, will not fail to take advantage of an opportunity offered of strengthening its power by the spoliation or even conquest of this territory.

I can thus imagine a moral politician, that is to say, one who understands the principles of statesmanship to be such as do not conflict with morals; but I cannot conceive of a political moralist who fashions for himself such a system of ethics as may serve the interest of statesmen.

These politicians, instead of adopting an open, straightforward way of doing things (as they boast), mix themselves up in intrigue. They get at the authorities in power and say what will please them; their sole bent is to sacrifice the nation, or even, if they can, the whole world. The principles which he makes use of here, although indeed he does not make them public, amount pretty much to the following sophistical maxims.

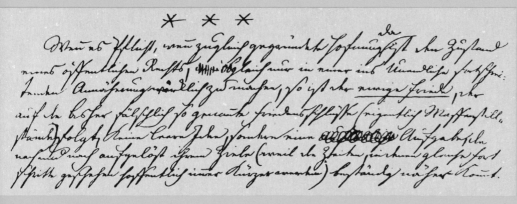

other states. At the same time, it is very advisable that this should be done. Hence the state will silently invite suggestion for this purpose, while at the same time keeping the fact secret. This amounts to saying that the state will allow philosophers to discuss freely and publicly the universal principles governing the conduct of war and establishment of peace.

brought into accord, then the idea of any antagonism between them is absurd, and the question of how best to make a compromise between the two points of view ceases to be even raised. Although the saying, "Honesty is the best policy," expresses a theory which, alas, is often contradicted in practice, yet the likewise theoretical maxim, "Honesty is better

1. *Fac et excusa.* Seize the most favorable opportunity for arbitrary usurpation—either of the authority of the state over its own people or over a neighboring people; the justification of the fact and extenuation of the use of force will come much more easily and gracefully.

*Below:* U.N. Headquarters, New York. The League of Nations and the United Nations are realizations of moral-political concepts from Kant's manifesto *Perpetual Peace.*

2. *Si fecisti, nega.* As for any crime you have committed, such as has, for instance, brought your people to despair and thence to insurrection, deny that it has happened owing to any fault of yours. Say rather that it is all caused by the insubordination of your subjects, or, in the case of your having usurped a neighboring state, that human nature is to blame; for, if a man is not ready to use force and steal a march upon his neighbor, he may certainly count on the latter forestalling him and taking him prisoner.

In all these twistings and turnings of an immoral doctrine of expediency which aims at substituting a state of peace for the warlike conditions in which men are placed by nature, so much at least is clear;—that men cannot get away from the idea of right in their private any more than in their public relations; and that they do not dare (this is indeed most

strikingly seen in the concept of an international law) to base politics merely on the manipulations of expediency and therefore to refuse all obedience to the idea of a public right. On the contrary, they pay all fitting honor to the idea of right in itself, even although they should, at the same time, devise a hundred subterfuges and excuses to avoid it in practice, and should regard force, backed up by cunning, as having the authority which comes from being the source and unifying principle of all right. It will be well to put an end to this sophistry, if not to the injustice it extenuates, and to bring the false advocates of the mighty of the earth to confess that it is not right but might in whose interest they speak, and that it is the worship of might from which they take their cue, as if in this matter they had a right to command. In order to do this, we must first expose the delusion by which they deceive themselves and others; then discover the ultimate principle from which their plans for a perpetual peace proceed; and thence show that all the evil which stands in the way of the realization of that ideal springs from the fact that the political moralist begins where the moral politician rightly ends and that, by subordinating principles to an end or putting the cart before the horse, he defeats his intention of bringing politics into harmony with morals.

If it is our duty to realize a state of public right, if at the same time there are good grounds for hope that this ideal may be realized, although only by an approximation advancing *ad infinitum,* then perpetual peace, following hitherto falsely so-called conclusions of peace, which have been in reality mere cessations of hostilities, is no mere empty idea. But rather we have here a problem which gradually works out its own solution and, as the periods in which a given advance takes place towards the realization of the ideal of perpetual peace will, we hope, become with the passing of time shorter and shorter, we must approach ever nearer to this goal.

*Kant's* Perpetual Peace *was published twelve times during his lifetime, twelve times between 1805 and 1914, and several dozen times since World War I. It received an important supplement in the essay by the young Friedrich Gentz (who is frequently cited by Henry Kissinger and others),* On the Perpetual Peace, 1800. *Gentz had assisted Kant in reading the galley proofs of the* Critique of Judgment. *In contrast to Fichte's* Geschlossener Handelsstaat *(an intensely socialistic treatise in favor of tariff protection, and a model for modern totalitarian states), Gentz declared: "Total unity between the peoples of this world is the principal prerequisite for true human culture. Whoever tries to prevent or even forbid free communication between nations and individuals, as Fichte does, destroys the basis of peace." This was written in 1800. The educated middle classes of the nineteenth and twentieth century recognized Kant as a philosopher only, taking no notice of his political work. Nevertheless his peace manifesto had an immense*

*effect and stimulated the peace movement all over the world. The League of Nations founded after World War I, the United Nations, the European Economic Community, as well as the longing for a United Europe reaching from the Atlantic coast to the Urals: They all drew sustenance from Kant's ideas.*

# The Code Napoléon

The Constitution enacted by the French National Assembly on 3 September 1791 stipulated a uniform law system for all France. This postulate was ignored for years. Finally, on 18 July 1800, Napoleon, who had become First Consul by the coup d'état of 9 November 1799, appointed a commission, with himself as chairman, to draft a law code within six months. This commission included the most eminent lawyers of France, among them François Tronchet, who had defended King Louis XVI; the later Minister of Culture Jean Portalis, who had defended clergymen under Danton; and also Jean-Jacques de Cambacérès, the Minister of Justice, who as Deputy had submitted drafts in 1793, 1794, and 1796, all of which had failed to gain approval. In December 1800, the Code, comprising 2,281 sections,

The red-white-and-blue cockade, designed by Lafayette, is used here to decorate a document of the Revolutionary government.

was essentially complete. On 14 July 1801, the anniversary of the storming of the Bastille, Napoleon announced the decision to adopt the Code, and on 20 March 1804 it was finally enacted as the *Code Civil des Français*. In 1807 a few sections were revised, and the name was changed to *Code Napoléon*.

## BARBARIAN INSTITUTIONS HAVE FALLEN

The background of the *Code Napoléon,* renamed the *Code Civil* after the Emperor's fall in 1815, can be traced to the seventeenth century. France's courts of law, called parliaments, had a great tradition in the administration of justice. However, there was no general French law system, just a hodgepodge of different regional codes and legal traditions. Between 1789 and 1800, some 14,000 new orders were decreed, many at variance with existing laws. Two years before his appointment as First Consul, Napoleon wrote to newly appointed Foreign Minister Talleyrand: "We are a nation with three hundred codes of law, yet without a law."

The *Code Civil des Français* is the first modern law code of Europe. Its guiding light was the faith in reason, which demands, and makes possible, reasonable and rational laws. The Code finally fixes in terms of law the great postulates of the French Revolution: personal freedom, freedom of conscience, freedom of industry, and equality before the law. The State is secular,

*Left:* Embossed medal commemorating the promulgation of the *Code Civil* in 1804.

*Left center:* Napoleon as First Consul, 1799. Painting by Antoine Gros.

*Below:* Debate over the *Code Civil* in the State Assembly presided over by the First Consul.

and so marriage is a State matter. A Corsican, Napoleon had grown up under Roman law, under which the woman is subject to the man. The First Consul prevailed against the revolutionary-minded "suffragists" on his commission. And so, in the *Code Civil,* we find the famous Section 213, which has been upheld until far into the twentieth century: "The husband owes protection to his wife, the wife obedience to her husband." Likewise, the principle of the father's authority over his children is given statutory force.

In his proclamation on the adoption of the *Code Civil,* Napoleon declared on 14 July 1801: "Frenchmen, let this day be appointed to commemorate an age of hope and glory: Barbarian institutions have fallen, and you have ceased to be divided into two nations: one condemned to humiliation, the other destined for rank and greatness. Your property has been freed as has your life; feudalism is abolished, and with it that unfettered abuse with which centuries had burdened you. . . . A civil code, the result of careful and thorough consideration, shall henceforth protect your property and your rights."

"Two nations. . . ." Decades after the French Revolution, Friedrich Engels and, later, Benjamin Disraeli saw England split into "two nations," the rich and the poor. This division into two factions epitomizes the tragic and ominous conflict that has dominated the nineteenth and twentieth centuries, and that Napoleon tried to avoid.

### OF THE PUBLICATION, THE EFFECTS, AND THE APPLICATION OF THE LAWS IN GENERAL

**2.**
The law ordains for the future only; it has no retrospective operation.

**3.**
The laws of police and public security bind all the inhabitants of the territory. Immovable property, although in the possession of foreigners, is governed by the French law.
The laws relating to the condition and privileges of persons govern Frenchmen, although residing in a foreign country.

**4.**
The judge who shall refuse to determine under pretext of the silence, obscurity, or insufficiency of the law, shall be liable to be proceeded against as guilty of a refusal of justice.

**5.**
The judges are forbidden to pronounce, by way of general and legislative determination, on the causes submitted to them.

### OF THE ENJOYMENT AND PRIVATION OF CIVIL RIGHTS

**7.**
The exercise of civil rights is independent of the quality of citizen, which is only acquired and preserved conformably to the constitutional law.

**8.**
Every Frenchman shall enjoy civil rights.

**12.**
The foreigner who shall have married a Frenchman, shall follow the condition of her husband.

**13.**
The foreigner who shall have been permitted by the government to establish his domicile in France, shall enjoy in that country all civil rights so long as he shall continue to reside there.

**17.**
The quality of Frenchman shall be lost, 1st, by naturalization in a foreign country; 2d, by accepting, without the author-

Creators of the Code (*from left to right*): Jean-Jacques de Cambacérès, François Tronchet, Jean Portalis.

ity of government, public employments bestowed by a foreign power; 3dly, by adoption into any foreign corporation which shall require distinctions of birth; 4thly by any settlement made in a foreign country, without intention of return. Commercial establishments shall never be considered as having been made without intention of return.

### 19.

A Frenchwoman, who shall espouse a foreigner, shall follow the condition of her husband.

If she become a widow, she shall recover the quality of Frenchwoman, provided she already reside in France, or that she return thither under the sanction of government, and declare at the same time her intention to fix there.

### 21.

The Frenchman who, without the authority of the government, shall engage in military service with a foreign power, or shall enroll himself in any foreign military association, shall lose his quality of Frenchman.

He shall not be permitted to re-enter France without the permission of the government, nor to recover the quality of Frenchman except by complying with the conditions required of a foreigner in order to become a citizen; and this without affecting the punishments denounced by the criminal law against Frenchmen who have borne or shall bear arms against their country.

### OF MARRIAGE

### 144.

A man before the age of 18, and a woman before 15 complete, are incapable of contracting marriage.

### 145.

The government shall be at liberty nevertheless, upon weighty reasons, to grant dispensations of age.

### 148.

The son who has not attained the full age of 25 years, the daughter who has not attained the full age of 21 years, cannot contract marriage without the consent of both parents; in case of disagreement, the consent of the father is sufficient.

### 165.

The marriage shall be celebrated publicly, before the civil officer of the domicile of one of the two parties.

### 203.

Married persons contract together, by the single act of marriage, the obligation of nourishing, supporting, and bringing up their children.

### 204.

A child has no action against his father and mother for an establishment in marriage or otherwise.

### 205.

Children owe a maintenance to their fathers and mothers, and other ancestors who are in want thereof.

### 212.

Married persons owe to each other fidelity, succor, assistance.

### 213.

The husband owes protection to his wife, the wife obedience to her husband.

### 214.

The wife is obliged to live with her husband, and to follow him to every place where he may judge it convenient to reside: the husband is obliged to receive her, and to furnish her with every thing necessary for the wants of life, according to his means and station.

### 215.

The wife cannot plead in her own name, without the authority of her husband, even though she should be a public trader, or non-communicant, or separate in property.

### 226.

The wife may make a will without the authority of her husband.

### 227.

Marriage is dissolved,
1st. By the death of one of the parties;

2d. By divorce lawfully pronounced; 3d. By condemnation become final of one of the married parties to a punishment implying civil death.

### 228.

A woman cannot contract a new marriage until ten months have elapsed from the dissolution of the preceding one.

### OF DIVORCE

### 229.

The husband may demand a divorce on the ground of his wife's adultery.

### 230.

The wife may demand divorce on the ground of adultery in her husband, when he shall have brought his concubine into their common residence.

### 231.

The married parties may reciprocally demand divorce for outrageous conduct, ill-usage, or grievous injuries, exercised by one of them towards the other.

### 232.

The condemnation of one of the married parties to an infamous punishment, shall be to the other a ground of divorce.

### 233.

The mutual and unwavering consent of the married parties, expressed in the manner prescribed by law, under the conditions, and after the proofs which it points out, shall prove sufficiently that their common life is insupportable to them; and that there exists, in reference to them, a peremptory cause of divorce.

### 272.

The suit for divorce shall be extinguished by the reconciliation of the parties, whether occurring subsequently to the facts which might have authorized such suit, or subsequently to the petition.

### 275.

The mutual consent of married persons shall not be admitted, if the husband have not reached twenty-five years, or if the wife be under twenty-one.

At the First Consul's request, the painter Jacques Louis David, in 1800, created this stylized view of the progressive, revolutionary leader.

He shall not be permitted to make this proof by witnesses, until he shall have already made a commencement of proof in writing.

### OF PATERNAL POWER

**371.**
A child, at every age, owes honor and respect to his father and mother.

**372.**
He remains subject to their control until his majority or emancipation.

**373.**
The father alone exercises this control during marriage.

**374.**
A child cannot quit the paternal mansion without the permission of his father, unless for voluntary enlistment after the full age of eighteen years.

### OF MINORITY, GUARDIANSHIP, AND EMANCIPATION

**420.**
In every guardianship there shall be a supplementary guardian, nominated by the family-council. His functions shall consist in acting for the interests of the minor, when they shall be in opposition to those of the guardian.

### OF MAJORITY, INTERDICTION, AND THE JUDICIAL ADVISER

**489.**
An adult, who is in an habitual state of idiotcy, of insanity, or madness, must be interdicted, even though such state present some lucid intervals.

**490.**
Any person is competent to claim the interdiction of a relative. It is the same with one spouse with regard to the other.

**491.**
In the case of madness, if the interdiction is not claimed, either by the spouse or by the relatives, it must be claimed by the commissioner of government, who may

**276.**
The mutual consent shall not be received until two years from the marriage.

**277.**
It shall no longer be admissible after twenty years of marriage, nor where the wife shall have attained the age of forty-five years.

**295.**
Married parties who shall be divorced, for any cause whatsoever, shall never be permitted to be united again.

**297.**
In case of divorce by mutual consent, neither of the parties shall be allowed to contract a new marriage until the expiration of three years from the pronunciation of the divorce.

### OF PATERNITY AND FILIATION

**312.**
An infant conceived during marriage claims the husband as his father. The latter, nevertheless, may disavow such child, on proof that during the time which has elapsed from the three hundredth to the one hundred and eightieth day previous to the birth of the infant, he was either, by reason of absence, or by the effect of some accident, under a physical incapability of cohabiting with his wife.

**313.**
The husband shall not disavow an infant, on allegation of his natural impotence; he shall not disavow it even for cause of adultery, unless the birth has been concealed from him, in which case he shall be permitted to bring forward all the facts proper to show that he is not the father.

**315.**
The legitimacy of an infant born three hundred days after dissolution of marriage, may be contested.

**331.**
Children born out of wedlock, other than such as are the fruit of an incestuous or adulterous intercourse, may be legitimated by the subsequent marriage of their father and mother, whenever the latter shall have legally acknowledged them before their marriage, or shall have recognized them in the act itself of celebration.

**333.**
Children legitimated by subsequent marriage shall enjoy the same rights as if they were born in wedlock.

**340.**
Scrutiny as to paternity is forbidden. In the case of rape, when the period of such rape shall refer to that of conception, the ravisher may be declared, on the petition of the parties interested, the father of the child.

**341.**
Scrutiny as to maternity is admissible. The child who shall claim his mother, shall be bound to prove that he is identically the same child of whom she was delivered.

also claim it in cases of idiotcy or insanity against an individual who is unmarried, and without known relatives.

### Of Property

**545.**

No one can be compelled to give up his property, except for the public good, and for a just and previous indemnity.

**546.**

Property in a thing, whether real or personal, confers a right over all which it produces, and over all connected with it by accession, naturally or artificially. This right is termed the "right of accession."

**552.**

Property in the soil imports property above and beneath.

The proprietor may make above all kinds of plantations and buildings which he shall judge convenient, saving the exceptions established under the title "Of Servitudes and Services relating to Land." He may make beneath all buildings and excavations which he shall judge convenient, and draw from such excavations all the products which they are capable of furnishing, saving the restrictions resulting from the laws and statutes relating to mines, and from the laws and regulation of police.

**570.**

If an artisan or any person whatsoever has employed a material which did not belong to him, in order to form something of a new description, whether the material can or cannot be restored to its original shape, the proprietor thereof has a right to claim the thing which has been formed from it, on paying the price of the workmanship.

**571.**

If however the workmanship were so important, that it surpassed by much, the value of the material employed, the labor shall then be deemed the principal part, and the artificer shall have a right to retain the thing wrought, on paying the price of the material to the proprietor.

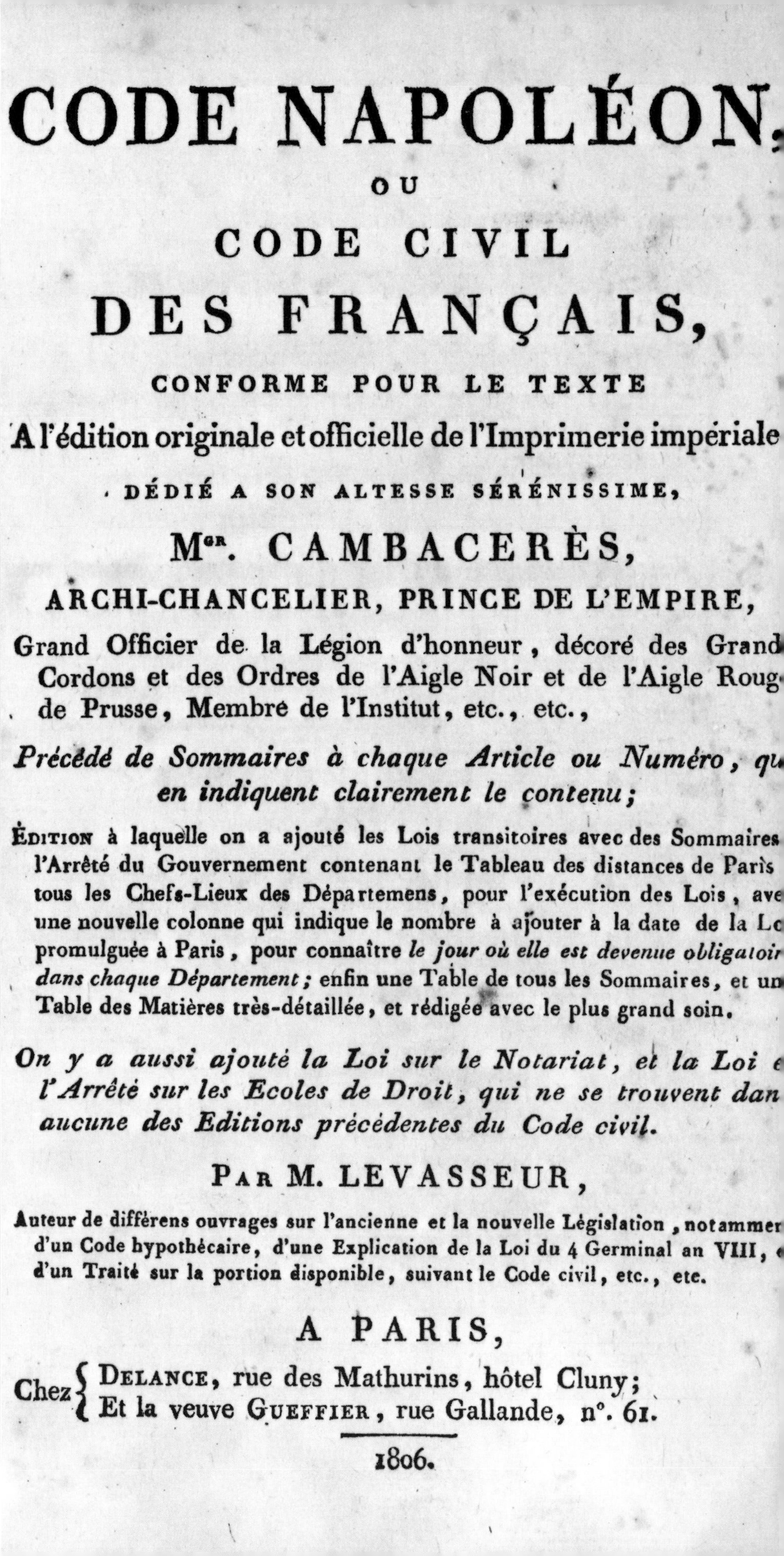

# CODE NAPOLÉON,

## OU

# CODE CIVIL DES FRANÇAIS,

### CONFORME POUR LE TEXTE

A l'édition originale et officielle de l'Imprimerie impériale

DÉDIÉ A SON ALTESSE SÉRÉNISSIME,

## Mᴳʀ. CAMBACERÈS,

### ARCHI-CHANCELIER, PRINCE DE L'EMPIRE,

Grand Officier de la Légion d'honneur, décoré des Grand Cordons et des Ordres de l'Aigle Noir et de l'Aigle Roug de Prusse, Membre de l'Institut, etc., etc.,

*Précédé de Sommaires à chaque Article ou Numéro, qu en indiquent clairement le contenu;*

ÉDITION à laquelle on a ajouté les Lois transitoires avec des Sommaires l'Arrêté du Gouvernement contenant le Tableau des distances de Paris tous les Chefs-Lieux des Départemens, pour l'exécution des Lois, ave une nouvelle colonne qui indique le nombre à ajouter à la date de la Lo promulguée à Paris, pour connaître *le jour où elle est devenue obligatoir dans chaque Département;* enfin une Table de tous les Sommaires, et un Table des Matières très-détaillée, et rédigée avec le plus grand soin.

*On y a aussi ajouté la Loi sur le Notariat, et la Loi e l'Arrêté sur les Ecoles de Droit, qui ne se trouvent dan aucune des Editions précédentes du Code civil.*

### Par M. LEVASSEUR,

Auteur de différens ouvrages sur l'ancienne et la nouvelle Législation, notammer d'un Code hypothécaire, d'une Explication de la Loi du 4 Germinal an VIII, d'un Traité sur la portion disponible, suivant le Code civil, etc., etc.

## A PARIS,

Chez { DELANCE, rue des Mathurins, hôtel Cluny;
Et la veuve GUEFFIER, rue Gallande, n°. 61.

1806.

## CONTRACTS OR CONVENTIONAL OBLIGATIONS

### 1109.

There can be no valid consent if such consent have been given through mistake, or have been extorted through violence or surreptitiously obtained by fraud.

### 1111.

Violence exercised toward him who has contracted the obligation, is a cause of nullity, although it have been exercised by a third person different from him for whose benefit the agreement has been made.

### 1113.

Violence is a cause of nullity of contract, not only when it has been exercised over the contracting party, but further when it has been so over his or her husband or wife, over their descendants or ancestors.

## CONTRACTS OF HIRING

### 1781.

The master is believed on his affirmation—For the proportion of wages;
For the payment of the salary for the year elapsed;
And for sums paid on account for the current year.

## DEPOSIT AND SEQUESTRATION

### 1955.

Sequestration is either conventional or judicial.

### 1956.

Conventional sequestration is a deposit made by one or more persons of a thing in dispute, in the hands of a third person, who binds himself to restore it, after the litigation terminated, to the person to whom the right to obtain it shall be adjudged.

## OF PRESCRIPTION

### 2262.

All actions, as well real as personal, are prescribed by thirty years, without compelling the party who alleges it to produce a document thereon, or without permitting an objection to be opposed to him derived from bad faith.

### 2271.

The actions of masters and instructors in sciences and arts, given by the month;
That by keepers of inns and taverns, on account of lodging and board which they supply;
That by artisans and work-people, for the payment of their daily labor, provisions, and salaries,
Are prescribed in six months.

### 2272.

The action by physicians, surgeons, and apothecaries for their visits, operations, and medicine;
That by officers of the court, for compensation for acts notified by them, and for commissions which they execute;
That by merchants, for commodities sold by them to private persons not merchants;
That by keepers of boarding-houses, for the price of the board of their pupils; and by other masters for the price of apprenticeship;
That by servants who are hired by the year, for the payment of their wages;
Are prescribed after a year.

### 2273.

The action by attorneys, for the payment of their costs and charges, is prescribed after two years, computing from the judgment on the process, or from the settlement by the parties, or from the revocation of the said attorneys. With regard to affairs not terminated, they cannot make demands for their costs and charges which shall extend more than five years backward.

### 2277.

Arrears of perpetual and life annuities,
Those of alimentary pensions;
The rents of houses, and the price of a lease of rural property;
Interest on sums lent, and generally every thing which is payable by the year, or at shorter periodical intervals;
Are prescribed after five years.

## THE EMPEROR'S LASTING GLORY

*What Napoleon had hoped for has now largely come true. His* Code Napoléon *and the subsequent codes (a new commercial code in 1806, a new procedural code in 1807, a new criminal code in 1810) have deeply influenced Europe's system of justice. As "the most successful law code of the nineteenth century," Napoleon's Code remained in force in the Old German Rhine provinces until the end of the nineteenth century. It is still valid in France, Belgium, and Luxembourg. It has left its mark on the civil law of Germany, the Netherlands, Switzerland, Italy, and Rumania. In America, the Code had a strong influence on Louisiana's civil code of 1825, which, although revised in part since that time, remains in effect today. Napoleon had longed to go to Latin America to lead the struggle for independence in Venezuela, Chile, and Peru and "form Latin America into a great empire." This remained just a dream, but his Code has been adopted by a number of Latin American states. Napoleon saw his Code as a charter of freedom for all the nations that came within the purview of his power. With this in mind, he wrote to his brother, the king of Westphalia, on 15 November 1807: "The benefits of the* Code Napoléon, *open court proceedings and the adoption of the jury system are to form the basis of your government. . . . Believe me, I have more faith in this as a means to expand and consolidate your reign than I have in the most splendid military victories."*

# The Communist Manifesto

In 1847 London's Central Committee of the "Communist Alliance" commissioned Karl Marx to write a manifesto on his convictions and objectives. By the beginning of 1848 this was submitted under the title *Manifesto of the Communist Party* and was published only a few weeks prior to the outbreak of the Paris revolution. Friedrich Engels, Marx's only lifelong friend, had given him a draft in the form of questions and answers, a sort of "catechism for Communists." Marx, finding this format too pedantic, blended Engels's thoughts into his Communist Manifesto. This unique document is a new gospel, messianic in tone, prophesying the historic triumph of the proletariat and promising "the old bourgeois society with its classes and class distinctions will be replaced by an association wherein the free development of each individual is the requirement for the free development of all."

*Right:* First edition of the Manifesto, 1848.

In 1845 Friedrich Engels published his *Situation of the Working Class in England,* based on his firsthand observations of workers' poverty and misery in Manchester. Engels, at the age of twenty-four, was profoundly moved, and indelibly marked, by these observations.

Manifest

der

Kommunistischen Partei.

Veröffentlicht im Februar 1848.

Proletarier aller Länder vereinigt euch.

London.

Gedruckt in der Office der „Bildungs-Gesellschaft für Arbeiter"
von J. E. Burghard.
46, Liverpool Street, Bishopsgate.

Now the revolution, which in turn was a
religious, philosophical, and political one,
has become an economic revolution.
Like all forms of revolution so far,
it means a break with the past,
it causes the overthrowing of existing order.
Without the complete overturning
of principles and dogmas
there cannot be a revolution,
only a mystification.

From "Toast to the Revolution" by P. J. Proudhon,
*Le Peuple,* 17 October 1848

## WORKERS OF THE WORLD, UNITE!

Marx and Engels were invited to attend a meeting in London on 29 November 1847, organized by the Fraternal Democrats in memory of the Polish revolution of 1830. In the same hall on Great Windmill Street, near the National Gallery, a ten-day congress began on the following day. Here three groups of German immigrants founded the Communist League, which succeeded the Union of the Just. At Engels's suggestion, it adopted the following principles: "It is the League's purpose to overthrow bourgeois society, to establish a proletarian government, to abolish the old bourgeois society based on class distinctions, and to establish a new classless society without private property." The motto of the Communist Union for the Education of Workers—"All men are brothers"—was replaced by Marx's war cry: "Workers of the world, unite."

After the conference Marx and Engels were asked to write a Communist Manifesto for the Communist Alliance. In this Manifesto there is clear evidence of the literary influence of the early radicals, who were thoroughly studied and later frequently damned by Marx; of the early utopian socialists; and of such enthusiastic individuals and bourgeois reformers as Babeuf, Saint Simon, Fourier, Owen, Proudhon, and Considérant. Karl Marx, a literary glutton, had thoroughly digested all of this. In terms of historical influence, however, the Communist Manifesto must be seen as the work of "the last Great Prophet" (to quote Isaiah Berlin). Marx's roots are to be found in two of the prophetic books of the Old Testament, Isaiah and Jeremiah. He is a descendant of the oldest lines of old Europe's Jewry—a heritage he took pains to renounce. "Marx's very radical break with the Judaism of his day, far from making a purely empirical interpretation of reality possible,

only led him—quite unconsciously—back to the oldest traditions of the Old Testament." (This was said by Franz Borkenau in 1956. Almost concurrently, such scholars as the Swiss Arnold Künzli and the Austrian Albert Massiczek have also laid stress on the biblical and Jewish elements in Marx's œuvre.) The "hells" observed and experienced by Engels and Marx helped shape the Communist Manifesto. Engels, the twenty-four-year-old son of a wealthy Rhenish textile manufacturer, was confronted with the English proletariat's infernal living conditions while working in his father's affiliated company in Manchester. He described these conditions with scientific detachment in his documentary work *The Situation of England's Working Class,* published in 1845 in Leipzig, and based largely on conservative parliamentary reports. In the large towns "the social war, the war of all against all . . . is openly declared." These wretched people lived almost naked, penned up like neglected animals, nearly dead from starvation. The description of Manchester is worse than Dante's pictures of hell: rivers of dirt and excrement, infant mortality, children five to seven years old working fourteen- to sixteen-hour shifts, day and night. Here the workers were nothing but "a mere instrument, a thing." Karl Marx ex-

perienced the same kind of hell in Paris in 1844. Deeply moved, he described the animal-like existence of workers "living in holes, poisoned by the pestilential stench of civilization." It is to these wretched people that the Communist Manifesto brings the good news of the victory of the proletariat over the bourgeoisie—and ultimately of the liberation of mankind.

At the same time the Communist Manifesto proclaims a new historic philosophy that no longer interprets history in retrospect but turns toward the future, so that man can find his true self: "Communism brings the positive abolition of private property as human self-estrangement, and therefore allows the true acquisition of human nature by and for human beings. This communism is a perfect naturalism-humanism and as such . . . the true solution of man's conflicts with nature and man, the true solution of the conflict between existence and being, . . . between freedom and necessity, between individual and species. It is the answer to the enigma of history and knows itself to be just that." These sentences—an interpretation of the Communist Manifesto—were written by Karl Marx in his *National Economy and Philosophy.* "The answer to the enigma of history": this was (and still is) the Communist Manifesto's most explosive effect.

## MANIFESTO OF THE COMMUNIST PARTY

### BOURGEOIS AND PROLETARIANS

. . . The history of all hitherto existing society is the history of class struggles. Freeman and slave, patrician and plebeian, lord and serf, guild-master and journeyman, in a word, oppressor and oppressed, stood in constant opposition to one another, carried on an uninterrupted, now hidden, now open fight, a fight that each time ended, either in a revolutionary re-constitution of society at large, or in the common ruin of the contending classes.

In the earlier epochs of history, we find almost everywhere a complicated arrangement of society into various orders, a manifold gradation of social rank. In ancient Rome we have patricians, knights, plebeians, slaves; in the Middle Ages, feudal lords, vassals, guild-masters, journeymen, apprentices, serfs; in almost all of these classes, again, subordinate gradations. . . .

The bourgeoisie, historically, has played a most revolutionary part.

The bourgeoisie, wherever it has got the upper hand, has put an end to all feudal, patriarchal, idyllic relations. It has pitilessly torn asunder the motley feudal ties that bound man to his "natural superiors," and has left remaining no other nexus between man and man than naked self-interest, than callous "cash payment." . . .

The bourgeoisie has torn away from the family its sentimental veil, and has reduced the family relation to a mere money relation.

The weapons with which the bourgeoisie felled feudalism to the ground are now turned against the bourgeoisie itself. . . .

In proportion as the bourgeoisie, i.e., capital, is developed, in the same proportion is the proletariat, the modern working class, developed—a class of labor-

125

ers, who live only so long as they find work, and who find work only so long as their labor increases capital. These laborers, who must sell themselves piecemeal, are a commodity, like every other article of commerce, and are consequently exposed to all the vicissitudes of competition, to all the fluctuations of the market.

### PROLETARIANS AND COMMUNISTS

. . . The distinguishing feature of Communism is not the abolition of property generally, but the abolition of bourgeois property. But modern bourgeois private property is the final and most complete expression of the system of producing

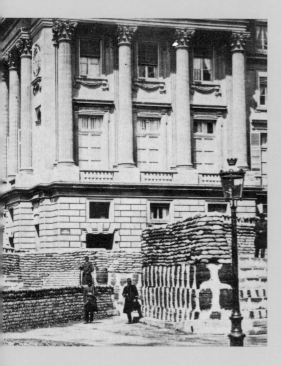

Karl Marx believed that the ideas of his Communist Manifesto were taking effect in the Paris Commune in the spring of 1871. Shown above are barricades erected by the rebels in the Rue de Rivoli, near the Place de la Concorde.

and appropriating products, that is based on class antagonisms, on the exploitation of the many by the few.

In this sense, the theory of the Communists may be summed up in the single sentence: Abolition of private property. . . .

You are horrified at our intending to do away with private property. But in your existing society, private property is already done away with for nine-tenths of the population; its existence for the few is solely due to its non-existence in the hands of those nine-tenths. . . .

In one word, you reproach us with intending to do away with your property. Precisely so; that is just what we intend. From the moment when labor can no longer be converted into capital, money, or rent, into a social power capable of being monopolized, i.e., from the moment when individual property can no longer be transformed into bourgeois property, into capital, from that moment, you say, individuality vanishes.

You must, therefore, confess that by "individual" you mean no other person than the bourgeois, than the middle-class owner of property. This person must, indeed, be swept out of the way, and made impossible.

Communism deprives no man of the power to appropriate the products of society; all that it does is to deprive him of the power to subjugate the labor of others by means of such appropriation.

The Communists are further reproached with desiring to abolish countries and nationality.

The working men have no country. We cannot take from them what they have not got. Since the proletariat must first of all acquire political supremacy, must rise to be the leading class of the nation, must constitute itself *the* nation, it is, so far, itself national, though not in the bourgeois sense of the word. . . .

In proportion as the exploitation of one individual by another is put an end to, the exploitation of one nation by another will also be put an end to. In proportion as the antagonism between classes within the nation vanishes, the hostility of one nation to another will come to an end.

### POSITION OF THE COMMUNISTS IN RELATION TO THE VARIOUS EXISTING OPPOSITION PARTIES

The Communists fight for the attainment of the immediate aims, for the enforcement of the momentary interests of the working class; but in the movement of the present, they also represent and take care of the future of that movement. . . .

In Germany they fight with the bourgeoisie whenever it acts in a revolutionary way, against the absolute monarchy, the feudal squirearchy, and the petty bourgeoisie.

But they never cease, for a single instant, to instill into the working class the clearest possible recognition of the hostile antagonism between bourgeoisie and proletariat, in order that the German workers may straightway use, as so many weapons against the bourgeoisie, the social and political conditions that the bourgeoisie must necessarily introduce along with its supremacy, and in order that, after the fall of the reactionary classes in Germany, the fight against the bourgeoisie itself may immediately begin.

The Communists turn their attention chiefly to Germany, because that country is on the eve of a bourgeois revolution that is bound to be carried out under more advanced conditions of European civilization, and with a much more developed proletariat, than that of England was in the seventeenth, and of France in the eighteenth century, and because the bourgeois revolution in Germany will be but the prelude to an immediately following proletarian revolution. . . .

The Communists disdain to conceal their views and aims. They openly declare that their ends can be attained only by the forcible overthrow of all existing social conditions. Let the ruling classes tremble at a Communistic revolution. The proletarians have nothing to lose but their chains. They have a world to win.

*Below:* First draft of the Communist Manifesto, in Marx's own hand.

*Far right:* Soviet revolutionary propaganda poster, 1919.

*Overleaf:* Bloody suppression of a Bolshevik demonstration in front of the St. Petersburg library, spring 1917.

The Communist Manifesto was originally published in English, French, German, Italian, Flemish, and Danish—but not in Russian: Marx did not think too highly of Russia and the Russians. Its impact, for quite a long time, was very slight. Marx and Engels themselves, as early as 1872, considered it somewhat obsolete. It was not until the years 1870–1872 that the Manifesto began very slowly to have some effect. It was finally translated into all major languages. Its effect was first felt in the "underdeveloped countries"—including Russia—whereas Marx, Engels, and even Lenin had hoped for the Great Revolution in industrialized Western Europe. Although this obvious misjudgment does not lessen the prophetic impetus of the Communist Manifesto, one can cite other faults inherent in Marxist doctrine. For example: "Does it require deep insight to understand that the peo-

ple's living conditions, their social relationships, their social existence bring about changes in their ideas, their views, their conceptions, in a word, their understanding?" Here we see a certain narrow "anthropology," the scanty picture of the "new man" that does not make enough allowance for such forces as the psyche's creative powers.

# Gandhi: The Power of Non-violence

Mahatma Gandhi's non-violence, a political program constructed on a deep religious foundation, has had broad-ranging influence for several decades. It arose in response to the subcontinent's struggle against British colonialism. Because India had supported the British Empire in World War I, mustering 1.2 million men as soldiers and workers, India nourished the hope of gaining independence after the war. Britain was not prepared, however, to make any noteworthy concessions, preferring to meet the threat of an Indian revolution by enacting harsh laws, setting up special courts, and proclaiming a state of emergency. On 13 April 1919 there occurred the massacre at Amritsar, in which British

On 13 April 1919 a political rally took place in Amritsar, inspired by Gandhi's policies, despite a ban proclaimed by Brigadier General Dyer. The demon-

stration was suppressed by force of arms. The result: 379 Indians killed and more than 1,200 wounded. The picture above shows the bank where the rally took place, destroyed by gunfire.

*Right:* Message in Gandhi's hand, written 4 May 1930: "I want world sympathy in this battle of Right against might."

I want world sympathy in this battle of Right against might.
Gandhi M K Gandhi
5ᵗʰ.4.'30

troops shot into a crowd of Indians, killing about four hundred and injuring more than a thousand persons. Reaction was of course intense all over India.

It was against this background that Gandhi worked and acted. Mohandas Karamchang Gandhi, having spent more than twenty years as a lawyer in South Africa, had personally experienced that country's discrimination against Asian people. It was in response to this situation that he first developed his theory of non-violent resistance, which he also made popular in India after his return home in 1914. When Britain refused to grant India autonomy after World War I, he became leader of the Congress party and began organizing passive resistance and the policy of civil disobedience against Britain.

The document presented here is of particular interest because it was published just one year after the massacre at Amritsar.

## RESTRAINT AND IMPERTURBABILITY

Gandhi was born at Probandar in the state of Bombay on 2 October 1869, into a merchant family of the Hindu caste. Both his father and grandfather held assignments as ministers to various small principalities. His mother was a deeply religious woman who educated her son Mohandas in her beliefs. In college he was tormented by serious spiritual and religious crises, and fleeing the spiritual

*Left:* Sermon on the Mount. Christ's teachings had an unmistakable impact on Gandhi.

*Right:* The "march to the sea," 1930, to break the British monopoly on salt.

ghetto of his environment, he went to England. There he became a lawyer, and in 1893 he went to South Africa. In that country's atmosphere of racial hatred he assumed his ultimate spiritual identity. He made thorough studies of India's religious literature as well as the Bible, and the Sermon on the Mount in particular impressed him deeply. He also read works by the Russian Tolstoi, the American Thoreau, and the Englishman Ruskin. This literary diversity laid the foundation of his religious ideology and also formed the basis for the methods of his later political activities. In 1914 he returned to India and on 20 May 1915 founded the community of the Sathyagraha-Ashrams, a training group consisting of twenty-five men and women dedicated to Sathyagraha, a way of life based on three tenets: truth, non-violence, and the willingness to suffer for one's fellow men rath-

two political forms: as non-cooperation and as civil disobedience. Both are a strategically planned disregard of laws judged to be false and unjust.

This meant open rebellion and revolution—without the use of violence. This struggle, in the years up to 1935, repeatedly brought Gandhi into grave conflict with the British occupation authorities. This struggle, despite frequent setbacks and defeats, made Gandhi a saint to his countrymen, the "Mahatma"—the man "whose soul is great."

Inspirers of Gandhi *(left to right):* Raychandbhai, Leo Tolstoi, Henry David Thoreau, John Ruskin.

er than inflict suffering. The concept of Sathyagraha, a Sanskrit word, means rooting oneself so deeply in a primitive sort of trust, in the unfathomable sea of creation and being, that an imperturbability results which is unshaken by hatred and terror and all other kinds of attack.

Gandhi practiced Sathyagraha in

Gandhi failed to realize his great dream of interior pacification of the Indian subcontinent, which was socially split by religion and caste. On 19 August 1947 India was divided into two independent states, Muslim Pakistan and Hindu India. On 30 January 1948 Mahatma Gandhi was assassinated by the radical Hindu nationalist Nathuram Godse, who considered Gandhi "a friend of Muslims" because the Mahatma had objected to the cruel Hindu persecution of Muslims.

## NON-VIOLENCE

When a person claims to be non-violent, he is expected not to be angry with one who has injured him. He will not wish him harm; he will wish him well; he will not swear at him; he will not cause him any physical hurt. He will put up with all the injury to which he is subjected by the wrong-doer. Thus Non-violence is complete innocence. Complete non-violence is complete absence of ill-will against all that lives. It therefore embraces even sub-human life, not excluding noxious insects or beasts. They have not been created to feed our destructive propensities. If we only knew the mind of the Creator, we should find their proper place in His creation. Non-violence is therefore in its active form good-will towards all life. It is pure Love. I read it in the Hindu Scriptures, in the Bible, in the Koran.

Non-violence is a perfect state. It is a goal towards which all mankind moves naturally though unconsciously. Man does not become divine when he personifies innocence in himself. Only then does he become truly man. In our present state, we are partly men and partly beasts and in our ignorance and even arrogance say that we truly fulfill the purpose of our species, when we deliver blow for blow and develop the measure of anger required for the purpose. We pretend to believe that retaliation is the law of our being, whereas in every scripture we find that retaliation is nowhere obligatory but only permissible. It is restraint that is obligatory. Retaliation is indulgence requiring elaborate regulating. Restraint is the law of our being. For highest perfection is unattainable without highest restraint. Suffering is thus the badge of the human tribe.

The goal ever recedes from us. The greater the progress, the greater the recognition of our unworthiness. Satisfaction lies in the effort, not in the attainment. Full effort is full victory.

Therefore though I realize more than ever how far I am from that goal, for me

Gandhi at the spinning wheel, showing by non-violent means how to become independent from British commercial power and trade monopoly.

The elderly Mahatma.

the Law of complete Love is the law of my being. Each time I fail, my effort shall be all the more determined for my failure. . . .

A drop of water must yield to the analyst the same results as a lakeful. The nature of my non-violence toward my brother cannot be different from that of my non-

violence to the universe. When I extend the love for my brother to the whole universe, it must still satisfy the same test.

A particular practice is a policy when its application is limited to time or space. Highest policy is therefore fullest practice. But honesty as policy while it lasts is not anything different from honesty as a creed. A merchant believing in honesty as a policy will sell the same measure and quality of cloth to the yard as a merchant with honesty as a creed. The difference between the two is that, while the political merchant will leave his honesty when it does not pay, the believing one will continue it, even though he should lose his all.

The political non-violence of the Non-cooperator does not stand this test in the vast majority of cases. Hence the prolongation of the struggle. Let no one blame the unbending English nature. The hardest fiber must melt in the fire of love. I cannot be dislodged from that position because I know it. When British or other nature does not respond, the fire is not strong enough, if it is there at all.

Our non-violence need not be of the strong, but it *has* to be of the truthful. We must not intend harm to the English or to our cooperating countrymen, if and whilst we claim to be non-violent. But the majority of us *have* intended harm, and we have refrained from doing it because of our weakness or under the ignorant belief that mere refraining from physical hurt amounted to a due fulfillment of our pledge. Our pledge of non-violence excludes the possibility of future retaliation. Some of us seem unfortunately to have merely postponed the date of revenge.

Let me not be misunderstood. I do not say that the policy of non-violence excludes the possibility of revenge when the policy is abandoned. But it does most emphatically exclude the possibility of future revenge after a successful termination of the struggle. Therefore, whilst we are pursuing the policy of non-violence, we are bound to be actively friendly to English administrators and their co-operators. I felt ashamed when I was told that in some parts of India it was not safe for Englishmen or well-known cooperators to move about safely. The disgraceful scenes that took place at a recent Madras meeting were a complete denial of non-violence. Those who howled down the Chairman because he was supposed to have insulted me, disgraced themselves and their policy. They wounded the heart of their friend and helper, Mr. Andrews. They injured their own cause. If the Chairman believed that I was a scoundrel, he had a perfect right to say so. Ignorance is no provocation. But a Non-cooperator is pledged to put up with the gravest provocation. Provocation there would be, when I act scoundrel-like. I grant that it will be enough to absolve every Non-cooperator from the pledge of Non-violence and that any Non-cooperator will be fully justified in taking my life for misleading him. . . .

But if Non-violence is to remain the policy of the nation, for its fair name and that of humanity, we are bound to carry it out to the letter and in the spirit.

And if we intend to follow out the policy, if we believe in it, we must then quickly make up with the Englishmen and the cooperators. We must get their certificate that they feel absolutely safe in our midst and that they may regard us as friends, although we belong to a radically different school of thought and politics. We must welcome them to our political platforms as honored guests. We must meet them on neutral platforms as comrades. We must devise methods of such meeting. Our non-violence must not breed violence, hatred and ill-will. We stand like the rest of fellow mortals to be judged by our works. A program of Non-violence for the attainment of Swaraj [liberation, independence] necessarily means ability to conduct our affairs on non-violent lines. That means inculcation of a spirit of obedience. Mr. Churchill, who understands only the gospel of force, is quite right in saying the Irish problem is different in character from the Indian. He means in effect that the Irish having fought their way to their Swaraj through violence will be well able to maintain it by violence, if need be. India, on the other hand, if she wins Swaraj in reality by Non-violence, must be able to maintain it chiefly by non-violent means. This Mr. Churchill can hardly believe to be possible unless India proves her ability by an ocular demonstration of the principle. Such a demonstration is impossible, unless Non-violence has permeated society so that people in their *corporate,* i.e. political, life respond to non-violence, in other words civil instead of military authority, as at present, gains predominance.

Swaraj by non-violent means can therefore never mean an interval of chaos and anarchy. Swaraj by non-violence must be a progressively peaceful revolution such that the transference of power from a close corporation to the people's representatives will be as natural as the dropping of a fully ripe fruit from a well-nurtured tree. I say again that such a thing may be quite impossible of attainment.

*Below:* Demonstration against the war in Vietnam. Youth all over the world formed such rallies to oppose the war that President Jimmy Carter was later to call an aberration, a case of "intellectual and moral bankruptcy."

But I know that nothing less is the implication of Non-violence. And if the present workers do not believe in the probability of achieving such comparatively non-violent atmosphere, they should drop the non-violent program and frame another which is wholly different in character. If we approach our program with the mental reservation that after all we shall wrest the power from the British by force of arms, then we are untrue to our profession of Non-violence. If we believe in our program, we are bound to believe that the British people are not unamenable to the force of affection, as they are undoubtedly amenable to force of arms. For the unbelievers, the Councils are undoubtedly the school of learning with their heavy program of humiliations spread over a few generations or a rapid but bloody revolution probably never witnessed before in the world. I have no desire to take part in such a revolution. I will not be a willing instrument for promoting it. The choice, in my opinion, lies between honest Non-violence with Non-cooperation as its necessary corollary, or reversion to responsive cooperation, i.e., cooperation *cum* obstruction.

*Gandhi continuously searched for a peaceful arrangement with the British government in India. In a letter addressed to the Viceroy he expressed the following sentiments: "If only I could make popular the use of strength of spirit, which is only another name for the power of love, instead of the use of brute force, I would present you an Indian nation that could defy the whole world. At all times—at opportune as well as inopportune moments—I shall try to be a personification of this eternal principle of suffering."*

*The two Indian nations, Hindu India and Muslim Pakistan, do not follow the path shown by Gandhi. But his theory and practice of non-cooperation and civil disobedience have nevertheless had worldwide impact. They lighted a fire that, although quenched again and again, continues to smolder beneath the surface of events: in North America, for example, in the various forms of civil rights movements and the youth movement or counterculture; in the passive resistance of young people in the Soviet Union, Poland, and Czechoslovakia; and in particular in Christian-inspired non-violent resistance.*

*This bearer of good news, whose significance in his own country has steadily declined, counts a growing number of spiritual sons and daughters today on other continents.*

# China's Declaration to All Nations

At the end of June 1925, when Tsai Yuan Pei, dean of Peking's National University, addressed his famous manifesto to the European powers, Japan, and America, his country was already torn by civil war. She was to continue living, fearing, fighting, and dying in that war for decades to come, and would find only temporary peace with the proclamation of the People's Republic of China on 1 October 1949. A central problem in the China of the nineteenth and twentieth centuries is the rule by "aliens" who have interfered so actively and aggressively in China's economic and political affairs. At the Washington conference of 1921–1922, the United States of America acknowledged China's autonomy, but England and Japan continued their policies in China because they feared the influence of Communism and were even afraid

The Boxer Rebellion was followed by a period of outwardly peaceful relations between China and the colonial pow-

ers. Foreign officers with experience in China continued to serve as instructors in the Chinese imperial army. In the background, China's first national flag.

Tsai Yuan Pei, 1867–1940.

So many deeds cry out to be done
And always urgently
The world rolls on.
Time presses;
Ten thousand years are too long.
The struggle is for this very morning,
and for this evening.
The Four Seas are rising.
Clouds and waters raging.
The Five Continents are rocking,
Wind and thunder roaring.
We must sweep away all creatures
harmful to human beings
And be invincible!

Mao Tse-tung, 1963

Two leaders of the Chinese revolution, Sun Yat-sen (seated) and his protégé Chiang Kai-shek, photographed around 1924.

of a Russian takeover. It was in the midst of this particularly critical situation that Tsai Yuan Pei addressed himself to the alien powers.

## ASIA TO THE ASIANS!

The more immediate cause of this great declaration was the exploitation of Chinese labor in Japanese-owned factories. This set off a general strike in 1925, supported by the Communists. Meanwhile, in Kobe, the aged and ailing founder of the First Chinese Republic, Sun Yat-sen, accused England of being chiefly responsible for the domination of Asian people by whites. After his death on 12 March of the same year, the country was flooded with pamphlets voicing hostility toward foreigners and Christians—emotions that continue to come to the surface in today's China—in such slogans as "Asia to the Asians" and "Down with Western imperialism."

The clashes started on 12 February 1925. Thirty thousand workers in thirteen Japanese cotton plants in Shanghai went on strike. The machines in the factories were

*Bottom*: The Western troops' high spirits and euphoria as they took to the field against the Chinese about 1900, and the white man's superiority complex toward Asians, are captured in this painting by Karl Röchling (*Attack by German Troops against Fort Haiku*).

*Below*: Western lady with two Chinese servants, around 1900.

taken by storm. Fighting spread to Canton, Peking, Tsingtau, as Chinese students, the pioneers and carriers of the Chinese revolution, joined the struggle. Obviously the University of Peking held a key position in this situation.

The objective of the Great National Movement was a "literary revolution" and the rebirth of China. Chinese intellectuals were beginning to listen to ideas from the West and even turned to the West for help.

For this reason the American philosopher John Dewey and the

## TSAI YUAN PEI: MANIFESTO OF THE CHINESE MOVEMENT

Our people are known throughout the world for their extremely peace-loving and orderly nature, and the concept that all men are brothers is firmly established in their consciousness. During the past decades we have acquired a deeper understanding of the essence of Western culture and have come to the conclusion that materialism and the struggle for existence has assumed more acute forms than here in China. We realize, however, that

Englishman Bertrand Russell were invited to give lectures. Almost all leading Chinese intellectuals were *liu-süeh-sheng*—students trained in foreign countries. Tsai Yuan Pei had returned from France in 1916 intending to reorganize Peking's university and to make it the source of the "cultural revolution."

technology and modern science are absolutely essential for our country. China has already sent thousands of students abroad, who later return and utilize the knowledge they have acquired for the benefit of our country. When American and European scholars visit China, they can always be sure of a friendly and worthy welcome.

Our relations with Great Britain are particularly close, since they have long been in existence and the English language is extremely widespread in China. With regard to Japan, this country originally took its culture from China and has blended this with Western teachings and traditions in more recent times. We Chinese can again derive great benefit from this. Our two countries are neighbors, the races and the writing are the same. Hence good relations ought to exist between China and Japan. So how can it be explained that current public opinion in China is so vehemently against Britain and Japan? I should like to offer an explanation for this situation.

There are in fact two reasons, one of which derives from long ago and the other from more recent date.

1. In the year 1842 Britain compelled China by force of arms to accede to the Treaty of Nanking. Since that time, China has often been obliged to sign unjust agreements of this kind. I only wish to draw attention to the most important and worst points from these treaties: consular jurisdiction, foreign leasing of land, foreign concessions, certain privileges, such as the right to station troops in China, free use of Chinese waterways, restrictions in the right to levy our own duties and many laws to protect and give preference to foreign goods and products in China. China is forced to deposit a part of its national income in foreign banks. Foreigners can establish their own schools in China without special concessions. We are muzzled and bound by foreign countries, from material relations to intellectual pursuits, from private business to the national economy. Following the gradual emergence of a national awareness, however, we can no longer remain subject to bonds of this kind. The situation can be compared to a volcano, which erupts when the internal stress becomes too great.

Entry of foreign troops into the Imperial City of Peking after the quelling of the Boxer Rebellion.

Chinese soldiers shown marching on the Great Wall toward the northeastern provinces to meet the Japanese invaders, 1937.

2. The following may be stated with respect to the more recent reasons: Chinese workers in the Japanese factories in Shanghai are very badly treated. The eight-hour working day has been introduced in all countries and the minimum daily wage is four marks (two Chinese dollars) in all civilized countries. But 12 to 13 hours per day are worked in the Japanese cotton spinning mills in Shanghai and Tsingtau, while the daily rate of pay is approximately 40 Chinese cents —or about 80 pfennigs. Although the Chinese people are extremely thrifty and undemanding, this wage is by no means adequate in view of the sharp rise in prices in recent years in China for foodstuffs and commodities. Long working hours are exceedingly harmful to the health of workers. If working conditions are compared with those in other countries, one can only wonder at such injustice. The treatment of Chinese workers by the Japanese inspectors in the companies mentioned is particularly severe. The workers quietly endured this treatment, until they were no longer able to tolerate it. On 12 February this year, the Chinese workers made the following demands of the managers of the Japanese works in Shanghai: increase in wages, reduction in working hours, and better treatment by the inspectors. The Japanese conceded nothing, however, and so the Chinese workers went on strike. On 12 April the Chinese workers at the Japanese factory in Tsingtau made similar demands and likewise began a strike when these were refused. Despite threats and various negotiations, no agreement was reached. On 28 February a Chinese worker at the Fong Tien factory in Shanghai was shot dead by a Japanese. On 15 May eleven Chinese workers at the Nei Wei works were shot by the Japanese. These shocking events led to a general strike. The Japanese must themselves bear the blame for this anti-Japanese movement. Workers in all countries are allowed the right to strike. Demonstrations of sympathy for those on strike are also generally permitted. On 30 May this year Chinese students in Shanghai demon-strated following the death of Chinese workers in Japanese factories. Yet the British police opened fire on the demonstrators and seven Chinese were killed. On 1 and 2 June, further demonstrations were held. The British police again reacted violently and many Chinese were again injured. The British maintain they have to act in this way, but on the thirteenth of this month the Chinese government was informed by telegram from American sources that the British police had acted over-hastily. On 15 June, a Mr. Samuel, a British citizen from Shanghai, confirmed by telegram that all those killed had been shot in the back. This provides evidence that they had been fleeing from the British police. The latter consider the life of a Chinese worthless, however. In the meantime, the Chinese government has opened negotiations with the diplomatic representatives of the foreign powers, in order to prevent brutality of this kind on Chinese citizens, but on 12 June British volunteers in Hankow killed eight Chinese demonstrators and wounded many others with machine-gun fire. China must take drastic action to defend herself from attacks of this kind. Britain alone bears the responsibility for the present situation.

When Japan and Britain have inflicted so much violence on us, we can only ask: What have we done to these two countries? We defend ourselves by not cooperating with them and by boycotting their goods. We do not take up arms against them, but persist in passive resistance. Anyone with a healthy understanding of human nature must realize that the Chinese people are too peace-loving and too weak. According to my information, our movement enjoys little sympathy in the outside world. A lot is said in this twentieth century about justice and universal human rights, but now when Japan and Britain have behaved so badly in China no country comes to our aid, but rather supports England and Japan! This we cannot understand with the best possible will!

Three misconceptions are held in the West: many say that the present movement is akin to the Boxer Rebellion of 1900. It is clear that this is a fallacy. The Boxer Rebellion occurred when populists in Northern China rose against local Christians, who they considered had treated them unjustly. From this there grew a movement against everything foreign. The Boxers believed they could silence foreign guns with magic spells and some Manchurian officials held the view that following the expulsion of the foreigners, the efforts of the young Chinese imbued with European ideas would come to nothing. They thought that once the foreigners had left China, the country would finally be permanently free of them. That was twenty-five years ago.

Yet there can no longer be any doubt about the powers held by foreign nations in China. At that time, many people really wanted foreigners killed, but this view is not held by anyone here, we just

national movement has now spread to the whole of China. All this demonstrates that the present movement has nothing in common with the Boxer rising. Many again tend to think of the movement as Bolshevist inspired and believe it should therefore be suppressed. This, too, is a totally false and ridiculous attitude. The question of whether Bolshevism is good for a country or not has not yet been answered. If, however, a country wished to adopt Bolshevist tenets as an experiment, it would be its own business, with which other countries would not be able to interfere. The Soviet Union is the birthplace of Bolshevism and yet other countries maintain diplomatic relations with it and do not venture to protest against its form of government. Industry is not yet developed in China and there are no marked class distinctions, hence Bolshevism is inconceivable for China. The danger of Bolshevization is far greater in

March a "Workers' Federation against Communism" was founded in Shanghai before the city council. On the occasion of the May 1st celebrations this year, a telegram from thirty-seven workers was published in the newspaper *General Daily of the Workers' Federation,* in which they called for a second General Assembly against Communism. Even following the events in Shanghai, many associations in Shanghai declared their opposition to Communism on 9 June this year. It is clear from this that the Chinese workers are absolutely against Communism and Bolshevism. Those who only go by appearances and believe that the exchange of declarations of understanding between Russia and China and the expressions of condolence conveyed to China by the Soviet government signify a sign of the Bolshevization of China, do not take into account that international acts of politeness bear no relation to the current politi-

wish to disassociate ourselves from the symbol of protest against Japan and Great Britain. The Boxer movement bore a general character of hostility to foreigners, the movement now is only directed against Britain and Japan. The Boxer Rebellion only took place in the provinces of Chihli and Shansi, the

the countries of Europe. They should therefore pay more attention to themselves in this respect and not worry about China. If the general strike in China is held to be Bolshevist inspired, why is the same view not held about similar labor movements in other countries?

I should like to list a few facts: On 20

cal orientation. This only concerns the customary courtesy as practiced between governments. In international affairs Russia has abrogated all former unjust treaties and concluded a new treaty, which is based entirely on justice and equality. This, of course, has caused public opinion in China to take a favorable attitude

*Left:* Mao Tse-tung around 1936.

*Below right:* During a work break, Chinese farm workers study Mao's teachings in the Red Book.

A LANDMARK

toward Russia. We only know that Russia is displaying considerable friendliness toward China, but do not inquire about the internal situation in that country. If Japan and Britain were to behave in a similar manner toward us, would we be expected to assume their form of constitution, i.e. a monarchy, out of friendship to them?

It might be thought abroad that Britain and Japan could put an end to the movement by exerting pressure on the Chinese central government in Peking. This, too, is a misconception. Foreign powers did, indeed, once obtain a large number of privileges from China in this way, but these are things of the past. In those days the Chinese central government was very strong and the people played little part in politics. Since the Revolution of 1911, however, the Chinese have become conscious of their political responsibilities and government is now less centralized. If the policies of the central government accord with the will of the people, they can be implemented; otherwise, even if the central government wished to yield to pressure from foreign powers, the provincial governments would offer resistance and even if certain provincial governments should sanction the actions of the central government, they would have the entire Chinese population against them. Hence the obligations extorted from the central government would be illusory, since a government of this kind would have no credibility. Thus, for example the Chinese people opposed the signing of the Treaty of Versailles, although the Chinese government wanted to give way under pressure from

Japan. The former strategy of compulsion against China no longer corresponds to modern realities. Why do not Britain and Japan try a new approach in their China policies viable for both parties?

I hope that both Britain and Japan will themselves feel that they have acted unjustly and that other powers will endeavor to modify their attitude toward China. Japanese factory owners must reduce the hours worked by our nationals in China to eight per day and set wages at a level which ensures a dignified existence, as well as putting an end to the harsh treatment of their Chinese workers. If that is done, the general strike will cease immediately and output will increase despite shorter working hours. Why do not the Japanese follow the example set by American and European companies? Britain must punish its police authorities in Shanghai and ban unprovoked attacks on innocent Chinese citizens. Compensation must be made for those killed. If the British would behave toward us as they do toward their own countrymen, we might believe in their sense of fair play.

I hope in addition that Britain, Japan, and other foreign powers, by studying the question more thoroughly, will themselves realize the injustice of the old treaties, annul these, and supersede them with new agreements based on the principle of equality and reciprocity. China will then develop in freedom, utilize its energies peacefully, and be able to cooperate on a friendly basis with other powers, in order to achieve mutually beneficial objectives. This will not only be to the advantage of China, but to the whole world. Whatever is good for both sides is of more value than that which only benefits one.

From the bottom of my heart and after mature consideration, I dedicate the above to Britain, Japan, and the other major powers!

*This manifesto, in the year 1925, proclaimed the following principles: All over the world our peoples are known to love peace and order, and to hold the deep-rooted belief that all men are brothers. During the past decades we have developed a better understanding of occidental culture and are now convinced that materialism and the struggle for existence are more severe in Western countries than in China. Tsai Yuan Pei implores the West—almost prophetically—not to misunderstand the close diplomatic relations between China and the Soviet Union, because China will always go its own way. The dean of Peking's university draws attention to British and Japanese acts of violence in China and then implores England, Japan, and all world powers to cancel the old and unfair treaties and to replace them with "new agreements based on the principle of equality and reciprocity" because "this will not only be to the ad-*

*vantage of China, but to the whole world."*

*It is hardly necessary, today, to stress the extraordinary importance of peaceful relations between 900 million Chinese and the peoples of other nations, especially of the Western world. Thus, 1925 was a landmark in the opening of China to the West.*

139

# The Atlantic Charter

One day in June 1812 the emperor Napoleon called together his Grande Armee and on 24 June he ordered it to advance toward Russia. On almost the same day in the month of June 1941, Adolf Hitler gathered his huge army for an attack on Russia, without any previous declaration of war. His army consisted of 153 German divisions, among them 19 tank divisions and 14 motorized divisions, 600,000 motor vehicles, 3,580 tanks, 7,481 guns, and a total of 3.2 million men. This German war machine was joined, more or less voluntarily, by the Rumanian army with 27 divisions and by Slovakian, Finnish, and Hungarian forces. On the morning of 22 June, German units crossed the Russian border at three different points, aiming at Leningrad, Moscow, and Kiev. With this unprovoked attack on the Soviet Union—in direct violation

Map showing Hitler's empire.

Winston Churchill (center).

President Franklin Delano Roosevelt (top right).

In War: Resolution.
In Defeat: Defiance.
In Victory: Magnanimity.
In Peace: Good will.

Winston Churchill

of the pact Hitler and Stalin had signed in 1939—the war that had begun with Hitler's invasion of Poland in the fall of 1939, and spread to Western Europe in the summer of 1940, now reached the dimension of a World War. Hitler hoped that, after a rapid victory over the Red Army, he would have a free rear and ample supplies of raw materials from western Russia. He could then turn to the West and force England to her knees. With the arrival of winter Hitler seemed to have reached his goal: At the beginning of December 1941, German advance troops were already able to see in the far distance the towers of the Kremlin. But despite enormous losses Soviet resistance was unbroken and a decision not yet reached. Then, on 6 December, the Russian units under General Zhukov forced German troops to retreat more than 100 kilometers. This first German defeat, within sight of Moscow—so similar to Napoleon's fate—was a ray of hope for all European countries occupied by German forces, a hope that their sufferings, fear, and suppression would yet reach an end.

As a result of the German attack on Russia and the first German victories, President Franklin D. Roosevelt and Prime Minister Winston Churchill, faced with the apparent defeat of the Soviet Union, arranged a meeting at sea off Argentia, Newfoundland. Here

*Below:* Battle in the Atlantic. German U-boats assail an Allied convoy.

With a smile of contempt a resistance fighter *(right)* awaits his execution.

*Bottom:* The Blitz—the terror of bombardment in London.

they agreed on 14 August 1941 on the Atlantic Charter, a political statement of the principles of peace and war.

An important adviser and participant in working out the Charter's final formulation was the Austrian constitutional law expert Hans Kelsen, who had also worked on the constitution of the first Austrian Republic in 1920 as well as the constitution of the Weimar Republic. Kelsen is recognized as a founder of pure jurisprudence.

obligations, to further the enjoyment by all States, great or small, victor or vanquished, of access, on equal terms, to the trade and to the raw materials of the world which are needed for their economic prosperity."

Both statesmen signed the Atlantic Charter on 14 August 1941. Six weeks later, on 24 September 1941, a common proclamation by British diplomats and the new Soviet allies took place at St. James's Palace in London. Applauded by British and

## TRAGEDY AND UTOPIA

Hans Kelsen was familiar with the tragic aftermath of certain demands contained in the Versailles Treaty that concluded World War I. As if attempting to avoid the same error, the fourth paragraph of the Atlantic Charter contained an appeal to the whole world: "The President of the United States of America and the Prime Minister . . . will endeavor, with due respect for their existing

American participants, the Soviet ambassador to London, Maisky, acknowledged the Atlantic Charter in the name of his government: "The Soviet Union is of the opinion that every nation is entitled to self-determination and territorial integrity of its country and that it has the right to choose the kind of social order and system of government it desires." With the "Declaration of United Nations," the principles of the Atlantic Charter were solemnly ratified on 1

*Right:* A Frenchman crosses the English Channel to join General de Gaulle.

*Below:* "In war: resolution": Surrender at the Warsaw Ghetto.

January 1942 by twenty-six allied countries, including the Soviet Union.

The Atlantic Charter won the approval of the entire free world. It was an inspiration to the soldiers of the allied forces, it kindled the spirit of resistance in occupied countries, it offered consolation to all those who suffered as well as an incentive to political courage and the hope for peace in a new, free world. But the hope proved vain. Future events were influenced less by the Atlantic Charter than by concrete stipulations dictated by Stalin at the conferences of the Big Three in Teheran, Yalta, and Potsdam. It is difficult, in the light of these events, to see the Atlantic Charter as anything more than a

all of the nations of the world, for realistic as well as spiritual reasons must come to the abandonment of the use of force."

But we must also realize that utopias exert strong ethical force, that they are real to the extent that they influence the process of world history. The terror in the wake of the bombing of Coventry, Rotterdam, Cologne, Dresden, and other cities, the soldiers' terror, the ter-

utopian dream. The time has come to take a critical look: wasn't this charter just a one-sided attempt to impose a world order largely defined by the two Allies, the United States and Great Britain, and by their particular concept of democracy, freedom, and independence? No less utopian was the demand in paragraph eight "that

ror in concentration camps and in the Warsaw ghetto, the deadly terror in extermination camps, and all the other forms of suffering this war inflicted—here was a force of such intensity that it could only be borne if answered by something as absolute as a utopia.

## THE CHARTER, 14 AUGUST 1941

The President of the United States of America and the Prime Minister, Mr. Churchill, representing His Majesty's Government in the United Kingdom, being met together, deem it right to make known certain common principles in the national policies of their respective countries on which they base their hopes for a better future for the world.

First, their countries seek no aggrandizement, territorial or other;

Second, they desire to see no territorial changes that do not accord with the freely expressed wishes of the peoples concerned;

Third, they respect the right of all peoples to choose the form of government under which they will live; and they wish to see sovereign rights and self government restored to those who have been forcibly deprived of them;

Fourth, they will endeavor, with due respect for their existing obligations, to further the enjoyment by all States, great or small, victor or vanquished, of access, on equal terms, to the trade and to the raw materials of the world which are needed for their economic prosperity;

Fifth, they desire to bring about the fullest collaboration between all nations in the economic field with the object of securing, for all, improved labor standards, economic advancement and social security;

Sixth, after the final destruction of the Nazi tyranny, they hope to see established a peace which will afford to all nations the means of dwelling in safety within their own boundaries, and which

*Below:* Hiroshima.

An angel *(below right),* survivor of the Dresden bombing.

will afford assurance that all the men in all the lands may live out their lives in freedom from fear and want;

Seventh, such a peace should enable all men to traverse the high seas and oceans without hindrance;

Eighth, they believe that all of the nations of the world, for realistic as well as spiritual reasons must come to the abandonment of the use of force. Since no future peace can be maintained if land, sea or air armaments continue to be employed by nations which threaten, or may threaten, aggression outside of their frontiers, they believe, pending the establishment of a wider and permanent system of general security, that the disarmament of such nations is essential They will likewise aid and encourage all other

practicable measures which will lighten for peace-loving peoples the crushing burden of armaments.

*Franklin D Roosevelt*

*Winston Churchill*

## SIGNPOST FOR THE FUTURE

*The Atlantic Charter is utopian in nature—a trait it shares with all the other great documents of mankind, those by Asia's sages, the Bible, the works of our Greek and Roman heritage, the writings of Kant. Like all these documents, the Atlantic Charter serves as a guide, a lighthouse in the ocean of world history that can guide all nations on their voyage into the future. This utopian character—the sense that today is not yet what it should be—does not lessen the importance of this and similar proclamations; they all announce the Copernican revolution necessary for the survival of the family of man. The earlier "si vis pacem, para bellum"—if you want peace, prepare for war—is*

*now altered to: Let us prepare for "a peace which will afford to all nations the means of dwelling in safety within their own boundaries." Although the political, ethical, and utopian pronouncements contained in the Atlantic Charter were ignored by statesmen when the war was over, their effect cannot be dismissed, not even by the most cynical Machiavellianism.*

# Scientists' Warning: The Franck Report

Albert Einstein, 1879–1955. On 2 August 1939 Einstein wrote a letter to President Roosevelt warning him about the danger of atomic weapons development in Germany. He suggested that the United States should undertake atomic research as a defensive measure.

*Right:* Atomic test explosion in the Pacific, 1946. The underwater detonation transforms a million tons of water into a spectacular spheroid.

On 2 August 1939 Albert Einstein addressed his famous letter to President Roosevelt urging him to produce an atomic weapon. Leo Szilard and Eugene Wigner, Hungarians living in exile, had persuaded Einstein to write this letter. Because they knew of the progress of Germany's atomic research, they were filled with anxiety for the future and fear of Hitler. But they did not know what we know today: that the work on the U.S. atomic bomb project had already begun prior to Einstein's letter. In a second letter to Roosevelt, on 25 March 1945, Einstein expressed his great concern for the future.

From 1945 to 1947 more than three thousand American scientists dared express their opposition to atomic weapons. They came together to form the Federation of American Scientists. Both the Jeffries Report of 18 November 1944 and the Franck Report of 11 June 1945 were decisive in forming this movement.

## An Urgent Appeal

Zay Jeffries was one of the leading metallurgists working for General Electric. His "Prospectus in Nucleonics" (the so-called Jeffries Report) was handed to Arthur H. Compton on 18 November 1944 to be forwarded to the government. He was inspired and morally supported in his work on this document by a thoughtful, versatile fellow scientist by the name of Eugene Rabinowitch.

The ethics of the Jewish faith—the Ten Commandments—and of Protestantism and Evangelism found a common expression in the collaboration of these two personalities. Rabinowitch had left Russia in 1917 as a boy and studied chemistry at the University of Berlin. Later he worked with James Franck on photosynthesis at Göttingen

James Franck, 1882–1964.

Our world faces a crisis, one whose
full significance has yet to be grasped. . . .
The unleashing of atomic power
has changed everything—except
our ways of thinking, and so we drift on
heedlessly toward a new disaster. . . .
The splitting of the atom need no more
annihilate humanity, need place
civilization in no graver danger,
than did the discovery of the safety match.
Its future development depends on
the level of their character, not on
the level of technology.

Albert Einstein, 1945,
on hearing of the bombing of Hiroshima

and emigrated in 1933 to England and in 1938 to the United States. There he worked at the Massachusetts Institute of Technology as a participant on "Met Lab," the metallurgic sub-project of the atomic bomb project. Rabinowitch, who by 1944 had a good mastery of English, assisted his older friend and colleague James Franck with the English wording of his report. Rabinowitch had also played a major part in the writing of Section VII of the Jeffries Report entitled "The Post War Organization of Nucleonics in America," in which he called for efforts for the establishment of effective supervision of all nuclear projects on an international level. He insisted that as soon as possible the peoples of the world should be informed of the dangers of the new scientific and technical developments and their possible control.

The Jeffries Report is a detailed prognosis on medical, agricultural, biological, and chemical possibilities in the use of nuclear energy. It foresees the technical peacetime uses of atomic energy as well as the dangers of atomic warfare. It con-

tains an urgent appeal for a global reorganization of international relations and social order: "Brotherhood, once a dream, is now a necessity"—a necessity for the survival of man.

Winner of the Nobel Prize in 1925, the German James Franck, a patriot and volunteer in World War I, was forced to leave Göttingen because of Hitler's attacks on scientific freedom. His first American post was at the Johns Hopkins University; then, in 1938, he moved on to the University of Chicago. His friend Rabinowitch was his closest collaborator on the Franck Report, which was sent to the Secretary of War on 11 June 1945.

This report foretells almost everything that has happened since: the atomic powers' ar-

Japanese empire, shown at its fullest expansion, in 1942.

maments race, and the resulting threats to peace—which still does not exist. But the report's most important message is the warning addressed to the government of the United States of America not to drop the atom bomb on Japan without prior notice. Franck suggests instead that a first atom bomb be exploded on an uninhabited island, with representatives of the United Nations as observers.

SUMMARY

The development of nuclear power not only constitutes an important addition to the technological and military power of the United States, but also creates grave political and economic problems for the future of this country.

Nucelar bombs cannot possibly remain a "secret weapon" at the exclusive disposal of this country for more than a few years. The scientific facts on which their construction is based are well known to scientists of other countries. Unless an effective international control of nuclear explosives is instituted, a race for nuclear armaments is certain to ensue following the first revelation of our possession of nuclear weapons to the world. Within ten years other countries may have nuclear bombs, each of which, weighing less than a ton, could destroy an urban area of more than ten square miles. In the war to which such an armaments race is likely to lead, the United States, with its agglomeration of population and industry in comparatively few metropolitan districts, will be at a disadvantage compared to nations whose population and industry are scattered over large areas.

We believe that these considerations make the use of nuclear bombs for an early unannounced attack against Japan inadvisable. If the United States were to be the first to realease this new means of indiscriminate destruction upon mankind, she would sacrifice public support throughout the world, precipitate the race for armaments, and prejudice the possibility of reaching an international agreement on the future control of such weapons.

Much more favorable conditions for the eventual achievement of such an agreement could be created if nuclear bombs were first revealed to the world by a demonstration in an appropriately selected uninhabited area.

In case chances for the establishment of an effective international control of nuclear weapons should have to be considered slight at the present time, then not only the use of these weapons against Japan, but even their early demonstration, may be contrary to the interests of this country. A postponement of such a demonstration will have in this case the advantage of delaying the beginning of the nuclear armaments race as long as possible. If, during the time gained, ample support can be made available for further development of the field in this country, the postponement will substantially increase the lead which we have established during the present war, and our position in an armament race or in any later attempt at international agreement would thus be strengthened.

On the other hand, if no adequate public support for the development of nucleonics will be available without a demonstration, the postponement of the latter may be deemed inadvisable, because enough information might leak out to cause other nations to start the armament race, in which we would then be at a disadvantage. There is also the possibility that the distrust of other nations may be aroused if they know that we are conducting a development under cover of secrecy, and that this will make it more difficult eventually to reach an agreement with them. If the government should decide in favor of an early demonstration of nuclear weapons, it will then have the possibility of taking into account the public opinion of this country and of the other nations before deciding whether these weapons should be used in the war against Japan. In this way, other nations may assume a share of responsibility for such a fateful decision.

To sum up, we urge that the use of nuclear bombs in this war be considered as a problem of long-range national policy rather than of military expediency, and that this policy be directed primarily to the achievement of an agreement permitting an effective international control of the means of nuclear warfare.

J. FRANCK, CHAIRMAN
D. J. HUGHES                G. T. SEABORG
J. J. NICKSON               J. C. STEARNS
E. RABINOWITCH             L. SZILARD

Atomic scientist Eugene Rabinowitch was a close friend of James Franck. He was actively involved in the writing of the Jeffries Report of 18 November 1944 as well as the Franck Report.

*Overleaf:* Hiroshima reduced to rubble. At right, the destroyed Exhibition Hall, whose ruins have been preserved intact as a memorial for future generations.

## A PROPHECY IGNORED

*The scientists' warnings were spoken in vain. In particular, Secretary of State James Byrnes and the "professional politicians," who as a rule are not richly endowed with intellectual capabilities, were opposed to these early insights. They are the representatives of the military-industrial complex, that close network of personalities from the armaments industry, the Pentagon, and politics.*

*The scientific community was soon torn by a major dispute. Many scientists allied themselves with the constantly growing armaments industry that provided them with such well-paid research jobs. From our viewpoint today, the Federation of American Scientists, between 1945 and 1947, can be considered a prelude to the awakening of the knowledge*

*Above:* Atomic generating station.

*Left:* Electron microscope, which permits the observation of radiation effects in reactor materials (steel, uranium, and aluminum, among others).

*and the conscience of mankind. These two reports—by Jeffries and by Franck—are milestones on the road leading from Hammurabi to the Ten Commandments and into the future. They prove that in situations of greatest psychic stress—in the middle of a World War—man's conscience emerges from the underground.*

# The Charter of the United Nations

The United Nations Organization is a political creation resulting from the disaster of World War II. Only "peace-loving nations" which had participated in the war against Germany prior to 1 March 1945 were to become members of this organization. Golo Mann said quite to the point: "Initially the United Nations was a war alliance taken over into times of peace, the alliance of the just that was to continue after the fall of the unjust." President Roosevelt was fond of speaking of the four "policemen—the USA, Great Britain, the Soviet Union, and China— who must enforce order on the 'small' of this world."

The rules of the United Nations are in their form an international treaty. They are the statute law of an international organization, that is, of a body under international law. The Charter was signed by fifty-one nations on 26 June 1945 after conclusion of the U.N. conference in San Francisco, and came into force on 24 October 1945. The rules provided for the acceptance of additional nations to the U.N. at any time.

## THE FAMILY OF MAN

The U.N. Charter is a culmination of the European struggle for freedom and human rights from the eleventh to the twentieth century and, more particularly, a reflection of the influences that struggle had on North America. The Charter would have been impossible without these struggles for the rights of groups, social classes, and later of individuals—without this specific experience of Euro-American white civilization. The languages of a great number of countries did not and still do not have words for "person," "personal freedom," "human rights," and "democracy." The genesis of the United Nations is also due in part to two more recent developments: One was the collective shock caused by the atrocities of World War II, and the other, the anxiety about the worldwide arms race.

The United Nations Charter outlines the purpose of the organization, stating that the primary objectives are the maintenance of international peace, the protection of human rights, the solving of economic and social problems in all countries, common measures and campaigns against threats to peace, acts of aggression, violators of peace. To ensure urgent international military actions, all member countries shall stand ready with a contingent of soldiers for such purpose. (A concrete example is the U.N. forces in the Near East.) As a supplement to the Charter,

The Detroit automotive workers, during a strike in 1937, call for the realization of human rights.

*Right.* The heirs of war.

General Secretaries of the U.N. *(left to right)*: Trygve Lie (1946–1952), Dag Hammarskjöld (1953–1961), Sithu U Thant (1962–1971), Kurt Waldheim (since 1972).

The United Nations General Assembly in full session, 1976 *(below)*. Today the organization numbers 147 member nations.

the U.N. on 10 December 1948 adopted the Universal Declaration of Human Rights. According to this Declaration, it is the responsibility of all members to preserve the freedom, justice, peace of "all members of the family of man." Like an echo of the great American and European declarations of human rights in the eighteenth century, this charter declares that all human beings are born free, with equal rights and duties. They are endowed with reason and conscience and shall act in a mutual spirit of brotherhood. Everyone has a right to life, freedom, and personal safety. Slavery

On 12 March 1976, Amnesty International published two photographs of scenes of torture in Uruguay, the first such pictures to reach the United Nations Human Rights Commission. One of them *(below)* pictures a man suffering the *bandera* or "banner": the photograph was taken after he had been hanging by his wrists for three hours.

and the slave trade are forbidden. No one shall be subject to torture or other acts of degradation. Everyone has the right to appeal to a national court if his human rights are violated. No one shall be subject to arbitrary arrest. No one shall be forced to go into exile.

## FROM THE U.N. CHARTER

WE THE PEOPLES
OF THE UNITED NATIONS

   determined
to save succeeding generations from the scourge of war, which twice in our lifetime has brought untold sorrow to mankind, and to reaffirm faith in fundamental human rights, in the dignity and worth of the human person, in the equal rights of men and women and of nations large and small, and to establish conditions under which justice and respect for the obligations arising from treaties and other sources of international law can be maintained, and to promote social progress and better standards of life in larger freedom,
   and for these ends
to practice tolerance and live together in peace with one another as good neighbors, and
to unite our strength to maintain international peace and security, and
to ensure, by the acceptance of principles and the institution of methods, that armed force shall not be used, save in the common interest, and
to employ international machinery for the promotion of the economic and social advancement of all peoples,
   have resolved to combine our efforts to accomplish these aims
Accordingly, our respective Governments, through representatives assembled in the city of San Francisco, who have exhibited their full powers found to be in good and due form, have agreed to the present Charter of the United Nations and do hereby establish an international organization to be known as the United Nations.

CHAPTER I
PURPOSES AND PRINCIPLES

Article 1

The Purposes of the United Nations are:
1. To maintain international peace and security, and to that end: to take effective collective measures for the prevention and removal of threats to the peace, and for the suppression of acts of aggression or other breaches of the peace, and to bring about by peaceful means, and in conformity with the principles of justice and international law, adjustment or settlement of international disputes or situations which might lead to a breach of the peace;
2. To develop friendly relations among nations based on respect for the principle of equal rights and self-determination of peoples, and to take other appropriate measures to strengthen universal peace;
3. To achieve international cooperation in solving international problems of an economic, social, cultural, or humanitarian character, and in promoting and encouraging respect for human rights and for fundamental freedoms for all without distinction as to race, sex, language, or religion; and
4. To be a center for harmonizing the actions of nations in the attainment of these common ends.

UNESCO food distribution in southern Chad.

*Below:* U.N. forces in the Sinai, near the Gidi Pass, overseeing the maintenance of the armistice.

## CHAPTER II
## MEMBERSHIP

### Article 4

1. Membership in the United Nations is open to all other peace-loving states which accept the obligations contained in the present Charter and, in the judgment of the Organization, are able and willing to carry out these obligations.

## CHAPTER V
## THE SECURITY COUNCIL

### Composition

### Article 23

1. The Security Council shall consist of fifteen Members of the United Nations. The Republic of China, France, the Union of Soviet Socialist Republics, the United Kingdom of Great Britain and Northern Ireland, and the United States of America shall be permanent members of the Security Council. The General Assembly shall elect ten other Members of the United Nations to be non-permanent members of the Security Council, due regard being specially paid, in the first instance to the contribution of Members of the United Nations to the maintenance of international peace and security and to the other purposes of the Organization, and also to equitable geographical distribution.

### FUNCTIONS AND POWERS

### Article 24

1. In order to ensure prompt and effective action by the United Nations, its Members confer on the Security Council primary responsibility for the maintenance of international peace and security, and agree that in carrying out its duties under this responsibility the Security Council acts on their behalf.

## CHAPTER IX
## INTERNATIONAL ECONOMIC AND SOCIAL CO-OPERATION

### Article 55

With a view to the creation of conditions of stability and well-being which are necessary for peaceful and friendly relations among nations based on respect for the principle of equal rights and self-determination of peoples, the United Nations shall promote:

a. higher standards of living, full employment, and conditions of economic and social progress and development;
b. solutions of international economic, social, health, and related problems; and cultural and educational co-operation;
c. universal respect for, and observance of, human rights and fundamental freedoms for all.

## CHAPTER XVI
## MISCELLANEOUS PROVISIONS

### Article 103

In the event of a conflict between the obligations of the Members of the United Nations under the present Charter and their obligations under any other international agreement, their obligations under the present Charter shall prevail.

## AN ENDURING HOPE

*In today's world, when people in a great many countries are being tortured, when human rights are violated, the slave trade is prospering, heads of governments are guilty of massacres, and citizens fighting for human rights are expelled from their own countries—it is easy to be critical of the United Nations and to see the Declaration of Human Rights as just a large-scale proclamation without any positive practical force. A thousand times—even a million times—mankind's great laws have been violated, in the days of Hammurabi, the Old Testament, Solon and Plato, and later, at the time of the framing of the U.S. Constitution and the European liberal legal order. Violations of these laws continue, and will continue, to occur. The nature of all these great proclamations is prospective. They challenge man to use his energies in their realization, to cope with the daily difficulties of our surroundings, our nation, our (white, yellow, black, and brown) civilization. We must pay the price for our eventual evolution from barbarism, and thus we should rejoice in the knowledge that we have a personal share in bringing about this longed-for evolution.*

The Spanish Civil War and World War II changed Picasso from a morally committed artist into an eminently political, prominently active one. He demonstrated his uncomprising political involvement in such pictorial statements as his *Guernica* (which he placed on long-term loan in New York's Museum of Modern Art until such time as he should return to Spain), his diverse works on the subject of peace, and his *Massacre in Korea*. His politically inspired work reached its true artistic highpoint in the dual frescoes he painted in 1952 for the small chapel of

the castle of Vallauris, France, entitled *War* and *Peace*. Antonina Vallentin, in her study *Pablo Picasso*, written in close cooperation with the artist, says that the *Hymn to Peace (below)*, "which is the answer to the murky parade of *War,* develops—as does the painting *The Joy of Life*—in the form of a ballet," and the critic John Berger asserts, more soberly, that the fresco *Peace* "can be considered Picasso's last will and testament. We can read in this painting what he, as an old man, had to say about the human condition."

# Hirohito's New Year's Message

In his Imperial Proclamation and New Year's Message of 1 January 1946, the emperor Hirohito refers to the constitution given by Emperor Meiji at the beginning of the Meiji era (1872) as fundamental to Japanese government policy. For Hirohito had to keep in mind the Japanese people's deep-rooted, traditional beliefs as he prepared his proclamation, which he knew was a radical break with Japanese tradition. To soften the clash with the time-honored past, Hirohito used a technique that was later employed by Pope John XXIII in his revolutionary encyclical *Pacem in Terris*—for John too was breaking with certain inveterate, sacred traditions. Both men, therefore, chose leaders of the past as "patron saints" for the new era: the Pope evoked Pope Pius XII, and Hirohito referred to Emperor Meiji, who, to save the Empire, made Japan accessible to Western civilization in technical, industrial, and economic respects.

The sun goddess Amaterasu. According to Japanese tradition she is the ancestor of the Japanese imperial dynasty. This ancestry ensures the "divinity" of each successive emperor.

Emperor Hirohito, born 1901.

Gazing after the
company of soldiers,
my heart ached:
how carefree
they marched. . . .

Poem by the Japanese Ishikawa Takuboku (1885–1912).

## THE BREAK WITH TRADITION

It is a long way through world history from the divine kings of Hammurabi's times and before, to the pharaohs who were bearers of divine justice, the kings who ruled Old Europe by divine right until World War I, and finally to the dramatic proclamation in which the emperor Hirohito renounced his imperial divinity. This renunciation is preceded by the words "Love of the family and love of the country are especially strong in this country. With more of this devotion should we now work toward love of mankind." The emperor voices his conviction that the people "will prove themselves worthy of their best tradition."

For Hirohito as for his country, the war ended under the most dramatic circumstances. Certain influential and powerful Japanese politico-military groups intended, like Hitler, to fight to the last man. After the atomic explosions of 6 and 9 August 1945, some of these reactionary extremists were even threatening to assassinate the emperor in a desperate effort to prevent surrender. Thus, on 15 August, with two major cities reduced to rubble, and in danger to his own life, the emperor Hirohito broadcast the radio message "End of war." On 2 September 1945, aboard the U.S. *Missouri* off Tokyo, the ceasefire was proclaimed. On 24 December, the eve of the commemoration of the birth of Jesus Christ, a decree by General MacArthur called for abrogation of the Japanese laws governing the state religion. This decree would have been a meaningless piece of paper, like thousands of similar decrees, were it not for the emperor Hirohito's courage. For the emperor dared to break with Japan's most sacred tradition, the belief that the Tenno or Emperor is the descendant of the sun queen

Guard figure from the Todai-ji temple in Nara *(left)* symbolizes the religious veneration of the emperor, who is not supposed to come into contact with the daily lives of his people. Despite dangerous opposition, Hirohito overcame these taboos and carried out the humanizing of the Japanese imperial office.

*Below right:* First voyage by the emperor to the wreckage of Hiroshima, where he appeared for the first time in full view of the Japanese people.

Amaterasu ("Shining from the Heavens"). The constitution of 1889, still under the spell of that tradition, had exalted the emperor's "holiness and invulnerability."

It was on 1 January 1946 that the emperor Hirohito proclaimed the opening-up of Japan's people and her culture to the unity of mankind. By reminding his people of their roots—in traditions that are old but no longer magical—the emperor helped them to face the tasks of the future.

Mutsuhito Meiji, Emperor of Japan, 1867–1912, weakened the nobles' feudal reign and opened up Japan to Western influences.

*Right:* The first manuscript page of the emperor Hirohito's 1946 New Year's Message; the subsequent pages are shown below. The original document is kept in the Japanese National Archives.

## IMPERIAL RESCRIPT, 1 JANUARY 1946

In greeting the New Year, We recall to mind that Emperor Meiji proclaimed, as the basis of our national policy, the Five Clauses of the Charter-Oath at the beginning of the Meiji Era. The Charter-Oath signified:—

1. Deliberative assemblies shall be established and all measures of government decided in accordance with public opinion.

2. All classes, high and low, shall unite in vigorously carrying on the affairs of State.

3. All common people, no less than the civil and military officials, shall be allowed to fulfill their just desires, so that there may not be any discontent among them.

4. All the absurd usages of old shall be broken through, and equity and justice to be found in the workings of nature shall serve as the basis of action.

Wisdom and knowledge shall be sought throughout the world for the purpose of promoting the welfare of the Empire.

The proclamation is evident in significance and high in its ideals. We wish to make this oath anew and restore the country to stand on its own feet again. We have to reaffirm the principles embodied in the Charter, and proceed unflinchingly towards elimination of misguided practices of the past, and keeping in close touch with the desires of the people, we will construct a new Japan through thoroughly being pacific, the officials and the people alike, attaining rich culture, and advancing the standard of living of the people.

The devastation of war inflicted upon our cities, the miseries of the destitute,

We feel deeply concerned to note that consequent upon the protracted war ending in our defeat, our people are liable to grow restless and to fall into the Slough of Despond. Radical tendencies in excess are gradually spreading and the sense of morality tends to lose its hold on the people, with the result that there are signs of confusion of thoughts.

We stand by the people and We wish always to share with them in their moments of joys and sorrows. The ties between Us and Our people have always stood upon mutual trust and affection. They do not depend upon mere legends and myths. They are not predicated on the false conception that the emperor is divine, and that the Japanese people are superior to other races and fated to rule the world.

Our Government should make every effort to alleviate their trials and tribulations. At the same time, We trust that the

the stagnation of trade, shortage of food, and the great and growing number of the unemployed are indeed heart-rending. But if the nation is firmly united in its resolve to face the present ordeal and to seek civilization consistently in peace, a bright future will undoubtedly be ours, not only for our country, but for the whole of humanity.

Love of the family and love of the country are especially strong in this country. With more of this devotion should we now work toward love of mankind.

people will rise to the occasion, and will strive courageously for the solution of their oustanding difficulties, and for the development of industry and culture. Acting upon a consciousness of solidarity and of mutual aid and broad tolerance in their civic life, . . . they will be able to render their contribution to the welfare and advancement of mankind. . . .

We expect Our people to join Us in all exertions looking to accomplishment of this great undertaking with an indomitable spirit.

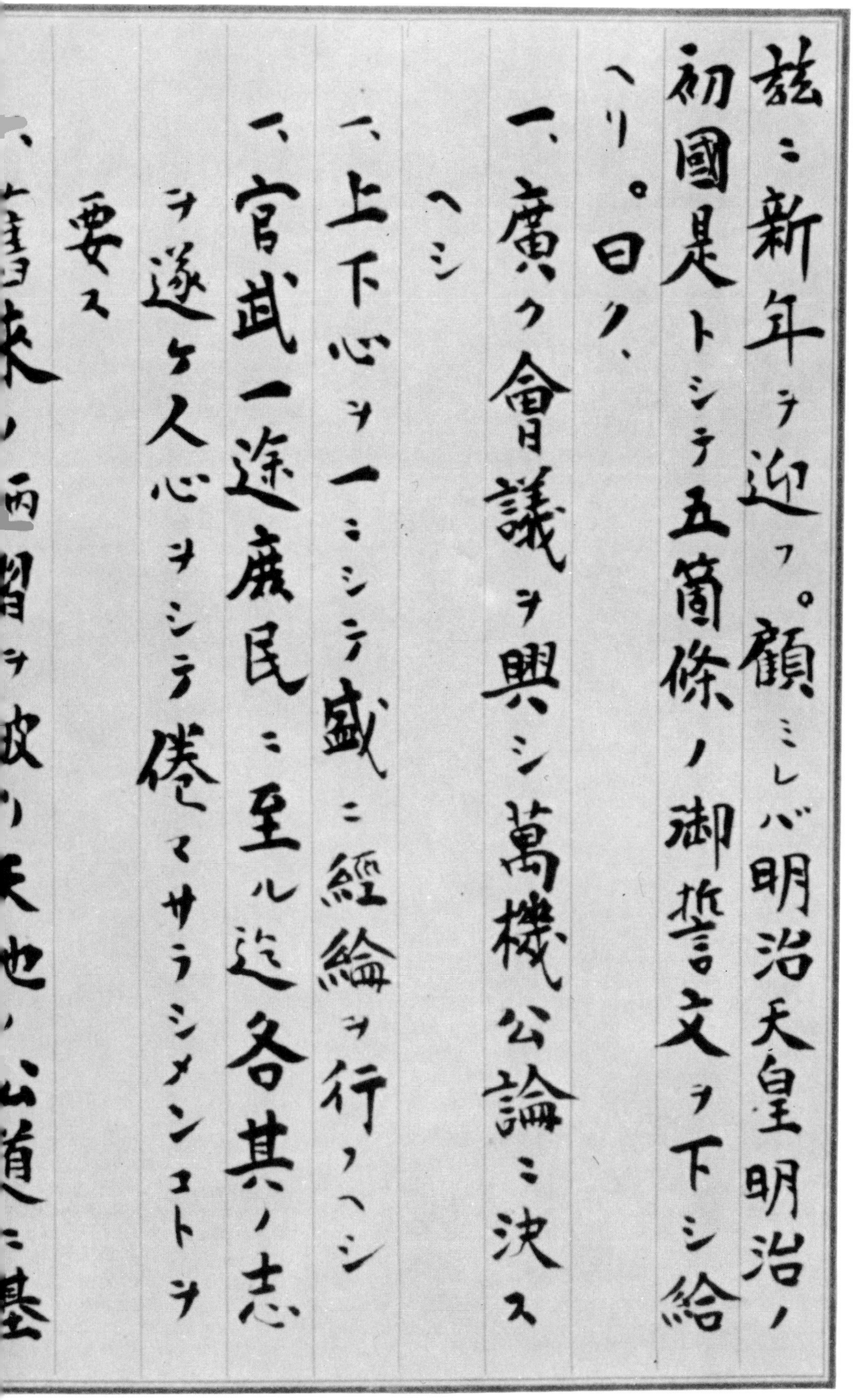

茲ニ新年ヲ迎フ。顧ミレバ明治天皇明治ノ初國是トシテ五箇條ノ御誓文ヲ下シ給ヘリ。曰ク、

一、廣ク會議ヲ興シ萬機公論ニ決スヘシ

一、上下心ヲ一ニシテ盛ニ經綸ヲ行フヘシ

一、官武一途庶民ニ至ル迄各其ノ志ヲ遂ケ人心ヲシテ倦マサラシメンコトヲ要ス

一、舊來ノ陋習ヲ破リ天地ノ公道ニ基

## A NEW JAPAN

In the war years (1937–1945), years in which Japan had tried by conquest to build up an empire in East Asia, she saw her population decrease by more than 1.5 million people. The war losses amounted, financially, to 67 billion yen. "Production had ground to a stop," writes Lucien Bianco, "communications were interrupted, there were famine and epidemics. The collapse was total, everything needed to be rebuilt." But "by 8 September 1951, when Japan signed the peace treaty at San Francisco, the nation represented by Yoshida bore no resemblance at all to pre-war Japan. It was an entirely new nation—if not a new people."

Today Japan is a leading power in many areas of world economics. Her export drives—so necessary in such a populous nation—are feared by her competitors. These drives—invasions of other continents—must be seen in the context of the difficulties confronting every national or international economy today. As an industrial power Japan has, like other modern nations, her share of drawbacks, including political corruption, and all the problems resulting from the struggle for survival, problems of basic sustenance, of maintaining prosperity and political stability as well as, of course, social equilibrium among great crowds of people living so close together.

A new people? The Japanese—who have never made a point of emphasizing their defeats—are at one and the same time a very old and a very young nation, on the one hand rooted in deep native instincts and traditions, on the other hand awake to the challenge of today's world and the world of tomorrow—as Japan's modern research equipment proves. The radical change for Japan, the breakthrough into the modern age, was made possible by Emperor Hirohito's proclamation. He served as a bridge spanning the millennia, leading toward a present in which Japan holds her own in a community of nations that is united in conflict as well as in peace.

# Voice of the Third World: Frantz Fanon

As the title for the appeal to oppressed nations he published in 1961, Frantz Fanon quoted the famous line from the "Internationale": "Awake, ye wretched of the earth!" The first section of his book, "Concerning Violence," is concerned with the situation of the colonized peoples, which is the exact opposite of the situation of the colonial master. There is no way that this reality can be disguised—as such conflicts often are disguised in the "developed" world. The colonial situation lacks the West's morality preachers, its false spurs to achievement—symbolized by the famous saga of the newsboy who becomes the richest man in the world—as well as its incitements to decorum and bourgeois uprightness.

In the colonies, peace and order are hammered into the heads of oppressed people by blows of billy clubs and by napalm bombs. The history the colonialist writes is not that of the pillaged country, but the history of his own nation. He writes it, for the most part, with naked force, and Fanon argues that

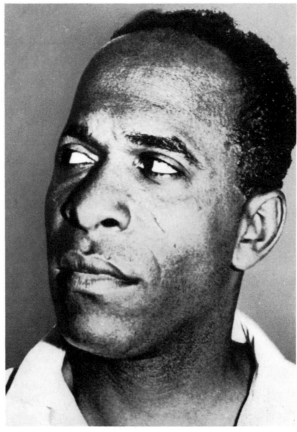

Frantz Fanon, 1925–1961.

Formerly our continent was buoyed up
by other means: the Parthenon, Chartres,
the Rights of Man, or the swastika.
Now we know what these are worth;
and the only chance of our being saved
from shipwreck is the very Christian sentiment
of guilt. . . . In the past we made history
and now it is being made of us.
The ratio of forces has been inverted;
decolonization has begun; all that
our hired soldiers can do is
to delay its completion.

Jean-Paul Sartre, Preface to
*The Wretched of the Earth*

the colonized man has no choice but to respond with violence. In the three subsequent sections ("Spontaneity: Its Strengths and Weaknesses," "The Pitfalls of National Consciousness," and "On Native Culture") the author describes the various phases in the development of national consciousness.

In the last section, "Colonial War and Mental Disorders," Frantz Fanon the psychiatrist analyzes patients from diverse clinics in Africa and provides concrete proof for his contention that the colonialists gradually destroy the identity of oppressed people.

## PSYCHIATRIST AND REVOLUTIONARY

In 1958, after severe internal unrest in France, Charles de Gaulle came back to power. In the same year, in Ghana's capital city of Accra, the first Pan-African Congress took place, an event that rekindled hopes of early independence in all colonized African countries. The Conference of Independent African States voted unanimously to lend full, active support to the struggle for Algerian independence then being carried on by the FLN (National Liberation Front). De Gaulle seemed at first to favor swift decolonization, but it soon became clear to Africans that what he had in mind was just a formal independence under the direction of the *Grande Nation*.

Frantz Fanon, a farmer's son born in Martinique in 1924, studied medicine and psychiatry in France. During World War II he joined the Partisans in the resistance against the German occupation. In 1953, repelled by the decadence and arrogance of the Western world, he migrated to Algeria, where he became chief of the psychiatric clinic of Blida-Joinville. Here he

Equipped with tropical helmet, pince-nez, parasol, and briefcase, a tourist sets out, around the turn of the century, to "conquer" Africa. Africans are carrying his luggage.

Algerian patriots enthusiastically wave the flag on 1 July 1962—the day Algeria won her independence. After his one-sided and therefore unsuccessful attempts at decolonization, De Gaulle adopted a more conciliatory attitude toward the former colony.

A soldier in the Portuguese army in Mozambique strides through a village bearing the head of an executed revolutionary.

Presidents of prominent African nations *(left to right)*: Kaunda of Zambia, Neto of Angola, Nyerere of Tanzania, Khama of Botswana, and Machel of Mozambique. They met in September 1976 to discuss possibilities for Zimbabwe's independence. They are supporting the country's independence drive with all means at their disposal.

was confronted with the direct consequences of colonization. He saw with his own eyes how the repressive mechanism of colonial power actually operated, even in the psychiatric clinics, which were filled with the victims of this oppression. Furious, in 1956 he wrote to the Governor General—the letter has since become famous—announcing his resignation in the most scathing terms. He immediately joined the National Liberation Front and became the most prominent spokesman for oppressed nations in the world. Shortly before his death he was ambassador of the GPRA (Provisional Government of the Algerian Republic) in Accra. He died of leukemia in New York in 1961 on the very day his *Wretched of the Earth* was published.

A year later the Algerians won their independence and gave an extraordinary impetus to the rest of the underdeveloped world. Even after his death, Frantz Fanon remains the great catalyst and the point of orientation for all the nations of the Third World. His name is evoked in the same breath with Che Guevara, Mao, Malcolm X.

# THE WRETCHED OF THE EARTH

## CONCERNING VIOLENCE

Decolonization, which sets out to change the order of the world, is, obviously, a program of complete disorder. But it cannot come as a result of magical practices, nor of a natural shock, nor of a friendly understanding. Decolonization, as we know, is a historical process: that is to say that it cannot be understood, it cannot become intelligible nor clear to itself except in the exact measure that we can discern the movements which give it historical form and content. Decolonization is the meeting of two forces, opposed to each other by their very nature, which in fact owe their originality to that sort of substantification which results from and is nourished by the situation in the colonies. Their first encounter was marked by violence and their existence together—that is to say the exploitation of the native by the settler—was carried on by dint of a great array of bayonets and cannons. The settler and the native are old acquaintances. In fact, the settler is right when he speaks of knowing "them" well. For it is the settler who has brought the native into existence and who perpetuates his existence. The settler owes the fact of his very existence, that is to say, his property, to the colonial system.

Decolonization never takes place unnoticed, for it influences individuals and modifies them fundamentally. It transforms spectators crushed with their inessentiality into privileged actors, with the grandiose glare of history's floodlights upon them. It brings a natural rhythm into existence, introduced by new men, and with it a new language and a new humanity. Decolonization is the veritable creation of new men. But this creation owes nothing of its legitimacy to any supernatural power; the "thing" which has been colonized becomes man during the same process by which it frees itself. In decolonization, there is therefore the need of a complete calling in question of the colonial situation. If we wish to describe it precisely, we might find it in the well-known words: "The last shall be first and the first last." Decolonization is the putting into practice of this sentence. That is why, if we try to describe it, all decolonization is successful. . . .

We have seen that it is the intuition of the colonized masses that their liberation must, and can only, be achieved by force. By what spiritual aberration do these men, without technique, starving and enfeebled, confronted with the military and economic might of the occupation, come to believe that violence alone will free them? How can they hope to triumph? The colonized races, those slaves of modern times, are impatient. They know that this apparent folly alone can put them out of reach of colonial oppression. A new type of relations is established in the world. The underdeveloped peoples try to break their chains, and the extraordinary thing is that they succeed. It could be argued that in these days of sputniks it is ridiculous to die of hunger; but for the colonized masses the argument is more down-to-earth. . . .

## THE PITFALLS OF NATIONAL CONSCIOUSNESS

History teaches us clearly that the battle against colonialism does not run straight away along the lines of nationalism. For a very long time the native devotes his energies to ending certain definite abuses: forced labor, corporal punishment, inequality of salaries, limitation of political rights, etc. This fight for democracy against the oppression of mankind will slowly leave the confusion of neo-liberal universalism to emerge, sometimes laboriously, as a claim to nationhood. It so happens that the unpreparedness of the educated classes, the lack of practical links between them and the mass of the people, their laziness, and, let it be said, their cowardice at the decisive moment of the struggle will give rise to tragic mishaps. . . .

The theoretical question that for the last fifty years has been raised whenever the history of underdeveloped countries is

under discussion—whether or not the bourgeois phase can be skipped—ought to be answered in the field of revolutionary action, and not by logic. The bourgeois phase in underdeveloped countries can only justify itself in so far as the national bourgeoisie has sufficient economic and technical strength to build up a bourgeois society, to create the conditions necessary for the development of a large-scale proletariat, to mechanize agriculture, and finally to make possible the existence of an authentic national culture. . . .

The duty of those at the head of the movement is to have the masses behind them. Allegiance presupposes awareness and understanding of the mission which has to be fulfilled; in short, an intellectual position, however embryonic. We must not voodoo the people, nor dissolve them in emotion and confusion. Only those countries led by revolutionary elite who have come up from the people can today allow the entry of the masses upon the scene of history. . . .

### ON NATIONAL CULTURE

When we consider the efforts made to carry out the cultural estrangement so characteristic of the colonial epoch, we realize that nothing has been left to chance and that the total result looked for by colonial domination was indeed to convince the natives that colonialism came to lighten their darkness. The effect consciously sought by colonialism was to drive into the natives' heads the idea that if the settlers were to leave, they would at once fall back into barbarism, degradation, and bestiality. . . .

Colonial domination, because it is total and tends to oversimplify, very soon manages to disrupt in spectacular fashion the cultural life of a conquered people. This cultural obliteration is made possible by the negation of national reality, by new legal relations introduced by the occupying power, by the banishment of the natives and their customs to outlying districts by colonial society, by expropriation, and by the systematic enslaving of men and women. . . .

A national culture under colonial domination is a contested culture whose destruction is sought in systematic fashion. It very quickly becomes a culture condemned to secrecy. This idea of a clandestine culture is immediately seen in the reactions of the occupying power which interprets attachment to traditions as faithfulness to the spirit of the nation and as a refusal to submit. This persistence in following forms of cultures which are already condemned to extinction is already a demonstration of nationality; but it is a demonstration which is a throwback to the laws of inertia. There is no taking of the offensive and no redefining of relationships. There is simply a concentration on a hard core of culture which is becoming shriveled up, inert, empty.

By the time a century or two of exploitation has passed there comes about a veritable emaciation of the stock of national culture. It becomes a set of automatic habits, some traditions of dress, and a few broken-down institutions. Little movement can be discerned in such remnants of culture; there is no real creativity and no overflowing life. The poverty of the people, national oppression, and the inhibition of culture are one and the same thing. . . .

But such a situation can only be transitory. In fact, the progress of national consciousness among the people modifies and gives precision to the literary utterances of the native intellectual. The continued cohesion of the people constitutes for the intellectual an invitation to go further than his cry of protest. The lament first makes the indictment; and then it makes an appeal. In the period that follows, the words of command are heard. The crystallization of the national consciousness will both disrupt literary styles and themes, and also create a completely new public. While at the beginning the native intellectual used to produce his work to be read exclusively by the oppressor, whether with the intention of charming him or of denouncing him, now the native writer progressively takes on the habit of addressing his own people.

*Today, Fanon's theses elicit worldwide agreement. Numerous nations have translated them into practice, with resounding success. Guinea Bissau, Angola, Mozambique, at the cost of their own blood, have won a place among the liberated countries of Africa, the continent that in 1914 was still almost completely in the hands of the colonial powers. Zimbawa, Nambia, and South Africa will soon follow; in Southeast Asia the Vietnamese won their independence after a ten-year struggle; and in South America as well the time is not far off when the desperate attempts of liberation movements will be crowned with success. For men like Fanon will raise their voices, again and again, never resting until the domination of man by man will have come to an end.*

*These pioneer fighters—all but unknown for the most part, and often vilified—are blazing a trail toward free human self-determination. For all the oppressed, and above all for their young people, this means overcoming illiteracy—the real as well as the spiritual kind—and also trusting in hope, mobilizing all their political and moral forces.*

# John XXIII: Pacem in Terris

On 11 October 1962, John XXIII opened the Second Vatican Council. Its first session ended on 8 December of the same year, and the second session began nine months later, on 29 September 1963. Between the two sessions, on Holy Thursday, 11 April 1963, in the fifth year of his pontificate, John XXIII published his famous encyclical *Pacem in Terris (Peace on Earth)*. This encyclical letter is the testament of a Pope who knew he was soon to die. His death came on 3 June 1963, just eight weeks after the publication of his encyclical. Its clear, simple style—innocent of all theological jargon—recalls the rustic, the man of the people. John hoped to give the Council fathers a fresh reminder of the great tasks that lay before them, and to guide his Church, once so isolated, back to the real world and its needs.

Angelo Giuseppe Roncalli, 1881–1963, became Pope John XXIII in 1958. His brief pontificate was historically decisive.

House in which Angelo Roncalli was born in the village of Sotto il Monte near Bergamo in northern Italy.

The prophets of gloom
keep telling us that,
compared with the past,
the present is bad
and getting worse.
But we see mankind embarking
on a new order,
and in this
we recognize a divine Plan.

John XXIII

### FARMBOY TO POPE

John XXIII, elected Pope in 1958, was born Angelo Giuseppe Roncalli, son of a farmer, on 25 November 1881 in the village of Sotto il Monte near Bergamo in northern Italy. He was ordained to the priesthood in 1904, was named secretary to the Bishop of Bergamo, who was to remain his spiritual father, and soon thereafter became professor of Church history, apologetics, and patrology in the Bergamo theological seminary. He served in World War I as a noncommissioned sanitation officer and as field chaplain—seeing firsthand the meaningless horrors of wartime, and their effect on his beloved countrymen.

The war over, he resumed his career—a slow and hard climb for this very homely, very friendly man, who was not in the least career conscious. It was typical of Roncalli that, even after becoming

Pope, he did not forget his unfortunate comrade from student days, Ernesto Buonaiuti—an outstanding church historian, former Docent at the University of Lausanne in Switzerland, and once well known throughout the

Visit to a prison in Rome, on Christmas Eve 1958, the first year of John XXIII's pontificate.

Slums in Rio de Janeiro. The Pope's appeals include a heartfelt call for the elimination of such misery.

world—who was excommunicated and proscribed by Pope Pius XII and whose works were placed on the Index of forbidden books.

In 1921 Angelo Roncalli was called to Rome to be professor of patrology at the Lateran School, and he then worked in the Papal Congregation for Missions. Pius XII named him apostolic Visitator in 1925, then made him a delegate to Bulgaria, where he came to know the Eastern Church. He was later Papal Nuncio in Ankara and, from 1944, in Paris. This man, although never taken seriously by the higher diplomats of the Roman Curia, accomplished an extraordinary feat: He persuaded De Gaulle to recon-

His election as Pope in 1958 was poorly received in certain Roman circles, where John had been an object of derision. This choice was seen as an unwelcome compromise at best, and John was referred to by some as an "interim" or "caretaker" Pope.

But with John XXIII began a new epoch for the Roman Catholic Church: an opening on the world, a step toward universal brotherhood. The encyclical *Pacem in Terris* speaks to "our time of the atom and of space exploration." It espouses the cause of democracy and the right of dissent, defends the rights of workers, women, oppressed races and minorities, favors disarmament and fair, adequate aid to economically underdeveloped countries. It associates itself with the U.N. Declaration of Human Rights of 10 December 1948. It recognizes that "it is not

cile himself with the French episcopate, most of whom had sided with Pétain and Vichy—and thus with the policy of collaboration. Named a cardinal in 1953, John was finally called to Venice as patriarch.

sufficient to be illumined by faith"; if men cannot overcome all their religious and ideological barriers and join together in active cooperation, then "peace must remain a hollow word."

## THE PAPAL ENCYCLICAL

### TO THE CLERGY AND FAITHFUL OF THE WHOLE WORLD, AND TO ALL MEN OF GOOD WILL

#### ORDER BETWEEN MEN

But first We must speak of man's rights. Man has the right to live. He has the right to bodily integrity and to the means necessary for maintaining a decent standard of living. In consequence, he has the right to be looked after in the event of ill-health, overwork, widowhood, old age, enforced unemployment, or when through no fault of his own he is deprived of the means of livelihood.

Moreover, man has a natural right to be respected. He has a right to his good name. He has a right to freedom in investigating the truth, and—provided no harm is done to the moral order or the common good—to freedom of speech and publication, and freedom to practice any profession. He has, too, the right to be accurately informed about public events. Also among man's rights is the right to be able to worship God in accordance with the right dictates of his own conscience, and to profess his religion both in private and in public.

Human beings have also the right to choose for themselves the kind of life which appeals to them. They can either found a family—in the founding of which both the man and the woman enjoy equal rights and duties—or embrace the priesthood or the religious life. In the economic sphere, it is evident that a man has not only the inherent right to be given the opportunity to work, but also to be allowed the exercise of personal initiative in the work he does.

Men are by nature social, and consequently they have the right to meet together and to form associations with their fellows.

Every human being has the right to freedom of movement and of residence within the confines of his own State. When there are just reasons in favor of it, he must be permitted to emigrate to other countries and take up residence there. The fact that he is a citizen of a particular State does not debar him from membership of the human family, or from citizenship of that universal society, the common, world-wide fellowship of men. Man's personal dignity involves his right to take an active part in public life, and to make his own contribution to the common welfare of his fellow citizens. Man as such, far from being the objective, passive element in society is rather its subject, its basis and its purpose; and so must he be esteemed.

## CHARACTERISTICS OF THE PRESENT DAY

There are three things which characterize our modern age.
In the first place we notice a progressive improvement in the economic and social condition of working men. They began by claiming their rights principally in the economic and social spheres, and then proceeded to lay claim to their political rights as well. Finally, they have turned their attention to acquiring the more cultural benefits of society. Today, therefore, working men all over the world are loud in their demands that they shall in no circumstances be subjected to arbitrary treatment, as though devoid of intelligence and freedom. They insist on being treated as human beings; and that, in every department of human society, whether economic, social, cultural or political.
Secondly, the part that women are now playing in political life is everywhere evident. This is a development that is perhaps of swifter growth among Christian nations, but it is also happening extensively, if more slowly, among nations that are heirs to different traditions and imbued with a different culture. Women are gaining an increasing awareness of their natural dignity. Far from being content with a purely passive role, or allowing themselves to be exploited, they are demanding both in domestic and in public life the rights and duties which belong to them as human persons.
Finally, we are confronted in this modern age with a form of society which is evolving on entirely new social and political lines. The long-standing inferiority complex of certain classes because of their economic and social status, sex, or position in the State, and the corresponding superiority complex of other classes, is rapidly becoming a thing of the past.

## RESPONSIBILITIES OF THE PUBLIC AUTHORITY

Any government which refused to recognize human rights or acted in violation of them, would not only fail in its duty; its decrees would be wholly lacking in binding force.
The public administration must give considerable care and thought to the question of social as well as economic progress, and to the development of essential services to keep pace with the expansion of the productive system. Such services include road-building, transportation, communications, drinking-water, housing, medical care, ample facilities for the practice of religion, and also recreational facilities. The government must also see to the provision of insurance facilities, to obviate any likelihood of a citizen's being unable to maintain a decent standard of living in the event of some misfortune, or some overwhelming increase in the burden of domestic responsibility. The government is also required to show no less energy and efficiency in the matter of providing opportunities for suitable employment, graded to the capacity of the workers. It must make sure that working men are paid a just and equitable wage, and are allowed a sense of responsibility in the industrial concerns for which they work. It must facilitate the formation of intermediate groups so that the social life of the people may become more creative and uninhibited. And finally, it must ensure that everyone has the means and opportunity of sharing as far as he can in the cultural benefits.

From a poster by Pablo Picasso, 1949.

## RELATIONS BETWEEN STATES

Nations are the subjects of reciprocal rights and duties. Their relationships, therefore, must likewise be harmonized in accordance with the dictates of truth, justice, willing cooperation, and freedom. The same law of nature that governs the life and conduct of individuals must also regulate the relations of political communities with one another. The idea that men, by the mere fact of their appointment to public office, are compelled to lay aside their own humanity is quite inconceivable. Their very attainment to this high-ranking office was due to their exceptional gifts and intellectual qualities, which earned for them their reputation as outstanding representatives of the body politic.
Some nations may have attained to a superior degree of scientific, cultural, and economic development. But that does not entitle them to exert unjust political domination over other nations. It means that they have a greater contribution to make to the common cause of social progress. There may be, and sometimes is, a clash of interests among States, each striving for its own advantage. When differences of this sort arise, they must be settled in a human way, not by armed force or by fraud or duplicity. There must be mutual assessment of the arguments and feelings on both sides, a mature and objective investigation of the situation, and an equitable reconciliation of opposing views.

## The Proper Balance between Population, Land and Capital

As everyone is well aware, there are some countries where the amount of arable land is out of all proportion to the population; other countries where natural resources exceed available supplies of agricultural machinery. It is imperative, therefore, that nations enter into collaboration with each other, and facilitate the circulation of goods, capital, and manpower.

We advocate in such cases the policy of bringing the work to the workers, wherever possible, rather than drafting workers to the scene of the work. In this way many people will be afforded an opportunity of raising their standard of living without being exposed to the painful necessity of uprooting themselves from their own homes, settling in a strange environment, and forming new social contacts.

## The Problem of Political Refugees

The deep feelings of paternal love for all mankind which God has implanted in Our heart make it impossible for Us to view without bitter anguish of spirit the plight of those who for political reasons have been exiled from their own homelands.

For this reason, it is no irrelevance here to draw the attention of the world to the fact that these refugees are persons and all their rights as persons must be recognized. Refugees cannot lose these rights; not even when they are deprived of citizenship of their own States.

And among man's personal rights we must include his right to enter a country in which he hopes to be able to provide more fittingly for himself and his dependents. It is therefore the duty of State officials to accept such immigrants and—so far as the good of their own community, rightly understood, permits—to further the aims of those who may wish to integrate themselves into a new society.

## Disarmament

We are deeply distressed to see the enormous stocks of armaments that have been, and continue to be, manufactured in the economically more developed countries. This policy is involving a vast outlay of intellectual and material resources, with the result that the people of these countries are saddled with a tremendous burden, and other countries are being deprived of the help they need for their economic and social development. The probable cause of this stock-piling of armaments is usually said to be the conviction that under modern conditions peace cannot be assured except on the basis of an equal balance of armaments. Hence, if one country increases its military strength, others are immediately roused by a competitive spirit to augment their own supply of armaments. And if one country is equipped with atomic weapons, others consider themselves justified in producing such weapons themselves, equal in destructive force. Consequently people are living in the grip of constant fear. They are afraid that at any moment the impending storm may break upon them with horrific violence. And they have good reasons for their fear, for there is certainly no lack of such weapons. While it is difficult to believe that anyone would deliberately assume responsibility for initiating the appalling slaughter and destruction that war would bring in its train, there is no denying that war could break out through some unexpected and unpremeditated act. Moreover, even though the monstrous power of modern weapons does indeed act as a deterrent, there is reason to fear that the very testing of nuclear devices for war purposes will, if continued, have disastrous consequences for various forms of life on earth.

Hence, justice, right reason, and the realization of man's dignity cry out insistently for a cessation to the arms race. The stock-piles of armaments which have been built up in various countries must be reduced all round and simultaneously by the parties concerned. Nuclear weap-ons must be banned. A general agreement must be reached on a suitable disarmament program. . . .

Everyone, however, must realize that it is impossible to stop the arms race, or to reduce armaments, or—and this is the main thing—ultimately to abolish them entirely, unless this process of disarmament be thorough-going and complete, and spring from inner conviction. Everyone must sincerely cooperate in the effort to banish fear from men's minds, and the anxious expectation of war. The preservation of peace will have to be dependent on a radically different principle from the one which is operative at the present time. True peace among nations must depend not on the possession of an equal supply of armaments, but solely upon mutual trust.

And yet, unhappily, we often find the law of fear reigning supreme among nations and causing them to spend enormous sums on armaments. Their object is not aggression, so they say—and there is no reason for disbelieving them—but to deter others from aggression. Nevertheless, we are hopeful that, by establishing contact with one another and by a policy of negotiation, nations will come to a better understanding of the natural ties that bind them together as men.

## Modern Developments

The United Nations Organization (U.N.O.) was established, as is well known, on June 6, 1945. To it were subsequently added lesser organizations consisting of members nominated by the public authority of the various nations and entrusted with highly important international commitments in the economic, social, cultural, educational, and health fields. The United Nations Organization has the special aim of maintaining and strengthening peace between nations, and of encouraging and assisting friendly relations between them, based on the principles of equality, mutual respect, and extensive cooperation in every field of human endeavor.

The Second Vatican Council, opened by John XXIII on 11 October 1962, marks a major turning point in the history of the Roman Catholic Church.

A clear proof of the farsightedness of this Organization is provided by the Universal Declaration of Human Rights passed by the United Nations General Assembly on December 10, 1948. The preamble of this Declaration affirms that the genuine recognition and complete observance of all the rights and freedoms outlined in the Declaration is an ideal to be pursued by all peoples and all nations.

It is therefore Our earnest wish that the United Nations Organization may be enabled progressively to adapt its structure and methods of operation to the magnitude and nobility of its tasks. May the day not be long delayed when every human being can find in this Organization an effective safeguard of his personal rights; those rights, that is, which derive directly from his dignity as a human person, and which are therefore universal, inviolable and inalienable. This is all the more desirable in that men today are taking an ever more active part in the public life of their own nations, and in doing so they are showing an increased interest in the affairs of all peoples. They are becoming more and more conscious of being living members of the universal family of mankind.

### AN IMMENSE TASK

Among the very serious obligations incumbent upon men of high principles, We must include the task of establishing new relationships in human society, under the mastery and guidance of truth, justice, charity, and freedom—relations between individual citizens, between citizens and their respective States, and finally between individuals, families, intermediate associations, and States on the one hand, and the world community on the other.

And upon all men of good will to whom We also address this Encyclical, We implore from God health and prosperity.

Given at Rome, at St Peter's, on Holy Thursday, the eleventh day of April, in the year 1963, the fifth of Our Pontificate.

John PP. XXIII

## A Voice and Its Echoes

Pacem in Terris *has made itself heard all over the world. Both Washington and Moscow listened; in Africa, Asia, Latin America people have appealed to it, and continue to appeal to it today, in the struggle against their own totalitarian regimes, in the struggle against the arms race and the disenfranchisement of men.*

*Today, if civil rights movements and champions of human rights are speaking out in the face of harsh repression—against all odds—in Eastern European countries, or in Latin America, this encyclical has helped to give them courage.* Pacem in Terris *was officially hailed by the Soviet Union and, in her wake, by the Communist regimes in Eastern Europe. There was surely a political-strategic motivation at work here, but what is odd about the dialectic of history is that man can never completely take back a word once he has uttered it publicly. And so the pledge to honor the demands of* Pacem in Terris *cannot be made completely in vain—once this word is spoken, it catches up with world leaders again and again, often in the most unlikely forms.*

*This document lives on in many ways. In the United States, congresses have been organized which meet periodically in Washington under the aegis "Pacem in Terris" in order to create an ongoing forum for this encyclical's demands for peace. Paraphrasing the encyclical's title, an international movement called "Pacem in Maribus" (Peace on the Seas) has been founded to keep the seas open, clean, and demilitarized.*

# The Pioneer 10 Plaque

The Pioneer 10 spacecraft, sent into space on 2 March 1972, the first man-made object to escape from the solar system into interstellar space, carries this pictorial plaque. It is designed to show scientifically educated inhabitants of some other star system—who might intercept it millions of years from now—when Pioneer was launched, from where, and by

God, creator of the firmament. The universe becomes knowable.

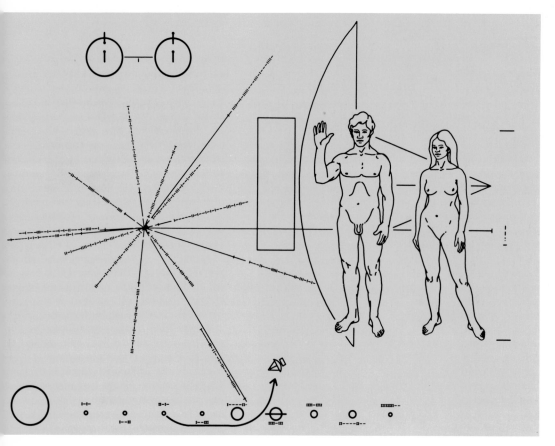

"1-" symbols at the ends of the lines are binary numbers that represent the frequencies of these pulsars at the time of launch of Pioneer relative to that of the hydrogen atom shown at the upper left with a "1" unity symbol. The hydrogen atom is thus used as a "universal clock" and the regular decrease in the frequencies of the pulsars will enable another civilization to determine the time that has elapsed since Pioneer 10 was launched. The hydrogen atom is also used as a "universal yardstick" for sizing the human figures and outline of the spacecraft shown on the right. The hydrogen wavelength—about 8 inches—multiplied by the binary number representing "8" shown next to the woman gives her height—i.e., 64 inches. The figures represent the type of creature that created Pioneer. The man's hand is raised in a gesture of good will. Across the bottom are the planets, ranging outward from the sun, with the spacecraft's trajectory arcing away from earth, passing Mars, and swinging by Jupiter.

what kind of beings. The design is etched into a gold-anodized aluminum plate, 152 by 229 millimeters (6 by 9 inches), attached to the spacecraft's antenna support struts in a position to help shield it from erosion by interstellar dust. The radiating lines at left represent the positions of 14 pulsars—cosmic sources of radio energy—arranged to indicate our sun as the home star of the launching civilization. The

Who was he, gazing on the stars' stage,
Who all unaware, even before
It could enter the thinker's mind,
Seized the bold idea of the
eternal Space?

Friedrich von Schiller, from the poem "The Artist"

### MESSAGE TO THE STARS

Since time immemorial, men have longed to penetrate "the heavens" or, in Plato's more precise terms, *"eis ton hyperouranion topon,"* the spaces above the stars. It was Paul-

Interplanetary spaceship Pioneer D on its launching pad, 8 November 1968. After successfully encircling the sun, Pioneer D became Pioneer 9. Its mission: to trace and measure radiance, magnetic fields, and energy particles.

ist Christians' great desire to rise to "the seven heavens." Gnostic throught strove to break through the roof above our earth in order to join the "All." Again and again, ever since Graeco-Roman times, space travel has provided subject matter for poems, political satire, and science fiction. In our own

come about only in a spirit of universal brotherhood.

The Pioneer 10 Plaque is free of all political, religious, ideological demands, appeals, proclamations. It bears no flags and no emblems. It has just one mission: to give a sign. A sign that is also an orientation concerning man's existence on

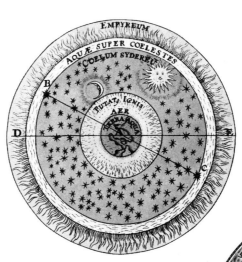

*Above:* Geocentric representation of the cosmos. The earth is surrounded by concentric layers that contain the stars, the moon, water, and fire.

Ptolemy *(above right)* broadened and refined this scheme.

*Right:* Heliocentric system as conceived by Copernicus. (The sun, rather than the earth, now occupies the center.) From *Atlas Coelestis,* by A. Cellarius, 1660.

day, with the "inner eye," some people hope by visions and trances to "lift themselves out of this earthly prison" up to heaven.

Prominent philosophical-religious thinkers in nineteenth-century Russia, speculating about space travel, spoke of man's mission to people the cosmos, to create artificial planets and islands in space. Such events, for these seers, would

this planet. Millions of years from now, this sign may reach other forms of life and give them a modest report: "Observe—here in the universe there were—there *are*—creatures endowed with reason, capable of sending this message out into space to testify to their scientific, technical, industrial, and intellectual capacities and accomplishments."

## Man's Ongoing Mission

*No one on earth can say whether this "Ecce Homo," this declaration of human existence, will ever arrive somewhere in space, whether it will reach living beings on other planets in other solar systems. To some persons, Pioneer 10 may even seem foolish, superfluous. Is there any point in proclaiming our existence into a void—into a dark, boundless future that, for all we know, may not exist?*

*However we may answer this question, the Pioneer 10 Plaque does testify to one thing: it demonstrates that our scientists and technicians believe in man's ongoing mission as a pioneer. It was in this same pioneering role that man first explored and settled the continents of this earth. Now, turning his view outward, a new Columbus, he presses on into space. Still tireless after crossing the world's oceans for a thousand years, he fits himself out with new tools and new ships and heads in a new directon. In this sense the Pioneer 10 Plaque confirms the oldest traditions of humanity. Hammurabi, Moses, all the authors and transmitters of the great human statements that we have inherited—did any of them know whether their good tidings would survive in the uncharted future, when and where their words might take effect, or how later generations might change or even deform them? These men's uncertainty, the risk they ran, was no less great than that of the Pioneer 10 Plaque. All these defiant gestures prove that man is an intrinsically transcendental creature who realizes himself to the extent that, step by step, flight by flight, he crosses the obstacles that nature and the elements have put in his way. At the same time he must also conquer the difficult obstacles that confront him from within, in order to become more human than he is today.*

# AFTERWORD

We look upon the evidence presented in this book not in terms of a review of the past but as "documents" in the original, Latin meaning of the word. And at the origin of the Latin word *documentum* stood the verb *docere,* which meant quite simply to teach, to show, to point out, to instruct. A *documentum* in classical Rome was anything that served to teach or demonstrate; it was proof, example, testimony, doctrine. This is the sense in which we wish our *documenta* to be understood: as the testimony of witnesses, as teachings that are still alive for us today and give us occasion to examine our own lives, our own time, our own political, social, moral, and religious circumstances and, in good and evil, without self-righteousness and without bias, our own consciences. We will realize then how far we still have to go to assimilate the truths of Lao-tse, Buddha, Moses, Jesus, Francis of Assisi, Nicholas of Cusa, Gandhi in our lives and in our time.

Among the celebrated fragments left by the German Romantic poet Novalis, probably the most curious of all our sources for German and European thought and feeling, we find under figure 1685 the very modern-sounding observation: "God is to be sought among men. It is in human events and in human thoughts and emotions that the Spirit of Heaven most clearly reveals itself."

In the documents reproduced in this book it is not directly God who is being sought, but they do reflect man's search for what the poet referred to in his private code as the "Spirit of Heaven." What he meant was the striving, for which there is evidence since the beginning of history, for a spiritually oriented humanity. This "spirit," this "mind"—as English prefers to call it—is no metaphysical abstraction, no merely notionally conceived entity; it is a part of man's objective being, seated in the depths of the human personality and stamping the human countenance. Locked in biological corporeality, it had a hard job before *homo sapiens* became aware of it. What followed this awareness we call the emergence of mankind, the evolution of humanity. The documents in our selection bear witness to stages in that evolution, stages at which law, ethics, morality, the state, and religion changed and became more human.

We must also remember that many documents have long since become myths to us, some of them continuing to affect us subconsciously, others being formed and transformed by consciousness. A classic example of the mythologization of a document is the "Bundesbrief" of the Swiss Confederation. In purely historical terms this is an extremely matter-of-fact text laying down a few legal principles to govern relations between the mountain farmers and the valley farmers along the Gotthard Pass and around the shores of Lake Lucerne. Fate, however, was to make this modest agreement the foundation charter of the Swiss state, and although its exact wording is known only to a few people, the "Bundesbrief" has for centuries possessed a mythological power that comes out with particular force whenever Switzerland is threatened from without—as two world wars have shown. And what is true of this document as far as Switzerland is concerned is true on a global scale of most of the documents of mankind. They live on, metamorphosed as myth, and in the mythic sense are omnipresent, regardless of their historicity.

If we think about this mythologization of documents at all, we realize something else: that myths very often act as substitutes for unwritten documents. For what are the myths of the Golden Age of Athens, of the *Pax Romana* under Augustus, of the Age of Charlemagne, of the period of the Hohenstaufen emperors, of the Florence of the Medici—what are they if not "unwritten documents," *documenta* in the Latin sense, evidence of our yearning for a glorious celebration of existence? So it need not surprise us that man creates myths in order not to have to look historical reality in the face. Phrases like "The Roaring Twenties" or "La Belle Epoque" are mythic concepts that draw a veil over the actual social misery of those very periods, suppressing unpleasant memories.

Which brings us to a fundamental problem regarding this book. Our selection of documents is colored by what I have called the "hope principle." It seeks to illustrate man's inborn urge to progress, and in doing so to represent the *"progressus populorum"* called for by Pope John XXIII, a universal progress in humanity on the part of all the peoples of the world, as a task by which our generation and our age are bound indissolubly to both past and future. This is why we have chosen not to document the historical reverses that this human will to progress has suffered again and again. The wealth of documented betrayals of human, political, and religious truths is incalculable. Landmarks on this backward road are the files of the Inquisition, the records of the trials of Joan of Arc and Galileo Galilei, and the documentary report that the Spanish Dominican Bartolomé de Las Casas gave to Emperor Charles V in Madrid in 1516 concerning the almost inconceivable cruelties practiced by the Spanish *conquistadores* and soldiers of fortune on defenseless Indians. And one of the most appalling documents in human history dates from our own century: the so-called "Wannseer Protokoll" that set in motion the "final solution of the Jewish question."

For the historian these documents of human betrayal are of inescapable significance. The aim of our book, however, is to demonstrate that despite all history's bleaker moments, despite all the manmade misery and suffering in this world, forces have always emerged and individuals arisen to overcome such misery and erect signposts pointing the way forward. Many of our documents reflect intellectual or other limits that could not be transcended at the time. Buddha took a one-sided view of the burdensome consequences of activity. Carried to its logical conclusion, his teaching would mean the end of all civilization and ultimately extinction for the human race. But the crisis facing today's immoderately active industrial society has taught us to see his teaching as a warning to us to take the necessary corrective action ourselves. Or another example: the *Code Napoléon* represented a greater step forward than we today are capable of assessing. Yet it preserved the classical, pagan principle that wives owed obedience to their husbands. Today we are trying in both legal and practical terms to replace this humiliating concept by that of partnership between man and woman. And what about the "limits" of the Sermon on the Mount? Politicians, even Christian politicians, prove daily in word and deed that the demands of the Sermon on the Mount are unusable as a constitutional basis for human society. But does that mean we are to give up trying to find God and the divine among men? Hammurabi did it; Jesus of Nazareth proclaimed the Kingdom of God as a "Kingdom of Man"; Paul professed unshakable faith in that kingdom; Francis of Assisi exemplified divine brotherhood in respect of man and all creation; Karl Marx sought to bring the divine truth of man, postponed to a paradisal "beyond," back down to earth. Neither Jesus nor Marx escaped fearful reverses. That nonetheless the "hope principle" still stands and shall continue to exert its historically proven force —such is our plea in this book.

XAVER SCHNIEPER

177

## DOCUMENTARY SEQUENCE

The historical table on these four pages gives an overview of the thirty documents contained in this book—a panoramic glimpse of the 3,600-year process of man's "becoming man"—that recalls the sequence of these texts and their closeness or remoteness to one another in time.

| ca. 1700 B.C. | ca. 1300 | ca. 590 | ca. 500 | ca. 480 | ca. 375 |
|---|---|---|---|---|---|
| **THE CODE OF HAMMURABI** | **THE TEN COMMAND-MENTS** | **THE LAWS OF SOLON** | **BUDDHA: TRUTH AND ENLIGHTENMENT** | **THE GREAT WISDOM OF CONFUCIUS** | **PLATO'S VISION OF TH[E] STATE** |
|  |  |  |  |  |  |
| Hammurabi founded the first state governed by the rule of law. Taking the law into one's own hands (e.g., blood vengeance) is prohibited. The law itself is given as divine revelation communicated by the king. | Statue of Moses by Michelangelo, in the church of San Pietro in Vincoli, Rome. The statue captures the spirit of the historical leader and lawgiver who organized the return of the Jews from Egypt. | Even Homer, who lived probably two hundred years before Solon, was thought of by later generations as the "educator" of the Greeks. The poet Solon deliberately sets out to become the political educator and shaper of the Athenian city-state. | Buddha's personality lives on as the prime example for his teaching in monastic communities which spread throughout East Asia. Buddha's ethos was historically the first to proclaim the idea of all-encompassing love. | Confucius seeks by teaching to stabilize the old patriarchal clan order and gives it a new spiritual aristocratic ethos, whose influence is still felt even in modern China. | According to Plato the ideal state, felt [to] be a living organi[sm] like that of the human being, will only materialize if [the] philosophers take power. |

---

## ACCOMPANYING EVENTS

None of these documents were caused or triggered by any single historical event, and yet each in some way represents and sums up its era. To give an idea of this political-social-cultural context, the lower half of the historical table includes a reference to major events or figures from the years in which each document was written down.

| ca. 1700 B.C. | ca. 1300 | ca. 590 | ca. 500 | ca. 480 | ca. 375 |
|---|---|---|---|---|---|
|  | The great age of Egyptian temple building. | The twins Romulus and Remus, rescued by a she-wolf, figure as the legendary founders of Rome ■. | | | Aristotle enters Pl[a]to's academy as a student. The brilli[ant] pupil finds himsel[f in] opposition to his [bril]less brilliant maste[r]. Woman as the ide[al] of beauty influen[ces] Greek art. Celtic tribes settle [in] Ireland. Opposing the Con[fu]cian family ethics, the Chinese Mo [Ti] calls for an all-en-compassing huma[n] love. |
| Palace of Knossos in Crete ■: labyrinthine layout. Temple of Stonehenge in England. Egypt conquers Nubia and parts of Palestine. |  Effigy of Egypt's King Tutankhamen ■.  |  Greek statue of Zeus ■ from the time of Solon. | Birth of Parmenides. This pre-Socratic philosopher from Elea (southern Italy) distinguishes between perception and thought: Only the latter can lead to truth. |  The philosophical school of Pythagoras ■ in Kroton (now Crotone, in southern Italy) is concerned with mathematics, music, and the general theory of harmonies. Heraclitus of Ephesus calls struggle the "father of all things," motivating the continual change of the world. Third Persian War: destruction of the Persian fleet in the battle of Salamis. |  |
| | | Rome is ruled by the Tarquinian kings of Etruscan descent. The Carthaginians establish Cadiz as a base on the Atlantic. | | | |

■ refers to an illustration

178

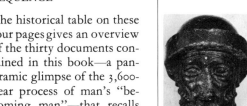

| 300 | ca. 25 A.D. | 57–58 | ca. 650 | 1215 | 1225–1226 | 1453 | 1517 |
|---|---|---|---|---|---|---|---|
| E TAO LAO-TSE | THE SERMON ON THE MOUNT | THE EPISTLE TO THE ROMANS | THE KORAN OF MOHAMMED | THE MAGNA CHARTA | ST. FRANCIS: CANTICLE OF THE SUN | NICHOLAS OF CUSA: DE PACE FIDEI | MARTIN LUTHER'S PROTEST |

ther Lao-tse was founder of hese Taoism, is pen question, his *Tao Te Ching* s most important ary monument, se influence is felt today.

Jesus of Nazareth sums up his message in the Sermon on the Mount: It is the charter for an empire free from laws and from oppression, and is focused on God the Father. This charter has remained an ideal.

St. Paul carries the gospel out into the pagan Roman world. This is historically the first time that the Christian faith claims universal validity. St. Paul's Epistle to the Romans states that the Christian justifies himself outside of the (Jewish) law by his faith alone.

At the time when the Germanic invasions gradually draw to a close, Mohammed lays the foundation for the Arab empire through his Koran, which declares the Arabian tribal god the One and Only God of the world.

The privileges and liberties obtained from King John of England by the barons and recorded in the Magna Charta mark the opening for the development of English democracy.

St. Francis of Assisi sought to live up to the teachings of the gospel. Unwittingly, he also practiced the teaching of Lao-tse, except that the personal God takes the place of Tao.

The call of Cusanus for "concord in religious belief" is a corollary of his view of God: God as the absolute "otherness" cannot be monopolized by any religion. Religions are variations of the worship of the one universal and unknowable God.

Reformers as early as the twelfth century including Gioacchino da Fiore, St. Francis, and Cusanus had striven to purify the Church. Finally, Luther, invoking St. Paul's Epistle to the Romans, brings about the Reformation.

---

ander the at ■, educated by totle, becomes of Macedonia wenty and founds mpire reaching Greece to India.

12 the Via ia ■ is built, the way linking ne with Brindisi, seaport for ece.

The emperor Augustus consolidates the *Pax Romana* in Rome. "Golden Age" of Roman literature.

Herod Antipas ■, son of Herod I the Great, is the man whom the gospels accuse of the "Slaughter of the Innocents." We do know that he had John the Baptist murdered.

Coin bearing the effigies of Agrippina the Younger and her son Nero ■. She later married the emperor Claudius, whom she poisoned to secure the throne for Nero. Nero orders the first

persecution of Christians. The apostles Paul and Peter are among the victims.

The library of Alexandria is destroyed by fire. The cultivation of Greek science is taken up by the Arabs.

In South America, the Indianic cultures develop and flourish: Olmecs 1700 B.C.– 400 A.D.; Mayas 1– 1500 A.D. (Pyramid of Huracan in Chichen Itza ■); Toltecs 900–1200; Aztecs 1200–1500. These cultures are later all destroyed by the Spanish conquerors.

Early in the thirteenth century, Genghis Khan ■ founds his empire and starts the period of Mongol invasions. Half of the world's people become his tributaries. From present-day Mongolia, his forces conquer southern Siberia, northern Persia, northern India, Russia, the Balkans, Poland and Silesia in the west, and China in the south. This empire last until the end of the thirteenth century.

St. Francis has his worldly counterpart in the splendid Emperor Frederick II of Hohenstaufen ■, 1215–1250.

The art of the troubadours in France and the minnesingers in Germany reaches its zenith ■.

In the fifteenth century, the world sets out for new shores. In Germany, Guten-

berg invents printing from type and publishes the first printed Bible ■. In Italy the Renaissance celebrates its first great triumphs. The Spaniards and Portuguese explore new seas. In 1492 Columbus discovers the American continent.

The Borgia Pope Alexander VI ■ gives Luther special cause to denounce papal corruption. Leonardo da Vinci ■ represents the intellectually independent Renaissance man.

179

| 1625 | 1776 | 1787 | 1789 | 1795 | 1804 | 1848 | 1920 |
|---|---|---|---|---|---|---|---|

## GROTIUS ON INTERNATIONAL ORDER

Hugo Grotius is a Christian humanist, and as such is predestined to reconcile his Christian outlook with natural law. His object is to humanize the arbitrary relations between nations and states and make them subject to rules of law.

The Thirty Years' War (1618–1648) devastates large areas of Germany. In France, Cardinal Richelieu ∎ as head of the *Conseil* moves against regionalism and the special interests of the aristocracy and Estates, and sets up the absolute monarchy. He takes advantage of the turmoil of the Thirty Years' War to seize the west bank of the Rhine for France.

## VIRGINIA DECLARATION OF RIGHTS

The struggle for human rights—taken up in the Age of Enlightenment first in England, then in France—which aims at liberating man from all arbitrary authority, celebrates its first world-historical victory in the Virginia Declaration of Rights.

The Age of Enlightenment receives its greatest literary formulation in the works of Johann Wolfgang von Goethe ∎. Traveling to Italy, he finds the way to a universal, aesthetically accented humanism, chiefly reflected in his dramatic plays *Tasso* and *Iphigenia*.

## THE UNITED STATES CONSTITUTION

The Virginia Declaration of Rights gave the cue for the American Declaration of Independence. The substance of those two declarations provides the foundation for the principles laid down in the United States Constitution.

Catherine II of Russia ∎, who had dethroned her consort Peter III and taken over as ruler in 1762, believes in enlightened absolutism. She carries out major reforms in administration, law, and education, and expands Russia's frontiers. Her efforts are impaired by corrupt court favorites.

## DECLARATION OF THE RIGHTS OF MAN

At the beginning of the French Revolution, the National Assembly, at the instance of General Lafayette, ratifies the Declaration of the Rights of Man and of Citizens, which soon has a profound political effect in all Europe.

At the height of the French Revolution, the political stage is chiefly dominated by

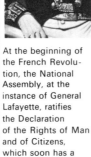

Danton and Marat. In January 1793, King Louis XVI is executed. In the following June, Danton as Minister of Justice is ousted by Robespierre ∎, who sets up a dictatorship which his opponents characterize as a reign of terror.

## KANT'S PEACE MANIFESTO

Kant's essay *Perpetual Peace* was inspired by the French Revolution and the human rights declarations. Kant had witnessed the three wars which Prussia had waged to seize Silesia. In his view of the world of values, there is no ethical justification for war.

In 1795 the Chinese Emperor Ch'ien Lung ∎ died. His 63-year reign saw the Chinese empire at its largest. His death also marks the end of the great period of Chinese science (1716, *K'ang-hi,* a Classical Chinese dictionary; 1725, the great encyclopedia of Chinese science).

## THE CODE NAPOLÉON

The law code of Napoleon I has decisively influenced civil law in Europe and in other parts of the world. In particular, it laid the statutory basis for the patriarchalism of the ensuing bourgeois age.

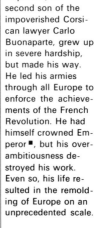

Napoleon, the second son of the impoverished Corsican lawyer Carlo Buonaparte, grew up in severe hardship, but made his way. He led his armies through all Europe to enforce the achievements of the French Revolution. He had himself crowned Emperor ∎, but his over-ambitiousness destroyed his work. Even so, his life resulted in the remolding of Europe on an unprecedented scale.

## THE COMMUNIST MANIFESTO

The Communist Manifesto of Marx and Engels is the radical antithesis to the deceptive optimism of the bourgeois age. It demonstrates that even the word is a history-forming force and a weapon of incalculable effect.

In 1848 the post-Napoleonic settlement of the "Holy Alliance" made at the Congress of Vienna in 1815 is shaken by popular risings in Berlin ∎, Munich, Paris, Vienna, and elsewhere.

## GANDHI: THE POWER OF NON-VIOLENCE

Gandhi's program of non-violence forms the historical foundation on which India gained her independence. Against Gandhi's intention, however, India was to be divided into two states after World War II.

Through Gandhi, policy of non-violence grows into a weapon which those in power often fear more than they do violent revolt, which can be countered with open violence. Non-violent also the women's suffragist demonstration in England ∎, which though beaten down by the police, ultimately succeeds.

| | 1941 | 1945 | 1945 | 1946 | 1961 | 1963 | 1972 |
|---|---|---|---|---|---|---|---|

| 25 | 1941 | 1945 | 1945 | 1946 | 1961 | 1963 | 1972 |

**HINA'S ECLARATION O ALL ATIONS**

**THE ATLANTIC CHARTER**

**SCIENTISTS' WARNING: THE FRANCK REPORT**

**THE CHARTER OF THE UNITED NATIONS**

**HIROHITO'S NEW YEAR'S MESSAGE**

**VOICE OF THE THIRD WORLD: F. FANON**

**JOHN XXIII: PACEM IN TERRIS**

**THE PIONEER 10 PLAQUE**

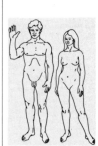

e statements of i Yuan Pei, rec- of Peking's tional University, irectly reflect the sery which the itics of the great wers wrought in ina from the mid- eteenth century il Japan's defeat World War II.

This Charter, formulated by Roosevelt and Churchill, is a document which in substance evinces an attitude of political humanism. However, the principles of the Atlantic Charter have been thoroughly betrayed since World War II, by great and small powers alike.

Since the atomic bomb destroyed Hiroshima on 6 August, the debate over the sense of science which gives military power the means for indiscriminate annihilation of human life has not come to rest.

On 26 June the United Nations Charter is proclaimed in San Francisco to "spare coming generations the scourge of war." The great expectations (held in particular by President Roosevelt) have failed to materialize.

The emperor Hirohito, in his New Year's message, demythicizes the Japanese imperial house and thus creates the opening for a constitutional monarchy on the Western democratic model.

The French psychiatrist Frantz Fanon, the Argentine physician Ernest Che Guevara, and the Brazilian bishop Dom Helder Camara, along with many other intellectuals, speak out against the oppression and exploitation of the Third World.

For the first time, a Pope appeals to "all men of good will," regardless of their religion. He calls upon the community of mankind to put into effect social justice and political freedom. This is the only way to assure peace.

The space probe Pioneer 10, sent out into space with unknown destination, testifies to man's hopes of finding living beings of kindred spirit in distant worlds.

---

In February, at the Yalta Conference ■, Churchill, Roosevelt, and Stalin divide Europe into "spheres of influence".

On 13 August, at the instance of Walter Ulbricht, president of the East German State

On 21 July 1969 the first man lands on the moon. The photograph of our earth ■, taken by men on the moon, impressively illustrates the efforts man is making to conquer new horizons.

*Le Monde entier parle du*

**ANIFESTE DU URRÉALISME**

*par*

**POISSON SOLUBLE**

**NDRÉ BRETON**

*Qu'est-ce que le Surréalisme?*

e 1920s produce a ge number of his- ically influential nifestoes: the nifesto of Futur- ; the Manifesto Surrealism ■; and political manifes- f National cialism in Hitler's in Kampf. The cade is marked by Russian Revolu- n.

6 April 1941: German invasion of Yugoslavia and Greece. 22 June: Germany invades Soviet Russia with an army of 3.2 million men, supported by the armies of Rumania, Slovakia, Finland, and Hungary. 7 December: Japan's raid on the U.S. fleet at Pearl Harbor ■. Bertolt Brecht's *Mother Courage and Her Children* has its world première at the Schauspielhaus in Zurich.

The destruction of Hiroshima ■ and Nagasaki compels Japan to capitulate.

In World War II, at least 50 million civilians and nearly 30 million soldiers were killed. According to minimum estimates, 7 million human beings were murdered in the concentration and extermination camps.

On 1 October the sentences are pronounced in the Nuremberg trial ■. Twelve of the accused are sentenced to death for "crimes against peace." The leader corps of the NSDAP and the SS are declared "criminal organizations." Italy, voting under a plebiscite, disowns its royal house for its association with fascism, and proclaims the Republic.

DAS IST MAUER

Council, a wall ■ is built through Berlin, dividing the city into East and West. The wall becomes a political issue which heavily burdens Germany's internal relations.

On 22 November, President John F. Kennedy ■ is assassinated in Dallas. That very year, he had visited Europe and met Soviet Prime Minister Nikita Khrushchev. Lyndon B. Johnson becomes the new U.S. President.

# SOURCES

## THE DOCUMENTS

The thirty documents in this work, almost all of which are too lengthy for complete reproduction, appear in excerpted form. These English-language versions have been taken from the following sources.

Hammurabi, "The Code," in Robert Francis Harper, *The Code of Hammurabi King of Babylon* (Chicago: The University of Chicago Press, Callaghan; London: Luzac and Co., 1904), pp. 12–97.

Solon, "Elegies" and other works, in *Elegy and Iambus,* 2 vols., ed. and trans. J.M. Edmonds (Cambridge, Mass.: Harvard University Press, 1968), pp. 117–133, 149–151. Reprinted by permission.

Buddha, "Of Dual View-points," in *Woven Cadences of Early Buddhists (Sutta Nipata),* trans. E.M. Hare (Oxford: Oxford University Press, 1945), pp. 108–114. Reprinted by permission.

Confucius, "Father and Son in Court" in *The School Sayings of Confucius,* ed. and trans. R.P. Kramers (Leiden, Holland: E.J. Brill, 1949), pp. 206–207. By permission.

Confucius, *Confucian Analects,* ed. and trans. James Legge (New York: Dover Publications, 1971), portions of pp. 149–322. By permission.

Plato, *The Republic,* trans. Desmond Lee (Harmondsworth and Baltimore: Penguin Books, 1955), pp. 276–280. By permission.

Lao-tse, *Tao Te Ching,* trans. D.C. Lau (Harmondsworth and Baltimore: Penguin Books, 1963), pp. 57, 59, 67, 74, 75, 88, 89, 107. By permission.

Mohammed, *The Koran,* trans. J.M. Rodwell (London: J.M. Dent & Sons, 1909, 1974), pp. 27–29, 130–134, 342, 350, 366–367. By permission.

"Magna Charta," in A.E. Dick Howard, *Magna Carta: Text and Commentary* (Charlottesville: University Press of Virginia, 1964), pp. 3ff. By permission.

Francis of Assisi, "The Canticle of the Sun," in *The Little Flowers of St. Francis of Assisi,* trans. Raphael Brown (London: Everyman's Library, 1960). By permission.

Nicholas of Cusa, "Concerning Concord in Religious Belief" *(De Pace Fidei),* in *Unity and Reform: Selected Writings of Nicholas de Cusa,* trans. and ed. John Patrick Dolan (Notre Dame, Ind.: University of Notre Dame Press, 1962), pp. 195–198, 200–201, 236–237. By permission.

Martin Luther, "Ninety-five Theses," in J.H. Robinson and. M. Whitcomb, "The Period of the Early Reformation in Germany," in *Translations and Reprints from the Original Sources of European History* (Philadelphia: University of Pennsylvania, 1897), vol. 2, no. 6, pp. 6–12.

Hugo Grotius, *De Jure Belli ac Pacis Libri Tres,* trans. Francis W. Kelsey (Oxford: Clarendon Press, 1922), vol. 2, pp. 33–35, 38–40, 91–94, 140, 631, 862.

"Declaration of the Rights of Man and of Citizens," in Frank M. Anderson, *The Constitutions and Other Select Documents Illustrative of the History of France 1789–1901* (Minneapolis: H.W. Wilson Co., 1904), pp. 58–60.

Immanuel Kant, *Perpetual Peace,* from *Works of Kant* (Berlin: Preussische Akademie der Wissenschaften, 1900).

*The Code Napoléon verbally translated from the French,* by Bryant Barrett (London: W. Reed, 1811), vol. 1, from pp. 2–158, 304–305, 488–627.

Karl Marx and Friedrich Engels, *Manifesto of the Communist Party,* trans. Samuel Moore (Moscow: Progress Publishers, 1973), pp. 39–96.

Mahatma Gandhi, "Non-violence," in Gandhi's *Young India, 1919–1922* (Triplicane, Madras: S. Ganesan, 1922), pp. 285–297.

Emperor Hirohito, "Imperial Rescript" (New Year's Message), in the *Nippon Times,* Tokyo, 1 January 1946, p. 1. Reprinted by permission of the Emperor.

Frantz Fanon, *The Wretched of the Earth,* trans. Constance Farrington (New York: Grove Press, 1963), pp. 27, 36–37, 73–74, 148, 175, 199, 200, 210–211, 236–237. By permission.

John XXIII, *Pacem in Terris* (Paramus, N.J.: Paulist Press, 1963).

Biblical passages are taken from the King James edition.

Additional documents are reprinted from U.S. Government or state publications and from other sources in the public domain.

## ADDITIONAL QUOTED MATERIAL

"The Axial Period," quoted in the Introduction, is from Karl Jaspers, *The Origin and Goal of History,* trans. Michael Bullock (London: Routledge and Kegan Paul; New Haven: Yale University Press, 1953), pp. 1–2.

The poem quoted on page 62 is from *The Odes of Horace,* trans. James Michie (Harmondsworth and Baltimore: Penguin Books, 1964).

The lines by Mao Tse-tung quoted on page 134 are from his "In Reply to Comrade Kuo Mo-jo," in *Selected Works of Mao Tse-tung* (New York: International Publishers Co., 1954, 1956).

These passages are reprinted with the publishers' permission.

# FURTHER READING

## GENERAL

Adler, Mortimer: *Great Ideas from the Great Books.* New York: Washington Square Press, 1968.

Brinton, Crane: *The History of Western Morals.* New York: Harcourt, Brace, Jovanovich, 1959.

—: *Ideas and Men: The Story of Western Thought.* 2nd ed. Englewood Cliffs, N.J.: Prentice-Hall, 1963.

*Cambridge Ancient History.* 12 vols. Cambridge and New York: Cambridge University Press, 1972.

*Cambridge Modern History.* 13 vols. Cambridge and New York: Cambridge University Press, 1970.

Danielou, Jean, et al.: *Introduction to the Great Religions.* Notre Dame, Ind.: Fides, 1967.

Harmon, Mont J.: *Political Thought: From Plato to the Present.* New York: McGraw-Hill Book Co., 1964.

Jaspers, Karl: *The Great Philosophers.* 2 vols. New York: Harcourt, Brace, Jovanovich, 1971.

—: *The Origin and Goal of History.* New Haven, Conn.: Yale University Press, 1953.

Jurji, Edward J.: *Great Religions of the Modern World.* Princeton, N.J.: Princeton University Press, 1965.

Ling, Trevor: *The History of Religion East and West.* New York: Harper & Row, 1970.

Russell, Bertrand: *History of Western Philosophy.* New York: Simon and Schuster, 1945.

Spengler, Oswald: *The Decline of the West.* 2 vols. New York: Alfred A. Knopf, 1945.

Strauss, Leo, and Cropsey, Joseph: *History of Political Philosophy.* Chicago: Rand-McNally, 1963.

Toynbee, Arnold J.: *A Study of History.* 12 vols. Oxford and New York: Oxford University Press, 1935–1964. Abbreviated edition, ed. D.C. Somerville. 2 vols. Oxford and New York: Oxford University Press, 1947, 1957.

## THE CODE OF HAMMURABI

Boehl, F.M.T.: *King Hammurabi of Babylon in the Setting of his Time.* Amsterdam: 1946.

Driver, Godfrey R., and Miles, John C., eds.: *The Babylonian Laws.* 2. vols. New York and Oxford: Oxford University Press, 1955, 1956.

Edwards, Chileric: *Hammurabi's Code.* 2nd ed. Port Washington, N.Y.: Kennikat Press, 1971.

Gordon, Cyrus H.: *Hammurabi's Code: Quaint or Forward-Looking?* New York: Holt, Rinehart and Winston, 1972.

Kramer, Samuel N.: *The Sumerians: Their History, Culture and Character.* Chicago: University of Chicago Press, 1963.

Oppenheim, A. Leo: *Ancient Mesopotamia: Portrait of a Dead Civilization.* Chicago: University of Chicago Press, 1968.

## THE TEN COMMANDMENTS

Allen, Charles L.: *The Ten Commandments: An Interpretation.* Old Tappan, N.J.: Revell, 1965.

Bright, John: *A History of Israel.* 2nd ed. Philadelphia: Westminster Press, 1972.

Buber, Martin: *Moses: The Revelation and the Covenant.* New York: Harper & Row, 1948.

Fox, Emmet: *The Ten Commandments.* New York: Harper & Row, 1953.

Freud, Sigmund: *Moses and Monotheism.* New York: Random House, 1955.

Goldman, Solomon: *The Ten Commandments.* Chicago: University of Chicago Press, 1965.

Mendenhall, George E.: *Tenth Generation: The Origins of the Biblical Tradition.* Baltimore: Johns Hopkins University Press, 1972.

Rowley, Harold H.: *From Joseph to Joshua: Biblical Traditions in the Light of Archaeology.* Oxford and New York: Oxford University Press, 1950.

## THE LAWS OF SOLON

Bowra, C.M.: *Early Greek Elegists.* New York: Cooper Square Publishers, 1969.

—: *The Greek Experience.* New York: Praeger Publishers, 1970.

—: *Periclean Athens.* New York: Dial Press, 1971

Ehrenberg, Victor: *From Solon to Socrates: Greek History and Civilization during the Sixth and Fifth Centuries.* New York: Barnes and Noble, 1968.

Hignett, Charles: *History of the Athenian Constitution to the End of the Fifth Century B.C.* Oxford and New York: Oxford University Press, 1952.

Jaeger, Werner: *Paideia: The Ideals of Greek Culture.* 3 vols. Oxford and New York: Oxford University Press, 1943–1945.

Jones, A.H.: *Athenian Democracy.* New York: Barnes and Noble, 1964.

Linforth, Ivan M.: *Solon the Athenian.* New York: Academic Press, reprint of 1919 ed.

Woodhouse, William J.: *Solon the Liberator.* New York: Farrar, Straus and Giroux, 1965.

## BUDDHA: TRUTH AND ENLIGHTENMENT

Bapat, P.V., ed.: *Two Thousand Five Hundred Years of Buddhism.* Mystic, Conn.: L. Verry, 1960.

Conze, Edward: *Buddhism: Its Wisdom and Development.* New York: Harper & Row, 1951.

—, trans.: *Buddhist Scriptures.* Harmondsworth and Baltimore: Penguin Books, 1959.

Gard, Richard A.: *Buddhism.* New York: Simon and Schuster, 1961.

Humphreys, Christmas: *Buddhism.* Rev. ed. Harmondsworth and Baltimore: Penguin Books, 1962.

Morgan, Kenneth W., ed.: *Path of the Buddha: Buddhism Interpreted by Buddhists.* New York: Ronald Press, 1956.

Murti, T.R.: *The Central Philosophy of Buddhism.* 2nd ed. New York: Humanities Press, 1960

Pali Text Society: *Translation Series* (Buddhist Texts). London: Pali Text Society, 1909– .

## THE GREAT WISDOM OF CONFUCIUS

Creel, Herrlee G.: *Chinese Thought from Confucius to Mao Tse-tung.* Chicago: University of Chicago Press, 1971.

—: *Confucius and the Chinese Way.* New York: Harper & Row, 1965.

Fung Yu-lan: *A Short History of Chinese Philosophy.* Glencoe, Ill.: The Free Press, 1966.

Kramers, R.P., ed.: *The School Sayings of Confucius.* Leiden, Holland: E.J. Brill, 1949.

Legge, James, ed.: *Confucian Analects.* New York: Dover Publications, 1971.

Nivison, David S., and Wright, A.F., eds.: *Confucianism in Action.* Stanford, Cal.: Stanford University Press, 1969.

Shyrock, John K.: *Origin and Development of the State Cult of Confucius.* New York: Paragon Books, 1966.

## PLATO'S VISION OF THE STATE

Barker, Ernest: *Greek Political Theory.* New York: Barnes and Noble, 1947.

Burnet, John: *Greek Philosophy from Thales to Plato.* New York: St. Martin's Press, 1914.

Field, G.C.: *The Philosophy of Plato.* 2nd ed. Oxford and New York: Oxford University Press, 1969.

Grube, G.M.: *Plato's Thought.* Boston: Beacon Press, 1958.

Murphy, Neville R.: *Interpretation of Plato's Republic.* Oxford and New York: Oxford University Press, 1951.

Plato: *Collected Dialogues of Plato.* Edited by E. Hamilton and H.C. Huntington. Princeton: Princeton University Press, Bollingen Series, 1971.

—: *Portrait of Socrates: Being the Apology, Crito, and Phaedo.* Oxford and New York: Oxford University Press, 1938.

Thorson, Thomas L., ed.: *Plato: Totalitarian or Democrat.* Englewood Cliffs, N.J.: Prentice-Hall, 1963.

## THE TAO OF LAO-TSE

Creel, Herrlee G.: *What Is Taoism, and Other Studies in Chinese Cultural History.* Chicago: University of Chicago Press, 1970.

Kaltenmark, Max: *Lao-tze and Taoism.* Stanford, Cal.: Stanford University Press, 1969.

Lao-tse: *Tao Te Ching.* Translated by D.C. Lau. Harmondsworth and Baltimore: Penguin Books, 1963.

Waley, Arthur: *The Way and Its Power: A Study in the Tao Te Ching and Its Place in Chinese Thought.* New York: Grove Press, 1958.

Welch, Holmes: *Taoism: The Parting of the Way.* Boston: Beacon Press, 1966.

## THE SERMON ON THE MOUNT

Buttrick, George A.: *Christ and History.* Nashville, Tenn.: Abingdon Press, 1963.

Davies, William D.: *The Sermon on the Mount.* Cambridge and New York: Cambridge University Press, 1966.

Dibelius, Martin: *From Tradition to Gospel.* New York: Scribner's, 1935.

—: *Jesus.* 4th ed. New York: Walter DeGruyter, 1966.

Fox, Emmet: *The Sermon on the Mount.* New York: Harper & Row, 1934.

Schweitzer, Albert: *Quest of the Historical Jesus.* New York: Macmillan, 1968.

Streeter, Burnett H.: *The Buddha and the Christ.* Port Washington, N.Y.: Kennikat Press, 1970.

## THE EPISTLE TO THE ROMANS

Buttrick, George A.: *The Interpreter's Bible.* 12 vols. Vol. 9: *The Acts, Romans.* Nashville, Tenn.: Abingdon Press, 1921.

Dibelius, Martin: *Paul.* Philadelphia: Westminster Press, 1953.

Knox, John: *Chapters in a Life of Paul.* Nashville, Tenn.: Abingdon Press, 1950.

McNeile, Alan H.: *Introduction to the Study of the New Testament.* 2nd ed. Oxford and New York: Oxford University Press, 1953.

Schweitzer, Albert: *Mysticism of Paul the Apostle.* New York: Seabury Press, 1968.

Weiss, Johannes: *Earliest Christianity: A History of the Period A.D. 30–150.* 2 vols. Gloucester, Mass.: Peter Smith, 1970.


## THE KORAN OF MOHAMMED

Arberry, Arthur A.: *The Koran Interpreted.* New York: Macmillan, 1964.

Geodefroy–De Mombynes, Maurice: *Muslim Institutions.* New York: Barnes and Noble, 1968.

*The Koran.* Translated by J.M. Rodwell. London and New York: Everyman's Library, 1974.

Rahman, F.: *Islam.* New York: Holt, Rinehart and Winston, 1967.

Watt, W. Montgomery: *Muhammad: Prophet and Statesman.* Oxford and New York: Oxford University Press, 1961.

—: *What Is Islam?* New York: Praeger Publishers, 1968.


## THE MAGNA CHARTA

Holt, James C.: *The Magna Charta.* Cambridge and New York: Cambridge University Press, 1969.

Howard, A. Dick: *Magna Carta: Text and Commentary.* Charlottesville: University Press of Virginia, 1964.

Hunt, William, and Poole, Reginald, eds.: *The Political History of England.* 12 vols. New York: AMS Press, 1905–1913.

Painter, Sidney: *The Reign of King John.* Baltimore: Johns Hopkins University Press, 1949.

Petit-Dutaillis, Charles, and Lefebvre, Georges: *Studies and Notes Supplementary to Stubbs' Constitutional History.* New York: Barnes and Noble, 1968.

Thompson, Faith: *The First Century of Magna Charta: Why It Persisted as a Document.* New York: Atheneum, 1967.

—: *Magna Charta: Its Role in the Making of the English Constitution 1300–1629.* New York: Farrar, Straus and Giroux, 1971.


## ST. FRANCIS: CANTICLE OF THE SUN

Chesterton, Gilbert K.: *St. Francis of Assisi.* New York: Doubleday, 1957.

Francis of Assisi, St.: *The Little Flowers of St. Francis.* Translated by Raphael Brown. London and New York: Everyman's Library, 1971.

Jorgensen, Johannes: *St. Francis of Assisi.* New York: Doubleday, 1960

Knowles, David: *Religious Orders in England.* 3 vols. Cambridge and New York: Cambridge University Press, 1959.

Lambert, Malcolm D.: *Franciscan Poverty: The Doctrine of the Absolute Poverty of Christ and the Apostles in the Franciscan Order 1210–1323.* Naperville, Ill.: Allenson, 1971.


## NICHOLAS OF CUSA: DE PACE FIDEI

Cassirer, Ernst: *The Individual and the Cosmos in Renaissance Philosophy.* Philadelphia: University of Pennsylvania Press, 1972.

— et al., eds.: *The Renaissance Philosophy of Man.* Chicago: University of Chicago Press, 1948.

Jacot, Ernest F.: *Essays in the Conciliar Epoch:* Oxford and New York: Oxford University Press, 1953.

—: *The Fifteenth Century.* Oxford and New York: Oxford University Press, 1961.

Nicholas de Cusa: *Unity and Reform: Selected Writings of Nicholas de Cusa.* Edited by J.P. Dolan. Notre Dame, Ind.: University of Notre Dame Press, 1962.

Vansteenberghe, Edmond: *Cardinal Nicolas De Cues.* New York: Academic Press, 1920 reprint.


## MARTIN LUTHER'S PROTEST

Bainton, Roland: *The Age of the Reformation.* New York: Van Nostrand, 1956.

—: *Here I Stand: A Life of Martin Luther.* New York: New American Library, 1962.

—: *The Reformation of the Sixteenth Century.* Boston: Beacon Press, 1956.

Erikson, Erik H.: *Young Man Luther.* New York: W.W. Norton, 1958.

Kidd, Beresford J.: *Documents Illustrative of the Continental Reformation.* Oxford and New York: Oxford University Press, 1911.

Luther, Martin: *Luther's Works in English.* Edited by J. Pelikan and H.T. Lehmann. St. Louis, Mo.: Concordia Publishing Co., 1955– .

—: *Selected Writings.* Edited by T.G. Tappert. 4 vols. Philadelphia: Fortress Press, 1967.

Wentz, Abdel R.: *Basic History of Lutheranism in America.* Philadelphia: Fortress Press, 1955.


## GROTIUS ON INTERNATIONAL ORDER

Fleisher, Martin, ed.: *Machiavelli and the Nature of Political Thought.* New York: Atheneum, 1972.

Grotius, Hugo: *The Freedom of the Seas.* New York: Arno Press, 1972.

Knight, W.S.: *Life and Works of Hugo Grotius.* Dobbs Ferry, N.Y.: Oceana Publications, 1925.

Lauterpacht, Hersch: "The Grotian Tradition in International Law." *British Year Book of International Law,* vol. 23, 1946.

Machiavelli, Niccolò: *The Prince and Other Works.* Translated by A.H. Gilbert. New York: Hendricks House, 1964.

van Eysinga, W.J.M.: "Grotius resurgens," *Netherlands International Law Review,* vol. 7, 1953.

## VIRGINIA DECLARATION OF RIGHTS

Beard, Charles A., and Beard, Mary: *New Basic History of the United States.* New York: Doubleday, 1960.

Brant, Irving: *The Bill of Rights: Its Origin and Meaning.* New York: New American Library, 1967.

Commager, Henry S., and Nevins, Alan: *The Spirit of Seventy-six: The Story of the American Revolution as Told by Participants.* New York: Harper & Row, 1967.

Grigsby, Hugh B.: *The Virginia Convention of 1776.* New York: DaCapo Press, 1969.

Hand, Learned: *The Bill of Rights.* New York: Atheneum, 1964.

Schwartz, B.: *The Bill of Rights: A Documentary History.* 2 vols. New York: McGraw-Hill Book Co., 1971.


## THE UNITED STATES CONSTITUTION

Barnes, William R., et al., eds.: *The Constitution of the United States.* 9th ed. New York: Barnes and Noble, 1971.

Becker, Carl L.: *The Declaration of Independence: A Study in the History of Political Ideas.* New York: Alfred A. Knopf, 1942.

Borden, Morton, ed.: *George Washington.* Englewood Cliffs, N.J.: Prentice-Hall, 1969.

Hamilton, Alexander, et al.: *The Federalist.* Cambridge, Mass.: Harvard University Press, 1961.

Rossiter, Clinton: *Alexander Hamilton and the Constitution.* New York: Harcourt, Brace, Jovanovich, 1960.

—: *1787: The Grand Convention.* New York: New American Library, 1968.

Schwartz, Bernard: *Commentary on the Constitution of the United States.* 2 vols. New York: Macmillan, 1962.


## DECLARATION OF THE RIGHTS OF MAN

Aulard, François V.: *The French Revolution: A Political History, 1789–1804.* 4 vols. New York: Atheneum, 1910 reprint.

Brinton, Crane: *Decade of Revolution, 1789–1799.* New York: Harper & Row, 1960.

—: *The Jacobins.* New York: Atheneum, 1961.

De Tocqueville, Alexis: *The Old Regime and the French Revolution.* Translated by Gilbert Stuart. New York: Doubleday, 1955.

Durant, Will, and Durant, Ariel: *Rousseau and Revolution.* New York: Simon and Schuster, 1967.

Godechot, Jacques: *France and the Atlantic Revolution of the Eighteenth Century.* Glencoe, Ill.: The Free Press, 1965.

Michelet, Jules: *History of the French Revolution.* Translated by Charles Cocks. Chicago: University of Chicago Press, 1967.


## KANT'S PEACE MANIFESTO

Berlin, Isaiah: *The Age of Enlightenment: The Eighteenth-Century Philosophers.* New York: New American Library, 1958.

Kant, Immanuel: *Kant's Political Writings*. Edited by H. Reiss. Cambridge and New York: Cambridge University Press, 1960.

Korner, Stephan: *Kant*. 2nd ed. Harmondsworth and Baltimore: Penguin Books, 1955.

Paulsen, Friedrich: *Immanuel Kant: His Life and Doctrine*. New York: Frederick Ungar, 1963.


THE CODE NAPOLEON

Bainville, Jacques: *Napoleon*. Port Washington, N.Y.: Kennikat Press, 1970.

Gershoy, Leo: *The French Revolution and Napoleon*. New York: Appleton-Century-Croft, 1964.

Geyl, Pieter: *Napoleon: For and Against*. New Haven, Conn.: Yale University Press, 1949.

Godechot, Jacques, et al.: *The Napoleonic Era in Europe*. New York: Holt, Rinehart and Winston, 1971.

Lefebvre, Georges: *Napoleon: From Eighteen Brumaire to Tilsit, 1799–1807*. New York: Columbia University Press, 1969.

Napoleon Bonaparte: *The Code Napoléon*. Reprint. Baton Rouge, La.: Claitor's Publishing Division, 1960.


THE COMMUNIST MANIFESTO

Bloch, Ernst: *On Karl Marx*. New York: McGraw-Hill Book Co., 1971.

Fromm, Erich: *Marx's Concept of Man*. New York: Frederick Ungar, 1960.

Marx, Karl, and Engels, Friedrich: *Basic Writings on Politics and Philosophy*. Edited by L.S. Feuer. Gloucester, Mass.: Peter Smith, 1960.

Mayer, Gustav: *Friedrich Engels: A Biography*. New York: Howard Fertig, 1969.

Mehring, Frantz: *Karl Marx: The Story of His Life*. Ann Arbor: University of Michigan Press, 1962.

Wilson, Edmund: *To the Finland Station: A Study in the Writing and Acting of History*. New York: Doubleday, 1953.

Wolfe, Bertram D.: *Marxism: One Hundred Years in the Life of a Doctrine*. New York: Dial Press, 1964.


GANDHI: THE POWER OF NON-VIOLENCE

Andrews, C.F.: *Mahatma Gandhi's Ideas*. New York: Fernhill House, 1949.

Erikson, Erik H.: *Gandhi's Truth: On the Origins of Militant Nonviolence*. New York: W.W. Norton, 1969.

Gandhi, Mahatma: *Autobiography: The Story of My Experiments with Truth*. Boston: Beacon Press, 1957.

—: *The Essential Gandhi*. Edited by Louis Fisher. New York: Random House, 1961.

—: *Selected Writings*. Edited by Ronald Duncan. New York: Harper & Row, 1972.


CHINA'S DECLARATION TO ALL NATIONS

FitzGerald, Charles P.: *The Birth of Communist China*. New York: Praeger Publishers, 1966.

—: *China: A Short Cultural History*. 3rd ed. New York: Praeger Publishers, 1954.


Mao Tse-tung: *Mao: An Anthology of His Writings*. Rev. ed. New York: New American Library, 1971.

Schurmann, Franz, and Schell, Orville: *A China Reader*. Vol. 3. New York: Random House, 1971.

Schwartz, Benjamin I.: *Chinese Communism and the Rise of Mao*. Cambridge, Mass.: Harvard University Press, 1951.

Snow, Edgar: *Red Star over China*. Rev. ed. New York: Grove Press, 1968.

Sun Yat-sen: *Memoirs of a Chinese Revolutionary*. New York: AMS Press, 1927.


THE ATLANTIC CHARTER

Churchill, Winston L.: *The Second World War*. 6 vols. New York: Bantam Books, 1971.

Feis, Herbert: *Churchill, Roosevelt, Stalin: The War They Waged and the Peace They Sought*. 2nd ed. Princeton, N.J.: Princeton University Press, 1967.

Schlesinger, Arthur M., Jr.: *The Age of Roosevelt*. 3 vols. Boston: Houghton Mifflin, 1957–1960.

Stansky, Peter, ed.: *Churchill: A Profile*. New York: Hill & Wang, 1973.

Sulzberger, C.L.: *World War II*. Rev. ed. New York: American Heritage Press, 1970.

Wilson, Theodore A.: *The First Summit: Roosevelt and Churchill at Placentia Bay 1941*. Boston: Houghton Mifflin, 1969.


SCIENTISTS' WARNING: THE FRANCK REPORT

Einstein, Albert: *Out of My Later Years*. Westport, Conn.: Greenwood Press, 1950.

Feis, Herbert: *The Atomic Bomb and the End of World War II*. Rev. ed. Princeton, N.J.: Princeton University Press, 1970.

Harris, Jonathan: *Hiroshima: A Study in Science, Politics and the Ethics of War*. Reading, Mass.: Addison-Wesley Publishing Co., 1971.

Hersey, John R.: *Hiroshima*. New York: Alfred A. Knopf, 1946.

Junck, Robert: *Brighter than a Thousand Suns: A Personal History of the Atomic Scientists*. New York: Harcourt, Brace, Jovanovich, 1970.

Smith, Alice Kemball: *A Peril and a Hope: The Scientists' Movement in America, 1945–1947*. Cambridge, Mass.: The M.I.T. Press, 1965.


THE CHARTER OF THE UNITED NATIONS

Barros, James, ed.: *The United Nations: Past, Present and Future*. Glencoe, Ill.: The Free Press, 1972.

Goodrich, Leland M., et al., eds.: *The United Nations Charter: Commentary and Documents*. 3rd ed. New York: Columbia University Press, 1969.

Hammarskjold, Dag: *Markings*. New York: Alfred A. Knopf, 1964.

Higgins, Rosalyn: *United Nations Peacekeeping, 1946–1967*. 2 vols. Oxford and New York: Oxford University Press, 1969–1970.

Nicholas, H.G. *The United Nations as a Political Institution*. 4th ed. Oxford and New York: Oxford University Press, 1971.


HIROHITO'S NEW YEAR'S MESSAGE

Downs, Ray F., ed.: *Japan Yesterday and Today*. New York: Praeger Publishers, 1969.

Mosley, L.: *Hirohito*. Englewood Cliffs, N.J.: Prentice-Hall, 1966.

Reischauer, Edwin O.: *Japan: The Story of a Nation*. 4th ed. New York: Alfred A. Knopf, 1970.

Varley, Paul H.: *Japanese Culture: A Short History*. New York: Praeger Publishers, 1972.


VOICE OF THE THIRD WORLD: FRANTZ FANON

Cartey, Martin, and Kilson, Martin: *Africa Reader: Independent Africa*. New York: Random House, 1970.

Caute, David: *Frantz Fanon*. New York: Viking Press, 1970.

Fanon, Frantz: *Black Skin, White Masks*. New York: Grove Press, 1967.

—: *Dying Colonialism*. New York: Grove Press, 1967.

—: *Toward the African Revolution*. New York: Grove Press, 1968.

Gendzier, Irene: *Frantz Fanon: A Critical Biography*. New York: Pantheon Books, 1973.

Match, John: *Africa, the Rebirth of Self-Rule*. Oxford and New York: Oxford University Press, 1967.

Ottaway, David, and Ottaway, Marina: *Algeria: The Politics of a Socialist Revolution*. Berkeley: University of California Press, 1970.


JOHN XXIII: PACEM IN TERRIS

John XXIII: *Pacem in Terris*. Paramus, N.J.: Paulist Press, 1963.

—: *Pope John XXIII on Race and Racial Justice*. Paramus, N.J.: Paulist Press, 1970.

Miller, John H., ed.: *Vatican II: An Interfaith Appraisal*. Notre Dame, Ind.: University of Notre Dame Press, 1966.

Royidis, Emmanuel: *Pope John*. New York: Viking Press, 1961.

Rynne, Xavier: *Vatican Council II*. New York: Farrar, Straus and Giroux, 1968.


THE PIONEER 10 PLAQUE

Lanczos, C.: *Space through the Ages*. New York: Academic Press, 1970.

Sullivan, Walter: *We Are Not Alone: The Search for Intelligent Life on Other Worlds*. Rev. ed. New York: McGraw-Hill Book Co., 1966.

Von Braun, Wernher: *Space Frontier*. Rev. ed. New York: Holt, Rinehart and Winston, 1971.

# PICTURE CREDITS

H.H. Prince Sadruddin Aga Khan, Geneva: 67

Akademische Druck- und Verlagsanstalt, Graz: 22 (left)

Algerian Ministry of Information: 160 (right); 179 (top row, 3rd from right)

Alinari, Florence: 8 (left, top and middle); 28 (top left); 42 (right, Alinari-Anderson); 171 (top right); 176 (middle row, far right)

Alte Pinakothek, Munich: 86 (left)

Archiv für Kunst und Geschichte, Berlin: 84 (left); 116

Archive Photographique, Paris: 178 (middle row, 2nd from right)

Associated Press, Frankfurt: 101 (bottom); 137; 179 (middle row, 3rd from left)

Bettman Archive, New York: 177 (middle row, 4th from left)

Biblioteca Nacional, Madrid: 15

Biblioteca Reale, Turin: 177 (bottom row, far right)

Bibliothèque Nationale, Paris: 23; 41 (right); 68 (top); 96; 108 (top right); 122

Bildarchiv Bucher, Lucerne: 140 (left); 141 (middle); 142/143; 150 (right, Peter Wichmann); 179 (top row, 2nd from left and middle row, 2nd from left)

Bildarchiv Foto Marburg, Marburg: 85; 113

Bildarchiv Preussischer Kulturbesitz, Berlin: 123; 127 (left); 135 (bottom)

Bildverlag Herder, Freiburg i. Breisgau: 170 (top right)

Werner Bischof, Zurich: 157 (right)

Bodleian Library, Oxford: 24 (bottom row); 45 (left)

British Library, London: 64 (top right); 72/73

British Museum, London: 17 (right); 33 (2nd from left); 47 (bottom)

The John Carter Brown Library, Brown University, Rhode Island: 106

Bulloz, Paris: 178 (bottom row, 2nd from left)

Sekai Bunka Photo, New York: 158 (top)

Camerapix, London: 163 (top)

Camera Press, London; Photo: Jousuf Karsh: 144 (top right)

Camera Press, London: 147 (left and bottom right)

Monsignore Loris F. Capovilla, Loreto: 164 (bottom left)

Centre de Documentation Juive, Paris: 142 (bottom)

China Publishing Company, Taipei: 134 (top right)

Gilbert Darlington Collection, New York: 99 (top left)

De Antonis, Rome: 35; 154/155

George Eastman House Collection: Lewis W. Hine, New York: 10 (first four from left); 11 (bottom row, 2nd and 4th from left)

George Eastman House Collection, New York: 11 (far right)

Edinburgh University Library, Edinburgh: 64 (left); 177 (top row, 4th from left)

Editions du Seuil, Paris: 59

Forman-Frontier Film: 139 (top)

Fromenti, Paris: 177 (bottom row, 2nd from left)

Giraudon, Paris: 18 (Louvre); 26 (left, Anderson-Giraudon); 118 (2nd from left, Musée de la Légion d'Honneur); 176 (top row, 3rd from left); 177 (middle row, far left); 178 (top row, 3rd from right, Musée de la Légion d'Honneur); 178 (middle row, 2nd from left)

Gräfe und Unzer Verlag, Munich: 114

GraphischeSammlung Albertina, Vienna: 55 (right)

Gunston Hall Plantation, Board of Regents, Lorton, Va.: 98 (right); 178 (top row, 2nd from left)

Hale Observatories, Pasadena: 172/173

Dr. Hermann Hallauer, Bad Godesberg-Bonn: 80 (right); 177 (top row, 2nd from right)

Hamlyn Picture Library, London: 156 (left)

Hirmer Fotoarchiv, Munich: 21 (Louvre)

Holle Bildarchiv, Baden-Baden: 36 (right)

Horyu-Ji Temple, Nara; Photo: Tasaburo Yoneda: 32 (bottom row, far right)

By permission of the Houghton Library, Harvard University, Cambridge: 60

Dr. Martin Hürlimann, Zollikon: 37 (top)

IBA, Oberengstringen: 131 (bottom row, far right)

Imperial War Museum, London: 141 (bottom right)

Independence National Historical Park, Philadelphia: 102 (top right); 103

India Office Library, London: 130 (far left)

Keystone: 136; 143 (left); 144 (left); 147 (top right); 148/149; 151 (top row); 152; 153; 164 (top); 179 (top row, 3rd from left and 2nd from right); 179 (middle row, 3rd from right); 179 (bottom left)

Janet Le Caisne, Paris: 58

Library of Congress, Washington: 11 (3rd from left); 160 (left)

Louisiana Room, Louisiana State University Library, Baton Rouge; 119 (right)

Magnum, March Riboud, Paris: 161

Mansell Collection, London: 46 (left); 48; 70; 71; 74; 92 (right); 93; 94; 97 (top); 99 (top right); 102 (far left); 112 (left); 117 (top); 131 (bottom, 2nd from left); 177 (top row, 1st and 5th from left); 178 (top row, far left and 5th from left)

Aage Marcus, Hørsholm: 49 (left)

MAS, Barcelona: 68 (bottom); 92 (2nd from left)

Leonard von Matt, Buochs: 22 (right); 24 (top); 26 (top right); 27 (top); 32 (2nd from left); 43 (bottom left); 44; 54; 56; 57; 61; 77; 81; 86 (right); 91; 176 (top row, 2nd and 4th from left and middle row, 2nd from left); 177 (middle row, 3rd from left and far right; bottom row, far left; top row, 3rd from left)

Mauritius Verlag, Peter Mauritius, Mittenwald: 143 (right)

McDonnell Douglas Corporation: 7

Metropolitan Museum of Art, New York: 52 (left); 177 (top row, 2nd from left)

Ministry of I. & B., Government of India: 130 (2nd from left); 131 (top and bottom, far left); 133; 178 (top row, far right)

Mondadori Press, Milan: 179 (middle row, far right)

Monumenti Musei e Gallerie Pontificie, Vatican: 42 (left); 176 (top row, far right)

Bernhard Moosbrugger, Zurich: 83 (right); 164/165 (bottom); 168/169; 169 (right)

Musée Carnavalet, Paris: 118 (far left)

Courtesy Museum of Fine Arts, Boston: 38; 176 (top row, 2nd from right)

Museum Rietberg, Zurich: 50/51

NASA, Washington: 170 (bottom); 171 (far left); 179 (top row, far right)

National Archives, Tokyo: 156 (right); 158 (bottom); 159; 179 (top row, 4th from right)

The National Archives, Washington: 104; 128/129

National Institute of Archaeology and Art, Tunis: 66

National Museum, Stockholm: 84 (right); 177 (top row, far left)

Nelson Gallery–Atkins Museum, Kansas City: 33 (far left)

The New York Historical Society, New York: 99 (bottom)

The New York Public Library, New York: 4; 10 (far right)

Oakland Museum: History Division, New York: 11 (far left)

Herb Orth, Time Inc., New York: 102 (2nd from left); 178 (top row, 3rd from left)

Palace Collection, Taiwan: 178 (bottom row, 3rd from left)

Photopress, Zurich: 133 (right); 165 (top)

Photothèque Laffont, Paris: 90; 109 (right, Archives Nationales); 110/111 (Musée Carnavalet); 138 (Centre de Recherches Asiatiques)

Popperfoto, London: 37 (bottom right); 132

Presse-Agentur Dukas, Zurich: 69

Publisher's Archives, Lucerne: 6; 8 (right, from top to bottom); 27 (bottom); 36 (left); 37 (bottom left); 39; 40; 46 (top right); 47 (top); 55 (bottom); 87; 89; 107; 117; 127 (right); 130 (bottom); 134 (second from left); 135 (top); 137 (top); 142 (top); 157 (left); 162; 163 (bottom); 166; 171 (top left and bottom); 176 (middle row,

left and bottom row, far left and far right); 177 (middle row, 2nd and 3rd from right and bottom row, 2nd from right); 179 (top row, 1st and 4th from left and middle row, far left and 3rd from right)

Radio Times Hulton Picture Library, London: 105; 124 (left); 131 (bottom, 3rd from left)

Record Office House of Lords, London: 98 (left)

Réunion des Musées Nationaux, Paris: 16 (Louvre); 17 (left, Louvre); 32 (bottom, 2nd from right, Musée Guimet); 62 (Louvre); 109 (left, Musée de Versailles); 121 (Musée de Versailles); 176 (top row, far left, Louvre)

Rheinisches Landesmuseum, Bonn; Photo Schafgans: 52 (right)

Ringier Bilderdienst, Zurich: 179 (bottom row, far right)

Roger-Viollet, Paris: 30/31; 43 (right); 108 (2nd from left); 118 (top right); 119 (left); 120; 124 (right); 125; 134 (far left); 141 (top); 178 (top row, 4th from left and 2nd from right; bottom row, far left)

Dr. Erich Salomon: 97 (bottom)

SCALA, Florence: 11 (top); 32 (top right); 53; 76; 78; 130 (top right); 177 (top row, 3rd from right)

Dr. Xaver Schnieper, Kriens: 79

Seattle Art Museum, Washington: 65

Signal Corps, Atomic Energy Commission: 145

George Sirot, Paris: 126

Courtesy of the Smithsonian Institution, Freer Gallery of Art, Washington: 33 (right)

Staatliche Museen, Berlin: 25; 176 (bottom row, 2nd from left)

Staatsbibliothek Preussischer Kulturbesitz, Berlin: 178 (middle row, far right)

Städelsches Kunstinstitut, Frankfurt: 178 (middle row, far left)

Stadtbibliothek, Zurich: 112 (right)

Süddeutscher Verlag, Munich: 178 (bottom row, far right)

TAP, Athens: 28/29; 45 (right); 92 (far left)

Thomas Institute, Cologne: 82

Robert Tobler, Lucerne: 63

United Nations; M. Grant: 151 (bottom)

UPI, New York: 140 (top right); 150 (left)

Vautier-Decool, Paris: 8 (top middle)

Victoria and Albert Museum, London: 32 (bottom, far left)

Virginia State Library, Richmond: 100/101 (top); 108 (far left)

The Warden and Fellows of All Souls College, Oxford: 74 (bottom)

Werbeagentur Plan'x, Zurich: 2/3

Wildwood House Ltd., London: 49 (right)

Worcester Art Museum, Worcester: 8 (bottom left)

Reportage Photographique YAN, Toulouse: 177 (middle row, 2nd from left)


PICTURE CREDITS
FROM PUBLISHED WORKS

Edouard Chavannes: *Mission archéologique dans la Chine septentrionale*. Paris, 1909: 41 (left)

Anton Lübke: *Nicolaus von Cusa*. Munich, 1968: 80 (left); 83 (left)

*China Pictorial,* No. 2, 1968: 139 (right)

# INDEX